CONTENTS

Welcome to
Europe

Ten European cities. What could be more enticing? From the café philosophers and couture of Paris to the cosmopolitan street-life and royal pageantry of London. And from the ancient sun-drenched cobbles of Rome to the dazzling contemporary architecture of Berlin, Europe has it all. With Eyewitness Top 10 European Cities, it is yours to explore.

Paris: culture, charm and *je ne sais quoi*. Does city life offer anything better than exploring the chic shops of the Champs Elysées or the hip Marais district? Wandering Montmartre or sauntering in the footsteps of Pablo Picasso for an early-morning coffee or lazy Left Bank lunch? Seeing the *Mona Lisa* in the **Louvre**, the Impressionists at the **Musée d'Orsay**, or the spectacle of a sunset over the city from the **Sacré-Coeur**?

Then there's London, an inimitable city of palaces and pubs. Hotbed of theatre and mecca of shopping, it's the most cosmopolitan city on earth. Sip a cocktail in a rooftop bar, eat food from every corner of the planet, stroll along the Thames, stand rapt among the crowds at the Globe Theatre, and feel your mind spin with the exuberance and energy of art at the two **Tate** galleries and the **National Gallery**. It's all here, packed into the world's most energetic streetscape.

Little Amsterdam, with its olive-green canals, alternative vibe, enchanting Golden Age architecture, convivial bars and historic churches. Home to the world's largest collection of artworks by Vincent Van Gogh, the **Rijksmuseum's** magnificent collection of 17th-century Dutch art, and, of course, the heart-breakingly evocative **Anne Frank House**.

Barcelona: splendidly set on the shores of the Mediterranean. Stroll along lively **La Rambla**, wander the medieval stone labyrinth of the Barri Gòtic quarter, marvel at extraordinary Modernista architecture and the Surrealist paintings of Joan Miró. Reignite your passion for cool by seeking out contemporary design throughout the city and party all night in buzzing clubs.

Clockwise from top: **British Museum, London; bridge over the Singel, Amsterdam; view from Castelo de São Jorge, Lisbon; Spanish Steps, Rome; Sacré-Coeur, Paris; houses on Nyhavn, Copenhagen**

Lisbon, Europe's most intimate capital, draped over seven hills. The hub of a maritime empire, its wealth is preserved in flamboyant Manueline buildings such as the **Mosteiro dos Jerónimos** and the **Torre de Belém**. Ride quaint old trams, dawdle in vibrantly tiled street cafés and escape for a day to heavenly **Sintra**.

Rome, eternal city, exuberant feast for eyes, soul and stomach. Wander around the ancient ruins of the **Colosseum** and the **Roman Forum** or gaze at the intricate paintings lining Michelangelo's Sistine ceiling. Startling espresso, fabulous pasta and delectable *gelato* await the taste buds. Who could argue with visitors, artists, and pilgrims who've been flocking here seeking *la dolce vita* since antiquity?

Venice, the world's most improbable city, with beautiful palaces of stone filigree rising from the water. Rise before dawn to glimpse dazzling **Piazza San Marco** without the crowds and local boats unloading fresh produce at the **Rialto** market. Then study the art of the **Accademia** and **Guggenheim** before losing yourself in the atmospheric narrow back-streets.

Copenhagen, the birthplace of hygge. A charming, compact maritime city of opulent palaces, brightly painted town houses and contemporary architecture. See the sights of its splendid

Left to right then top to bottom: **Burano, Venice; stained-glass dome at the Palau de la Música Catalana, Barcelona; Berliner Dom, Berlin; Wallenstein Garden, Prague**

harbour, marvel at the magnificent grounds of Frederiksberg, explore the alternative culture of **Christiania** and cosy up in cafés.

Berlin: hip, historic and bursting with youthful energy. From Prussian powerhouse and Nazi bastion to Cold War zombie and now the vibrant capital of a reunited Germany. Stroll along refined **Unter den Linden**, walk beneath the towering **Brandenburger Tor** and see the astonishing new centre of **Potsdamer Platz**. Venture to riverside **Schloss Charlottenburg** for manicured green lawns and indulgent Baroque architecture.

Prague, a city of 100 spires and a bewitching castle. Easily navigable on foot, explore the shadowy cobbled lanes of Josefov, stroll past the pastel buildings lining the streets of Malá Strana, and cross the famous **Charles Bridge**. The birthplace of Franz Kafka and Václav Havel still throbs with culture, music and theatre, as well as decadent cafés and some very atmospheric beer cellars.

Whether you're staying for a weekend or a week, our Top 10 guide brings together the best the continent has to offer, from London to Lisbon and Berlin to Barcelona. Add detailed maps and inspiring photography, and you've got the essential pocket-sized travel companion. **Enjoy the book and enjoy Europe**.

Top 10 Paris

**Magnificent vaulting and stained-glass
windows, Sainte-Chapelle**

Exploring Paris

Paris has an inexhaustible wealth of things to see and do. Here are some ideas for how to make the most of your time. The city is relatively compact, so you should be able to do most of your sightseeing on foot, and you're never far from a metro station.

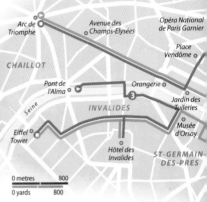

Musée d'Orsay is housed in a former railway station.

Key
— Two-day itinerary
— Four-day itinerary

Two Days in Paris

Day ❶
MORNING
Cross Pont Neuf over the River Seine to the Ile de la Cité and view the cathedral of **Notre-Dame** (see pp22–5), partially damaged by fire in April 2019, or visit lovely **Sainte-Chapelle** (see pp36–7). Continue south into the lively Latin Quarter and pause for lunch in a classic Left Bank bistro.

AFTERNOON
Meander through stylish St-Germain-des-Prés to the **Musée d'Orsay** (see pp18–21) and admire its spectacular collection of Impressionist paintings. From here it's a short walk to **Hôtel des Invalides** (see pp38–9) and the majestic **Eiffel Tower** (see pp26–7), stunningly lit up at night.

Day ❷
MORNING
Take in the views from atop the **Arc de Triomphe** (see pp30–31), then stroll the Avenue des Champs-Elysées and Jardin des Tuileries to the **Musée du Louvre** (see pp14–17).

AFTERNOON
Explore the hip Marais, stopping en route at the **Centre Georges Pompidou** (see pp32–3). Take a metro to Montmartre and walk up to **Sacré-Coeur** (see pp28–9) for panoramic sunset views.

Four Days in Paris

Day ❶
MORNING
Visit Montmartre's **Sacré-Coeur** (see pp28–9), then head down through Pigalle to Opéra National

The white basilica of **Sacré-Coeur** is the second-highest viewpoint in Paris.

Montmartre's leafy Place du Tertre is always crowded with artists at their easels or selling their work.

de Paris Garnier *(Pl de l'Opéra)* and elegant Place Vendôme.

AFTERNOON

Wander through the Jardin des Tuileries and visit Monet's exquisite *Water Lilies* at the Orangerie *(Jardin des Tuileries)*. Then stroll along the Avenue des Champs-Elysées to the **Arc de Triomphe** *(see pp30–31)*.

Day ❷
MORNING

Discover modern art at the **Centre Georges Pompidou** *(see pp32–3)*, then explore the 18th-century art collection at Musée Cognac-Jay *(8 Rue Elzévir)*. Enjoy a bistro lunch on Place des Vosges.

AFTERNOON

Check out the Marais district, then visit Ile St-Louis. Pass by **Notre-Dame** *(see pp22–5)*, before enjoying a concert at **Sainte-Chapelle** *(see pp36–7)*.

Day ❸
MORNING

Take a boat trip along the River Seine before a visit to the great Impressionists at the **Musée d'Orsay** *(see pp18–21)*.

AFTERNOON

Pay your respects to Napoleon at **Hôtel des Invalides** *(see pp38–9)* and then head to the **Eiffel Tower** *(see pp26–7)*.

Day ❹
MORNING

You'll have time to see all the star exhibits of the **Musée du Louvre** *(see pp14–17)* before heading off for lunch in the Latin Quarter.

AFTERNOON

Visit France's great and good at the **Panthéon** *(see pp34–5)*, explore the lovely Jardin des Plantes and end the day with live jazz at Caveau de la Huchette *(5 Rue de la Huchette)*.

🔟 Paris Highlights

From the Arc de Triomphe to the Eiffel Tower, Paris holds some of the world's most famous sights. These ten attractions should be top of the list for any first-time visitor, and remain eternally awe-inspiring.

Musée du Louvre ①

The world's most visited museum also contains one of the world's finest collections of art and antiquities (up to 1848). To complete the superlatives, it was once France's largest royal palace *(see pp14–17)*.

MONCEAU

⑥ AVE DE FRIEDLAND

AVENUE DES CHAMPS ELYSEES

AVE MARCEAU

CHAILLOT

PLACE DE LA CONCORI

AVE DU PRES. WILSON

Seine

QUAI D'ORSAY

AVE BOSQUET

INVALIDES

④ Parc du Champ de Mars

AVE DE SUFFREN

⑩

| 0 metres | 800 |
| 0 yards | 800 |

② Musée d'Orsay

This former railway station is one of the world's leading art galleries and, for many, reason alone to visit Paris *(see pp18–21)*.

Notre-Dame ③

This great Gothic cathedral, founded on the site of a Gallo-Roman temple, is a repository of art and history. It is also the geographical "heart" of France *(see pp22–5)*.

④ Eiffel Tower

More than seven million visitors a year ascend to the top of this most famous Paris landmark for the spectacular views. It was erected for the Universal Exhibition of 1889 *(see pp26–7)*.

Sacré-Coeur ⑤

The terrace in front of this monumental white-domed basilica in Montmartre affords one of the finest free views over Paris *(see pp28–9)*.

6 Arc de Triomphe
Napoleon's triumphal arch, celebrating battle victories, stands proudly at the top of the Champs-Elysées and, along with the Eiffel Tower, is one of the city's most iconic structures *(see pp30–31)*.

7 Centre Georges Pompidou
Home to France's National Museum of Modern Art, the building itself is a fascinating work of contemporary art *(see pp32–3)*.

8 Panthéon
The great and the good of France, including Voltaire, are buried in the Panthéon *(see pp34–5)*.

9 Sainte-Chapelle
Known as "a gateway to heaven", this exquisite church was built to house relics collected by St Louis on his Crusades *(see pp36–7)*.

10 Hôtel des Invalides
The glowing golden dome of the Hôtel des Invalides church is unmistakable across the rooftops of Paris. It houses Napoleon's tomb *(see pp38–9)*.

🔟 ⭐ Musée du Louvre

One of the world's most impressive museums, the Louvre contains some 35,000 priceless objects. It was built as a fortress by King Philippe-Auguste in 1190, but Charles V (1364–80) made it his home. In the 16th century François I replaced it with a Renaissance-style palace and founded the royal art collection with 12 paintings from Italy. Revolutionaries opened the collection to the public in 1793. Shortly after, Napoleon renovated the Louvre as a museum.

1 Venus de Milo
This iconic statue of Greek goddess Aphrodite – later known as Venus by the ancient Romans – is the highlight of the museum's Greek antiquities. It dates from the end of the 2nd century BC and was discovered on the Greek island of Milos in 1820.

2 Mona Lisa
Arguably the most famous painting in the world, Leonardo da Vinci's portrait of a Florentine noblewoman with an enigmatic smile *(see p17)* has been beautifully restored. Visit early or late in the day.

3 Marly Horses
Coustou's famous rearing horses being restrained by horse-tamers were sculpted in 1745 for Louis XIV's Château de Marly. Replicas stand near the Place de la Concorde.

4 Slaves
Michelangelo (1475–1564) sculpted *Dying Slave* **(left)** and *Rebellious Slave* (1513–20) for the tomb of Pope Julius II in Rome. The unfinished figures seem to be emerging from their "prisons" of stone.

5 Glass Pyramid
The unmistakable glass pyramid, designed by I M Pei, became the Louvre's new entrance in 1989. Stainless steel tubes make up the 21-m-high (69-ft) frame **(above)**.

6 Medieval Moats
An excavation in the 1980s uncovered the remains of the medieval fortress. You can see the base of the towers and the drawbridge support under the Cour Carrée.

7 The Winged Victory of Samothrace
This Hellenistic treasure (3rd–2nd century BC) stands atop a stone ship radiating grace and power. It was created to commemorate a naval triumph at Rhodes.

8 The Raft of the Medusa

The shipwreck of a French frigate three years earlier inspired this gigantic early Romantic painting (left) by Théodore Géricault (1791–1824) in 1819. The work depicts the moment when the survivors spot a sail on the horizon.

9 Perrault's Colonnade

The majestic east façade by Claude Perrault (1613– 88), with its paired Corinthian columns, was part of an extension plan commissioned by Louis XIV.

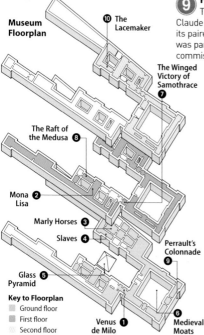

Museum Floorplan

10 The Lacemaker

The Winged Victory of Samothrace **7**

The Raft of the Medusa **8**

Mona Lisa **2**

Marly Horses **3**

Slaves **4**

Perrault's Colonnade **9**

Glass Pyramid **5**

Key to Floorplan
- Ground floor
- First floor
- Second floor

Venus de Milo **1**

Medieval Moats **6**

10 The Lacemaker

Jan Vermeer's (1632–75) masterpiece (above), painted around 1665, gives a simple but beautiful rendering of everyday life and is the highlight of the Louvre's Dutch collection.

NEED TO KNOW

MAP D4 ■ Musée du Louvre, 75001 ■ 01 40 20 53 17 ■ www.louvre.fr

Open 9am–6pm Mon, Thu, Sat & Sun, 9am–9.45pm Wed & Fri; closed Tue, public hols

Adm €17; free 1st Sun of month (except Apr–Sep); under-18s free; under-26s (EU only) free

■ For a light lunch, try Le Café Marly in the Richelieu Wing or the food court in Carrousel du Louvre. For a more special option book at the Café Grand Louvre below the pyramid.

■ To beat the queues buy tickets in advance online. Choose a date and a 30-minute window to access the museum. Tickets are also available at machine kiosks at the Porte des Lions entrance at the west end of the Denon Wing (except Friday) or at the Office de Tourisme at 25 Rue des Pyramides.

Gallery Guide

The foyer is under the pyramid. Those with tickets are given priority access at the pyramid. Alternatively, buy tickets at the Carrousel du Louvre entrance (99 Rue de Rivoli) or Porte des Lions. The Sully, Denon and Richelieu wings lead off from the foyer. Painting and sculpture are displayed by country, plus galleries for objets d'art, antiquities and prints. The Petit Galerie, in the Richelieu wing, is a temporary exhibition area aimed at children.

Louvre Collections

Ancient Egyptian vase

1 French Paintings
This superb collection ranges from the 14th century to 1848 and includes works by such artists as Jean Watteau, Georges de la Tour and J H Fragonard.

2 French Sculpture
Highlights include the Tomb of Philippe Pot by Antoine le Moiturier, the Marly Horses (see p14) and works by Pierre Puget.

3 Egyptian Antiquities
The finest collection outside Cairo, featuring a Sphinx in the crypt, the Seated Scribe of Sakkara, huge sarcophagi, mummified animals, funerary objects and intricate carvings depicting everyday life in Ancient Egypt.

4 Greek Antiquities
The wondrous art of Ancient Greece here ranges from a Cycladic idol from the third millennium BC to Classical Greek marble statues (c.5th century BC) to Hellenistic works (late 3rd–2nd centuries BC).

5 Oriental Antiquities
A stunning collection includes a re-created temple of an Assyrian king and the Codex of Hammurabi (18th century BC), mankind's oldest written laws.

6 Italian Paintings
French royalty adored the art of Italy and amassed much of this collection (1200–1800). It includes many works by Leonardo da Vinci.

7 Italian Sculpture
Highlights of this collection, dating from the early Renaissance, include a 15th-century Madonna and Child by Donatello and Michelangelo's Slaves (see p14).

8 Dutch Paintings
Rembrandt's works are hung alongside domestic scenes by Vermeer and portraits by Frans Hals.

9 Objets d'Art
The ceramics, jewellery and other items in this collection span history and the world.

10 Islamic Art
This exquisite collection, which spans 13 centuries and three continents, is covered by an ultra-modern glass veil.

Museum Floorplan

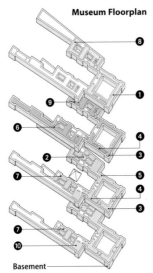

Basement

LEONARDO DA VINCI AND THE MONA LISA

Leonardo da Vinci, Renaissance man extraordinaire, was not only an artist but also a sculptor, engineer, architect and scientist. His many interests included the study of anatomy and aerodynamics.

Born in Vinci, Republic of Florence, Italy, to a wealthy family, Leonardo da Vinci (1452–1519) took up an apprenticeship under artist Andrea del Verrocchio, then served the Duke of Milan as an architect and military engineer, during which time he painted the *Last Supper* mural (1495). On his return to Florence, to work as architect to Cesare Borgia, he painted his most celebrated portrait, the *Mona Lisa* (1503–06). It is also known as *La Gioconda*, allegedly the name of the model's aristocratic husband, although there is ongoing speculation regarding the identity of the subject. The work, in particular the sitter's mysterious smile, shows mastery of two techniques: *chiaroscuro*, the contrast of light and shadow, and *sfumato*, subtle transitions between colours. It was the artist's own favourite painting and he took it with him everywhere. In 1516 François I brought them both to France, giving da Vinci the use of a manor house in Amboise in the Loire Valley, where he died three years later.

Mona Lisa, da Vinci's enigmatic portrait

TOP 10
LOUVRE RESIDENTS

1 Charles V (1364–80)

2 Henri II (1547–49)

3 Catherine de' Medici (1519–89)

4 Henri IV (1589–1610)

5 Louis XIII (1610–43)

6 Louis XIV (1643–1715)

7 Anne of Austria (1601–66)

8 Guillaume Coustou, sculptor (1677–1746)

9 Edmé Bouchardon, sculptor (1698–1762)

10 François Boucher, artist (1703–70)

TOP 10 ⭐ Musée d'Orsay

This wonderful collection covers a variety of art forms from the years 1848 to 1914, and includes a superb Impressionists section. Its setting, in a converted railway station, is equally impressive. Built in 1900, in time for the Paris Exposition, the station was in use until 1939, when it was closed and largely ignored, although it was the location for Orson Welles' 1962 film *The Trial*. It was later used as a theatre and as auction rooms, and in the mid-1970s was considered for demolition. In 1977, the Paris authorities decided to save the imposing station building by converting it into this striking museum.

1 The Building
The former railway station that houses this museum **(left)** is almost as stunning as the exhibits. The light and spacious feel on stepping inside, after admiring the magnificent old façade, takes one's breath away.

2 Van Gogh Paintings
The star of the collection is Vincent Van Gogh (1853–90) and the most absorbing of the canvases on display is the 1889 work showing the artist's *Bedroom at Arles* **(right)**. Also on display are some of the artist's self-portraits, painted with his familiar intensity (Rooms 71 and 72).

3 Le Déjeuner sur l'Herbe
Edouard Manet's (1832–83) controversial painting (1863) was first shown in an "Exhibition of Rejected Works". Its bold portrayal of a classically nude woman enjoying the company of 19th-century men in suits brought about a wave of criticism (Room 29).

4 Olympia
Another Manet portrayal (1865) of a naked courtesan, receiving flowers sent by an admirer, was also regarded as indecent, and shocked the public and critics, but it was an important influence on later artists (Room 14).

5 Blue Waterlilies
Claude Monet (1840–1926) painted this stunning canvas (1919) on one of his favourite themes. His love of waterlilies led him to create his own garden at Giverny in order to paint them in a natural setting. This work inspired many abstract painters later in the 20th century (Room 36).

6 Degas' Statues of Dancers
The museum has an exceptional collection of works by Edgar Degas (1834–1917). Focusing on dancers and the world of opera, his sculptures range from innocent to erotic. *Young Dancer of Fourteen* (1881) was the only one exhibited in the artist's lifetime **(left)** (Room 31).

7 Jane Avril Dancing

Toulouse-Lautrec's (1864–1901) paintings define Paris's *belle époque*. Jane Avril was a famous Moulin Rouge dancer and featured in several of his works, like this 1895 canvas **(left)**, which Toulouse-Lautrec drew from life, in situ at the cabaret (Room 10).

8 Dancing at the Moulin de la Galette

One of the best-known paintings of the Impressionist era, this 1876 work by Pierre-Auguste Renoir (1841–1919) was shown at the Impressionist exhibition in 1877. Its exuberance captures the look and mood of Montmartre and is one of the artist's masterpieces (Room 32).

9 La Belle Angèle

This portrait of a Brittany beauty (1889) by Paul Gauguin (1848–1903) shows the influence of Japanese art on the artist. It was bought by Degas, to finance Gauguin's first trip to Polynesia (Room 72).

10 Café Campana

Offering a rest from all the impressive art, the museum's café, renovated by the Campana Brothers, is delightfully situated behind one of the former station's huge clocks. A break here is an experience in itself and the food is good too.

NEED TO KNOW

MAP C4 ■ 1 Rue de la Légion d'Honneur, 75007 ■ 01 40 49 48 14 ■ www.musee-orsay.fr

Open 9:30am–6pm Tue–Sun (Thu till 9:45pm); closed 1 May, 25 Dec

Adm €14 (under-18s free, under-26s EU only free); €11 for 18–25s non-EU; free first Sun of month; to beat queues, buy tickets online or at the Office de Tourisme

■ The busy restaurant is open for lunch, plus dinner on Thursdays; closed Monday. For a snack or a drink try the upper level café (Café Campana) or the self-service mezzanine café just above.

■ Music concerts are often held. Call 01 53 63 04 63. Concert tickets include free museum entry.

Gallery Guide
As soon as you enter the gallery, collect a map. The ground floor houses works from the early to mid-19th century, as well as striking Oriental works, decorative arts and a bookshop. The middle level includes Naturalist, Symbolist and Post-Impressionist paintings, and sculpture terraces. The upper level is home to the Impressionist galleries. The museum also features temporary exhibitions focusing on 19th-century artists, such as Manet, Renoir and Degas.

Musée d'Orsay Collections

 The Impressionists
One of the best Impressionist collections in the world. Admirers of Manet, Monet and Renoir will not be disappointed.

 The Post-Impressionists
The artists who moved on to a newer interpretation of Impressionism are equally well represented, including Matisse, Toulouse-Lautrec and the towering figure of Van Gogh.

3 School of Pont-Aven
Paul Gauguin was at the centre of the group of artists associated with Pont-Aven in Brittany. His work here includes the carved door panels known as the *House of Pleasure* (1901).

 Art Nouveau
Art Nouveau is synonymous with Paris, with many metro stations retaining entrances built in that style. Pendants and glassware by René Lalique (1860–1945) are among the examples on display here.

5 Symbolism
This vast collection includes works by Gustav Klimt (1862–1918) and Edvard Munch (1863–1944), and

Gallery Floorplan

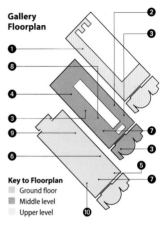

Key to Floorplan
▢ Ground floor
▢ Middle level
▢ Upper level

James Whistler's (1834–1903) portrait of his mother, dating from 1871.

 Romanticism
The Romantics wanted to heighten awareness of the spiritual world. One striking example is *The Tiger Hunt* (1854) by Eugène Delacroix (1798–1863).

7 Sculpture
The collection includes pieces by Auguste Rodin (1840–1917) and satirical carvings of politicians by Honoré Daumier (1808–79).

8 Naturalism
Naturalist painters intensified nature in their work. *Haymaking* (1877) by Jules Bastien-Lepage (1848–84) is a fine example.

9 Nabis
The Nabis Movement made art into a more decorative form. Pierre Bonnard (1867–1947) is one of its founding members.

10 Architecture
In the 19th century, architects were fascinated by the Roman water supply systems. This collection features architectural etchings and drawings – several on Paris.

Blue Dancers (1890), Edgar Degas

THE IMPRESSIONIST MOVEMENT

Regarded as the starting point of modern art, the Impressionist Movement is the best-known and best-loved art movement in the world – certainly if the crowds in the Musée d'Orsay are anything to go by. It began in France, and almost all its leading figures were French. Impressionism was a reaction against the formality and Classicism insisted upon by the Académie des Beaux-Arts in Paris, which was very much the art establishment, deciding what would or would not be exhibited at the Paris Salon. The term "impressionism" was coined by a critic of the style, who dismissed the 1872 Monet painting *Impression: Sunrise*,

now on display at the Musée Marmottan. The artists them- selves then adopted the term. The style influenced Van Gogh and was to have a lasting influence on 19th- and 20th-century art.

Cathedral at Rouen (1892–3), Claude Monet

TOP 10 IMPRESSIONISTS

1 Claude Monet (1840–1926)

2 Edouard Manet (1832–83)

3 Pierre-Auguste Renoir (1841–1919)

4 Edgar Degas (1834–1917)

5 Camille Pissarro (1830–1903)

6 Alfred Sisley (1839–99)

7 James Whistler (1834–1903)

8 Walter Sickert (1860–1942)

9 Mary Cassatt (1844–1926)

10 Berthe Morisot (1841–95)

On the Beach (1873), Edouard Manet

𝗧𝗢𝗣 𝟭𝟬 ⭐ Notre-Dame

The "heart" of the country, both geographically and spiritually, the Cathedral of Notre-Dame (Our Lady) stands on the Ile de la Cité. After Pope Alexander III laid the foundation stone in 1163, an army of craftsmen toiled for 170 years to realize Bishop Maurice de Sully's magnificent design. Almost destroyed during the Revolution, the Gothic masterpiece was restored in 1841–64 by architect Viollet-le-Duc. A devastating fire in 2019 toppled the cathedral's famous 96-m (315-ft) spire and caused part of the roof to cave in.

Notre-Dame

1 Flying Buttresses

The striking flying buttresses supporting the cathedral's east façade are by Jean Ravy. The best view is from Square Jean XXIII.

2 The Towers

The huge towers are 69 m (226 ft) high; 387 stairs within the north tower lead to great views. In 2013, new bells rang here to celebrate the cathedral's 850th birthday.

3 West Front

The glorious entrance to the cathedral **(above)** is through three elaborately carved portals. Biblical scenes, sculpted in the Middle Ages, depict the Life of the Virgin, the Last Judgment and the Life of St Anne. Above is the Gallery of Kings of Judaea and Israel.

4 Portal of the Virgin

The splendid stone tympanum **(right)** was carved in the 13th century and shows the Virgin Mary's death and coronation in heaven. However, the statue of the Virgin and Child that stands between the doors is a modern replica.

5 Galerie des Chimères

Lurking between the towers are the famous gargoyles *(chimères)* **(above)**, placed here to ward off evil.

6 Rose Windows

Three great rose windows adorn the north, south and west façades, but only the north window (left) retains its 13th-century stained glass, depicting the Virgin surrounded by figures from the Old Testament. The south window shows Christ encircled by the Apostles.

7 The Spire

The 19th-century spire was added by Viollet-le-Duc. Completely destroyed by fire in 2019, plans to build a new one are underway.

8 Statue of the Virgin and Child

Also known as Notre-Dame de Paris (Our Lady of Paris), this 14th-century statue was brought to the cathedral from the chapel of St Aignan. It stands against the southeast pillar of the transept, at the entrance to the chancel.

Cathedral Floorplan

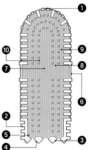

9 Treasury

Reliquaries, ancient manuscripts, and religious garments were housed in the sacristy. The Crown of Thorns, once on public view, was saved from the inferno.

10 Choirstalls

More than half of the original stalls commissioned by Louis XIV survive. Among the beautifully carved work on the 78 stalls are scenes from the Life of the Virgin.

NEED TO KNOW

MAP N4 ■ 6 Parvis Notre-Dame – Place Jean-Paul II, 75004 ■ 01 53 10 07 00 (towers); 01 42 34 56 10 (cathedral) ■ www.notredamedeparis.fr

The cathedral is currently closed to the public due to ongoing restoration work.

The Fire of Notre-Dame
On 15 April 2019 fire broke out near the cathedral's spire during renovation work. Watched by hundreds of onlookers, the fire quickly spread to the east and west along the roof, which was partially covered in scaffolding at the time. As the flames reached the Gothic towers, the spire collapsed and crashed through the vaulted roof. It took 500 firefighters more than 12 hours to extinguish the inferno. It is thought the cathedral was 30 minutes away from being all but destroyed had the fire engulfed the bell towers, causing them to fall. Many of the priceless treasures and artworks were rescued from the blaze and the 16 copper roof statues had already been removed due to the refurbishment. The vaulted stone ceiling and the cathedral's rose windows mostly survived. Within hours of the fire, donations from global corporations and business tycoons poured in to help fund the painstaking restoration and it is hoped Notre-Dame will be rebuilt within five years.

Famous Visitors to Notre-Dame

 Joan of Arc
The patriot Jeanne d'Arc (1412–31), who defended France against the invading English, had a posthumous trial here in 1455, despite having been burned at the stake 24 years earlier. She was found to be innocent of heresy.

 François II and Mary Stuart
Mary Stuart (Mary Queen of Scots; 1542–87) had been raised in France and married the Dauphin in 1558. He ascended the throne as François II in 1559 and the king and queen were crowned in Notre-Dame.

 Napoleon
The coronation of Napoleon (1769–1821) in Notre-Dame in 1804 saw the eager general seize the crown from Pope Pius VII and crown himself emperor and his wife, Josephine, empress.

Statue of Joan of Arc inside Notre-Dame

 Josephine
Josephine's (1763–1814) reign as Empress of France lasted only five years; Napoleon divorced her in 1809.

Pope Pius VII
In 1809 Pope Pius VII (1742–1823), who oversaw Napoleon's Notre-Dame coronation, was taken captive when the emperor declared the Papal States to be part of France. The pope was imprisoned at Fontainebleau, 50 km (30 miles) south of Paris.

 Philip the Fair
In 1302 the first States General parliament was formally opened at Notre-Dame by Philip IV (1268–1314), otherwise known as Philip the Fair. He greatly increased the governing power of the French royalty.

 Henry VI of England
Henry VI (1421–71) became King of England at the age of one. Like his father, Henry V, he also claimed France and was crowned in Notre-Dame in 1430.

Marguerite of Valois
In August 1572, Marguerite (1553–1589), sister of Charles IX, stood in the Notre-Dame chancel during her marriage to the Protestant Henri of Navarre (1553–1610), while he stood alone by the door.

Henri of Navarre
As a Protestant Huguenot, Henri's marriage to the Catholic Marguerite resulted in uprising and many massacres. In 1589, he became Henri IV, the first Bourbon king of France, and converted to Catholicism, stating that "Paris is well worth a Mass".

Charles de Gaulle
On 26 August 1944, Charles de Gaulle entered Paris and attended a Magnificat service to celebrate the liberation of Paris, despite the fact that hostile snipers were still at large outside the cathedral.

Charles de Gaulle visits Notre-Dame

SAVING NOTRE-DAME

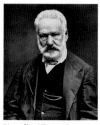

Novelist Victor Hugo

Paris's great cathedral has had a history of deterioration and restoration. When Victor Hugo's novel *Notre-Dame de Paris (The Hunchback of Notre-Dame)* was published in 1831, the cathedral was in a state of decay. Even for the crowning of Napoleon in 1804, the crumbling setting had to be disguised with ornamentation. During the Revolution, the cathedral was sold to a scrap dealer, though fortunately not demolished. Hugo was intent on saving France's spiritual heart and helped mount a campaign to restore Notre-Dame before it was too late; Eugène Emmanuel Viollet-le-Duc (1814–79) was the chosen architect. Repairs began again in 2019 before the cathedral was damaged by fire. Within 24 hours of the blaze, President Macron vowed to rebuild Notre-Dame and more than €800m was raised. At the same time, sales of Hugo's iconic novel rocketed, prompting French booksellers to ask for profits from renewed sales to be directed towards the restoration.

TOP 10
EVENTS IN NOTRE-DAME HISTORY

1 Construction of the cathedral begins (1163)

2 St Louis places the Crown of Thorns here temporarily (1239)

3 Construction is completed (1334)

4 Retrial of Joan of Arc (1455)

5 Revolutionaries loot the cathedral and make it a Temple of Reason (1789)

6 Crowning of Emperor Napoleon (1804)

7 Restoration work is completed (1864)

8 Mass for the Liberation of Paris (1944)

9 New bells with a medieval tone mark the 850th anniversary (2013)

10 Fire destroys the spire and roof (2019)

The Hunchback of Notre-Dame, Hugo's 1831 novel, tells the story of Quasimodo, a hunchbacked bell-ringer at Notre-Dame, who falls in love with gypsy girl Esmeralda.

TOP 10 ⭐ Eiffel Tower

The most distinctive symbol of Paris, the Eiffel Tower was much maligned by critics when it appeared on the city's skyline in 1889 as part of the Universal Exhibition, but its graceful symmetry soon made it the star attraction. A feat of engineering, at 324 m (1,062 ft) high, it was the world's tallest building until it was surpassed by New York's Chrysler Building in 1930. Despite its delicate appearance, the tower weighs 10,100 metric tons and French engineer Gustave Eiffel's construction was so sound that it never sways more than 9 cm (3.5 in) in strong winds.

Eiffel Tower

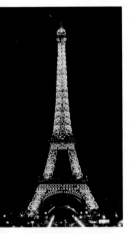

① Lighting
Some 20,000 bulbs and 336 lamps make the Eiffel Tower **(left)** a spectacular night-time sight. It sparkles like a giant Christmas tree for five minutes every hour from dusk until 1am.

② View from the Trocadéro
Day or night, the best approach for a first-time view of the tower is from the Trocadéro, which affords a monumental vista from the Chaillot terrace across the Seine.

③ Gustave Eiffel's Office
Located at the top of the tower is Gustave Eiffel's office, which has been restored to its original condition. It displays wax models of Thomas Edison and Eiffel himself.

④ First Level
You can walk the 345 steps up to the 57-m- (187-ft-) high first level and enjoy a meal at 58 Tour Eiffel. Renovated in 2014, this level includes glass floors and educational displays.

⑤ Viewing Gallery
At 276 m (906 ft), the stupendous view **(right)** from here stretches for 80 km (50 miles) on a clear day. You can also see Gustave Eiffel's sitting room on this level.

7 Champ-de-Mars

The long gardens of this former parade ground stretch from the base of the tower to the École Militaire (military school).

8 Ironwork

The complex pattern of the girders (above), held together by 2.5 million rivets, stabilizes the tower in high winds. The metal can expand up to 15 cm (6 in) on hot days.

9 Bust of Gustave Eiffel

This bust of the tower's creator, by Antoine Bourdelle, was placed below his remarkable achievement, by the north pillar, in 1929.

10 Hydraulic Lift Mechanism

The 1899 lift mechanism is still in operation and travels some 103,000 km (64,000 miles) a year. The uniformed guard clinging to the outside is a model.

6 Second Level

At 115 m (377 ft) high, this level is the location of Le Jules Verne restaurant (below), one of the finest in Paris for food and views. It is reached by a private lift in the south pillar.

THE LIFE OF GUSTAVE EIFFEL

Born in Dijon, Gustave Eiffel (1832–1923) was an engineer and builder who made his name building bridges and viaducts, and helped in the design of the Statue of Liberty. Eiffel was famous for the graceful designs and master craftsmanship of his many wrought-iron constructions. He once said that his famous tower was "formed by the wind itself". In 1890 he became immersed in the study of aerodynamics, and kept an office in the tower until his death, using it for experiments. In 1889, when the Eiffel Tower was erected, its creator was awarded the Légion d'Honneur.

NEED TO KNOW

MAP A4 ■ Champ de Mars, 75007 ■ 08 92 70 12 39 ■ www.tour eiffel.paris

Open Lift 9:30am–11:45pm daily; last adm for top 10:30pm (mid-Jun–1 Sep: 9am–12:45am; last adm 11pm); Stairs 9:30am–6:30pm daily; last adm 6pm (mid-Jun–early Sep: 9:30am–12:45am; last adm midnight)

Adm €10–€25 (stairs & lifts only); €5–€12.50 for under-18s; check website for various combos

■ There are restaurants and snack bars on levels 1 and 2, along with a Champagne bar on level 3.

■ Skip the queue and book the ticket online or opt for a tour (cultival.fr).

TOP 10 ⭐ Sacré-Coeur

One of the city's most photographed sights, the spectacular white basilica of Sacré-Coeur (Sacred Heart) watches over Paris from its highest point. The basilica was built as a memorial to the 58,000 French soldiers killed during the Franco-Prussian War (1870–71). It took 46 years to build and was finally completed in 1923 at a cost of 40 million francs (6 million euros). Priests still pray for the souls of the dead here, 24 hours a day, as they have since 1885. People flock here for the breathtaking panoramic views – at sunset, in particular, there are few sights in Paris more memorable.

1 Great Mosaic of Christ

A glittering Byzantine mosaic of Christ, created by Luc Olivier Merson between 1912 and 1922, decorates the vault over the chancel. It represents France's devotion to the Sacred Heart.

2 Crypt Vaults

The arched vaults of the crypt (above) house a chapel that contains the heart of Alexandre Legentil, one of the advocates of Sacré-Coeur.

3 Bronze Doors

The doors of the portico entrance are beautifully decorated with bronze relief sculptures depicting the Last Supper and other scenes from the Life of Christ.

4 The Dome

The distinctive egg-shaped dome of the basilica is the second-highest viewpoint in Paris after the Eiffel Tower. Reached via a spiral staircase, vistas from here can stretch as far as 48 km (30 miles) on a clear day.

5 Statue of Christ

The basilica's most important statue shows Christ giving a blessing. It is symbolically placed in a niche over the main entrance, above the two bronze equestrian statues.

6 Stained-Glass Gallery

One level of the great dome is encircled by stained-glass windows **(right)**. From here there is a beautiful view over the whole interior.

7 Bell Tower

The campanile, designed by Lucien Magne and added in 1904, is 80 m (262 ft) high. One of the heaviest bells in the world, the 19-ton La Savoyarde hangs in the belfry. Cast in Annecy in 1895, it was donated by the dioceses of Savoy.

8 Façade

Architect Paul Abadie (1812–1884) employed a mix of domes, turrets and Classical features in his design. The Château-Landon stone secretes calcite when wet and so keeps the façade bleached white **(left)**.

THE FRANCO-PRUSSIAN WAR

In 1870, as Prussia made moves to take over the rest of Germany, France was also threatened by its military power. Two Catholic businessmen in Paris made a vow to build a church dedicated to the Sacred Heart if France were spared the Prussian onslaught. France declared war on Prussia in July, but the country was ill-prepared and in September Napoleon III was captured. Parisians held fast – defending their city with homemade weapons and eating dogs, cats and rats. But by January 1871 they surrendered.

9 Equestrian Statues

Two striking bronze statues of French saints stand on the portico above the main entrance, cast in 1927 by Hippolyte Lefèbvre. One is of Joan of Arc, the other is of Louis IX, later canonized as St Louis.

10 The Funicular

To avoid the steep climb up to Sacré-Coeur, take the *funiculaire* cable railway **(below)** and enjoy the views at leisure. It runs from the end of rue Foyatier, near Square Willette.

NEED TO KNOW

MAP E1 ■ Parvis de la Basilique du Sacré-Coeur, 75018 ■ 01 53 41 89 00 ■ www.sacre-coeur-montmartre.com

Basilica: 6am–10:30pm daily, last entry 10:15pm

Dome: May–Sep: 8:30am–8pm; Oct–Apr: 9am–5pm; adm €8

■ Avoid the lunch crowds by heading to 23 Rue des Abbesses and grab a bite at Le St-Jean.

■ An evocative sung Mass takes place on Sundays at 11am.

🔟 ⭐ Arc de Triomphe

The best day to visit the world's most familiar triumphal arch is 2 December, the date that marks Napoleon's victory at the Battle of Austerlitz in 1805. Work began on the 50-m (164-ft) arch in 1806 but was not completed until 1836, due, in part, to Napoleon's fall from power. Four years later, Napoleon's funeral procession passed beneath it, on its way to his burial in Hôtel des Invalides (see pp38–9). Traffic is banned along the Champs-Elysées on the first Sunday of the month, making it easier to access and get that perfect photo of the Arc de Triomphe.

① Museum
Within the arch is a small but interesting museum which tells the history of its construction and gives details of various celebrations and funerals that the arch has seen over the years. The more recent of these are shown in a short video.

② Departure of the Volunteers in 1792
One of the most striking sculptures is on the front right base. It shows French citizens leaving to defend their nation against Austria and Prussia.

③ Triumph of Napoleon
As you look at the arch from the Avenue des Champs-Elysées, J P Cortot's high-relief on the left base shows the restored *Triumph of Napoleon*. It celebrates the Treaty of Vienna peace agreement signed in 1810, when Napoleon's empire was in its heyday.

④ Tomb of the Unknown Soldier
In the centre of the arch flickers the eternal flame on the Tomb of the Unknown Soldier (left), a victim of World War I buried on 11 November 1920. It is symbolically reignited every day at 6:30pm.

⑤ Viewing Platform
Take the lift or climb 284 steps to the top of the Arc de Triomphe to get a sublime view (below) of Paris and a sense of the arch's dominant position in the centre of the Place de l'Etoile. To the east is the Champs-Elysées and to the west is the Grande Arche de La Défense. There are another 40 steps after the lift.

Arc de Triomphe

7 Battle of Austerlitz
Another battle victory is shown on a frieze on the arch's north side. It depicts Napoleon's heavily outnumbered troops breaking the ice on Lake Satschan in Austria, a tactic which drowned thousands of enemy troops.

6 Battle of Aboukir
Above the *Triumph of Napoleon* carving is a scene **(above)** showing Napoleonic victory over the Turks in 1799. The same victory was commemorated on canvas in 1806 by the French painter Antoine Gros and is now on display at the Palace of Versailles *(Place d'Armes)*.

8 Frieze
A frieze running around the arch shows French troops departing for battle (east) and their victorious return (west).

THE GREAT AXIS

The Arc de Triomphe is the central of three arches; together they create a grand vision of which even Napoleon would have been proud. He was responsible for the first two, placing the Arc de Triomphe directly in line with the Arc de Triomphe du Carrousel in front of the Louvre *(see pp14–17)*, which also celebrates the victory at Austerlitz. In 1989, the trio was completed with the Grande Arche de La Défense. The 8km-long (5-mile) *Grand Axe* (Great Axis) runs from here to the Louvre's Pyramid.

9 General Marceau's Funeral
Marceau died in battle against the Austrian army in 1796, after a famous victory against them the previous year. His funeral is depicted in a frieze located above the *Departure of the Volunteers in 1792*.

10 Thirty Shields
Immediately below the top of the arch runs a row of 30 shields, each carrying the name of a Napoleonic victory.

NEED TO KNOW

MAP A2 ■ Place Charles-de-Gaulle, 75008 ■ 01 55 37 73 77 (enquiries) ■ www.paris-arc-de-triomphe.fr/en

Open Apr–Sep: 10am–11pm daily (to 10:30pm Oct–Mar; last adm 45 mins before closing); closed 1 Jan, 1 May, 8 May (am), 14 Jul (am), 11 Nov (am), 25 Dec and events

Adm €12; concession €9 (under-18s and EU 18–25s free)

■ Arrive early to see the golden tone of the stonework at its best.

■ Enjoy the old-world charm of Le Fouquet (99 Ave des Champs-Elysées). Expensive, but worth it.

■ Arch access is via the underground tunnel only.

★ Centre Georges Pompidou

Today it's one of the world's most famous pieces of modern architecture. However, when the Pompidou Centre opened in 1977, architects Richard Rogers and Renzo Piano startled everyone by turning the building "inside out", with brightly coloured pipes displayed on the façade. Designed as a cross-cultural arts complex, it houses the excellent Musée National d'Art Moderne (Modern Art Museum), as well as a cinema, library, shops and performance space. The outside forecourt is a popular gathering spot for tourists and locals alike.

1 Escalator
One of the building's most striking and popular features is the external escalator **(right)**, which climbs, snake-like, up the front of the Centre in its plexiglass tube. The view gets better and better as you rise high above the activity in the Centre's forecourt, before arriving at the top for the best view of all.

4 Bookshop
The ground-floor bookshop sells a range of postcards, posters of major works in the Modern Art Museum and books on artists associated with Paris.

2 Pipes
Part of the shock factor of the Pompidou Centre is that the utility pipes are outside the building **(above)**. Not only that, they are vividly coloured: bright green for water, yellow for electricity and blue for air conditioning.

3 Top-Floor View
The view from the top of the Pompidou Centre is spectacular. The Eiffel Tower is visible, as is Montmartre in the north and the monolithic Tour Montparnasse to the south. On clear days views can stretch as far as La Défense.

5 The Piazza
Visitors and locals gather in the open space in front of the Centre to enjoy a variety of street performers and the changing installations of sculptures, which are often related to shows at the Centre.

6 Stravinsky Fountain
This colourful fountain in Place Igor Stravinsky was designed by Niki de Saint-Phalle and Jean Tinguely as part of the Pompidou Centre development. Inspired by composer Stravinsky's ballet *The Firebird* (1910), the bird spins and sprays water.

8 Avec l'arc noir (With a Black Arch)

One of the pioneers of Abstract art, artist Vasily Kandinsky (1866–1944) promoted the use of non-naturalist geometric forms. His *Avec l'arc noir* (1912) features a black line that recalls the *douga* (wooden arch) of a Russian *troika* (carriage).

7 Man with a Guitar

Within the Modern Art Museum, this 1914 work **(above)** by artist Georges Braque (1882–1963) is one of the most striking of the Cubist Movement.

9 Brancusi's Studio

The Romanian sculptor Constantin Brancusi (1876–1957) left his entire studio to the state. It has been reconstructed **(left)** in the Piazza, and displays his abstract works.

NEED TO KNOW

MAP E4 ■ Pl Georges Pompidou 75004 ■ 01 44 78 12 33 ■ www. centrepompidou.fr

Museum: 11am–9pm Wed–Mon (11pm Thu); closed 1 May; adm €11–14; free 1st Sun of the month, under-18s free, under-26s free (EU only)

Brancusi's Studio: 2–6pm Wed–Mon

■ The centre's café is pleasant and has free Wi-Fi access. For something grander, head to Georges, the rooftop brasserie.

■ Buy tickets online to avoid the queues.

Centre Guide

The Centre is home to various institutions. The Museum of Modern Art (Mnam) is on levels 4 and 5; the cinema is on level 1. Check at the information desk or on the website for details about the temporary shows (level 6), rehangs of works and the contemporary art "happenings". Displays at the Mnam often change and some works are now shared with its sister institution in Metz.

10 Compositie n°3

Together with Piet Mondrian, Dutch painter Bart van der Leck (1876–1958) founded the De Stijl style, an abstract approach in which colours are limited and forms created with horizontal and vertical lines. The figurative basis for his work *Compositie n°3* is believed to have been harvesters.

TOP10 ⭐ The Panthéon

Paris's Panthéon is a fitting final resting place for the nation's great figures. Originally built as a church at the behest of Louis XV, it was completed in 1790 and was intended to look like the Pantheon in Rome, but more closely resembles St Paul's Cathedral in London. During the Revolution it was used as a mausoleum. Napoleon returned it to the Church in 1806 and it became a public building in 1885.

① Crypt
The crypt **(above)** is eerily impressive in its scale, compared to most tiny, dark church crypts. Here lie the tombs and memorials of worthy French citizens, including the prolific French writer Emile Zola.

② Frescoes of Sainte Geneviève
Delicate murals by 19th-century artist Pierre Puvis de Chavannes, on the south wall of the nave, tell the story of Sainte Geneviève, the patron saint of Paris. She is believed to have saved the city from invasion in 451 by Attila the Hun and his hordes through the power of her prayers.

③ Façade
The Panthéon's façade **(right)** was inspired by Roman architecture. The 22 Corinthian columns support both the portico roof and bas-reliefs.

④ Dome
Inspired by Sir Christopher Wren's design for St Paul's Cathedral in London, as well as by the Dôme Church at Hôtel des Invalides (*see p38*), this iron-framed dome **(right)** is made up of three layers. At the top, a narrow opening lets in only a tiny amount of natural light, in keeping with the building's sombre purpose.

⑤ Dome Galleries
A staircase leads to the galleries immediately below the dome itself, affording spectacular 360-degree views of Paris. The pillars surrounding the galleries are both decorative and functional, providing essential support for the dome.

⑥ Monument to Diderot
French philosopher Denis Diderot (1713–84) is honoured by this grand 1925 monument by Alphonse Terroir.

7 Foucault's Pendulum

In 1851 French physicist Jean Foucault (1819–68) followed up an earlier experiment to prove the earth's rotation by hanging his famous pendulum from the dome of the Panthéon. The plane of the pendulum's swing rotated 11 degrees clockwise each hour in relation to the floor, thereby proving Foucault's theory.

LOUIS BRAILLE

One of the most influential citizens buried in the Panthéon is Louis Braille (1809–52). Braille became blind at the age of three. He attended the National Institute for the Young Blind and was a gifted student. He continued at the Institute as a teacher and, in 1829, had the idea of adapting a coding system in use by the army, by turning words and letters into raised dots on card. Reading Braille has transformed the lives of blind people ever since.

Panthéon Floorplan

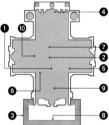

NEED TO KNOW

MAP E5 ■ Place du Panthéon, 75005 ■ 01 44 32 18 00 ■ www. paris-pantheon.fr/en

Open Apr–Sep: 10am–6:30pm daily; Oct–Mar: 10am–6pm daily; closed 1 Jan, 1 May, 25 Dec

Adm €9, concession €7 (under-18s & EU under-26s free)

■ La Crêperie (12 Rue Soufflot, open 7am–midnight, from 8am Sun) is an ideal pit stop for a crêpe or coffee.

■ Keep in mind that ticket sales stop 45 minutes before closing time, so be sure to arrive in plenty of time.

8 Pediment Relief

The bas-relief above the entrance shows a female figure, representing France, handing out laurels to the great men of the nation – the same way that Greeks and Romans honoured their heroes.

9 Tomb of Voltaire

A statue **(left)** of the great writer, wit and philosopher Voltaire (1694–1788) stands in front of his tomb.

10 Tomb of Victor Hugo

The body of the French author *(see p25)* was carried to the Panthéon in a pauper's hearse, at his own request.

TOP10 ★ Sainte-Chapelle

This Gothic masterpiece is considered the most beautiful church in Paris, not least for its 15 stained-glass windows soaring 15 m (50 ft) to a star-covered vaulted ceiling. It was built by Louis IX (1214–70) as a shrine for his holy relics of the Passion and completed in 1248. The church was damaged during the 1789 Revolution but restored in the mid-19th century.

1 Window of Christ's Passion
Located above the apse, this stained-glass depiction of the Crucifixion is the most beautiful window in the chapel.

2 Lower Chapel
Intended for use by the king's servants, and dedicated to the Virgin Mary, this chapel **(below)** is not as light and lofty as the Upper Chapel but is still a magnificent sight.

5 Upper Chapel Entrance
As you emerge, via a spiral staircase, into this airy space **(right)**, the effect of light and colour is utterly breath-taking. The 13th-century stained-glass windows, the oldest surviving in Paris, separated by stone columns, depict biblical scenes from Genesis right through to the Crucifixion. To "read" the windows, start in the lower left panel and follow each row left to right, from bottom to top.

6 The Spire
The open latticework and pencil-thin shape give the *flèche* (spire) a very delicate appearance. In fact, three earlier church spires burned down – this one was erected in 1853 and rises 75 m (245 ft) into the air.

3 Main Portal
Like the Upper Chapel, the main portal has two tiers. Its pinnacles are decorated with a crown of thorns as a symbol of the relics within.

4 Rose Window
The flamboyant rose window **(right)**, depicting St John's vision of the Apocalypse in 86 panels, was a gift from Charles VIII in 1485. The green and yellow hues are brightest at sunset.

7 St Louis' Oratory
In the late 14th century Louis XI added an oratory where he could watch Mass through a small grille in the wall. The chapel originally adjoined the Conciergerie, the former royal palace on the Ile de la Cité.

9 Seats of the Royal Family
During Mass, the royal family sat in niches located in the fourth bays on both sides of the chapel, away from the congregation.

RELICS OF THE PASSION

Louis IX, later St Louis, was the only French king to be canonized. While on his first Crusade in 1239, he purchased the alleged Crown of Thorns from the Emperor of Constantinople, and subsequently other relics, including pieces of the True Cross, nails from the Crucifixion and a few drops of Christ's blood, paying almost three times more for them than for the construction of Sainte-Chapelle itself. The relics resided in Notre-Dame and were rescued from the destructive fire in 2019.

8 Evening Concerts
Sainte-Chapelle has excellent acoustics. From March until November, classical concerts are held here several evenings a week.

10 Apostle Statues
Beautifully carved medieval statues of the 12 Apostles stand on pillars along the walls. Badly damaged in the Revolution, most have been restored: the bearded apostle **(right)**, fifth on the left, is the only original statue.

NEED TO KNOW

MAP E4 ■ 6 Blvd du Palais, 75001 ■ 01 53 40 60 97 ■ www.sainte-chapelle.fr/en

Open Apr–Sep: 9am–7pm; Oct–Mar: 9am–5pm (Opening hours can vary, check website for details)

Adm €10, concession €8; under-18s and 18–25s (EU only) free. Audio guides €3. Joint adm to Conciergerie (2 Boulevard du Palais) €15, concession €12; temp exhibits €1.50 extra; ticket sales stop 30 mins before closing.

■ To experience a little 1920s-style elegance,

try Brasserie des Deux Palais on the corner of Boulevard du Palais and Rue de Lutèce.

■ A pair of binoculars comes in handy if you want to catch a glimpse of the church's uppermost glass panels.

🔟 ⭐ Hôtel des Invalides

The *invalides* for whom this imposing Hôtel was built were wounded soldiers of the late 17th century. Louis XIV had the building constructed between 1671 and 1678, and veterans are still housed here, although only a dozen or so compared to the original 4,000. They share their home with arguably the greatest French soldier of them all, Napoleon Bonaparte, whose body rests in a crypt directly below the golden dome of the Dôme Church. Other buildings accommodate military offices, the Musée de l'Armée and smaller military museums.

1 Invalides Gardens

The approach to the Hôtel is across public gardens and then through a gate into the Invalides Gardens themselves. Designed in 1704, their paths are lined by 17th- and 18th-century cannons.

3 Golden Dome

The second church at the Hôtel was begun in 1677 and took 27 years to build. Its magnificent dome stands 107 m (351 ft) high and glistens as much now as it did when Louis XIV, the Sun King, had it first gilded in 1715.

4 Musée de l'Armée

The Army Museum *(129 Rue de Grenelle)* is one of the largest collections of militaria in the world **(left)**. Enthusiasts will be absorbed for hours, and even the casual visitor will enjoy the exhibits. The Département Moderne, which traces military history from Louis XIV to Napoleon III, is also worth a visit.

Dôme Church Ceiling 2

The colourful, circular painting on the interior of the dome **(right)** above the crypt is *Saint Louis in Glory*, painted in 1692 by the French artist Charles de la Fosse. Near the centre is St Louis, who represents Louis XIV, presenting his sword to Christ in the presence of the Virgin Mary and angels.

7 Napoleon's Tomb

Napoleon's body was brought here from St Helena in 1840, some 19 years after he died. He rests in grandeur in a cocoon of six coffins **(left)**, almost "on the banks of the Seine" as was his last wish.

Hôtel des Invalides Floorplan

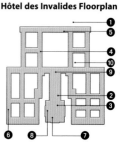

5 Hôtel des Invalides

One of the loveliest sights in Paris, the Classical façade of the Hôtel **(below)** is four floors high and 196 m (645 ft) end to end. Features include the dormer windows with their variously shaped shield surrounds.

8 Church Tombs

Encircling the Dôme Church are the imposing tombs of great French military men, such as Marshal Foch and Marshal Vauban, who revolutionized military fortifications and siege tactics.

9 St-Louis-des-Invalides

Adjoining the Dôme Church is the Invalides complex's original church, worth seeing for its 17th-century organ, on which the first performance of Berlioz's *Requiem* was given.

10 Musée des Plans-Reliefs

Maps and models of French forts and fortified towns are displayed here. Some of them are beautifully detailed, such as the oldest model on display, of Perpignan, dating from 1686.

6 Musée de l'Ordre de la Libération

The Order of Liberation, France's highest military honour, was created by Général de Gaulle in 1940 to acknowledge contributions during World War II. The museum details the history of the honour and the wartime Free French movement.

NEED TO KNOW

MAP B4–C4 ■ 129 Rue de Grenelle, 75007 or Place Vauban, 75007
■ 08 10 11 33 99
■ www.invalides.org

Open Apr–Oct: 10am–6pm daily (Nov–Mar: 10am–5pm); closed first Mon of the month (except Jul–Sep), 1 Jan, 1 May, 1 Nov, 25 Dec

Adm €12 adults; €10 concessions; under-18s free; under-26s (EU only) free

■ Le Café du Musée, between the Varenne metro station and the Musée Rodin (77 Rue de Varenne), is known for its various cocktails. It is a lovely spot for a drink.

Hôtel Guide

Approach from the Seine for the best view, and then walk around to the ticket office on the south side. You will need a ticket for the museums and to see Napoleon's Tomb. If time is short, concentrate on the Musée de l'Armée, before walking through to the cobbled courtyard in front of the Dôme Church.

Top 10 Restaurants

1 **Café de la Paix**
Historic café

2 **Carette**
French staples

3 **Le Jules Verne**
Located in the Eiffel Tower

4 **Taverne Henri IV**
Simple plates

5 **Les Ombres**
Fine dining

6 **Café Constant**
Modern French fare

7 **Le Hangar**
Friendly bistro

8 **Au Moulin à Vent**
Classic French cuisine

9 **Marché des Enfants Rouges**
Food market

10 **Les Deux Magots**
Iconic Parisian café

0 metres   1000
0 yards   1000

Top 10 London

The Great Court,
British Museum

Exploring London

For things to see and do, visitors to London are spoiled for choice. Whether you're here for a short stay or you just want a flavour of this great city, you need to make the most of your time. Here are some ideas for two and four days of sightseeing in London.

Shakespeare's Globe is a replica of the original Globe Theatre.

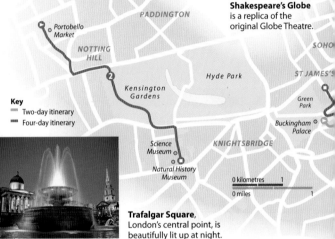

PADDINGTON

Portobello Market

NOTTING HILL

SOHO

Kensington Gardens

Hyde Park

ST JAMES'S

Green Park

Buckingham Palace

Key
— Two-day itinerary
--- Four-day itinerary

Science Museum

Natural History Museum

KNIGHTSBRIDGE

0 kilometres   1
0 miles   1

Trafalgar Square, London's central point, is beautifully lit up at night.

Two Days in London

Day ❶
MORNING
Take a Beefeater tour of the **Tower of London** *(see pp72–5)*, then visit St Paul's Cathedral *(see pp76–9)*.
AFTERNOON
Cross Millennium Bridge, for a panorama of the River Thames. Explore **Tate Modern** *(see pp64–5)* then catch a play at Shakespeare's Globe *(21 New Globe Walk)*.

Day ❷
MORNING
Begin at **Buckingham Palace** *(see pp60–61)* and, if it's August or September, tour the State Rooms. Afterwards, head to **Westminster Abbey** *(see pp68–9)* to see the monuments of English monarchs.

AFTERNOON
After lunch, spend 2 hours at the **National Gallery** *(see pp52–3)* in Trafalgar Square. Then take a "flight" on the **London Eye** *(see pp62–3)*.

Four Days in London

Day ❶
MORNING
Start with a full morning exploring the **Tower of London** *(see pp72–5)*, then cross imposing Tower Bridge and stroll along the river past HMS *Belfast (The Queen's Walk)*.
AFTERNOON
Take lunch at Borough Market *(8 Southwark St)*, just around the corner from the towering **Shard** *(see p63)*. Roam **Tate Modern** *(see pp64–5)* then catch a play at Shakespeare's Globe *(21 New Globe Walk)*.

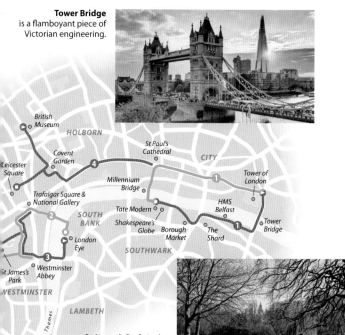

Tower Bridge is a flamboyant piece of Victorian engineering.

St James's Park, in the heart of London, is popular for its well-groomed flower beds and great views.

Day ❷

MORNING
Begin in Notting Hill, with a morning turn around Portobello Road market. Walk south from there through the stately expanse of Kensington Gardens.

AFTERNOON
Exit the park into South Kensington's museum quarter, for an afternoon exploring the **Science Museum** (see pp58–9) and the **Natural History Museum** (see pp56–7).

Day ❸

MORNING
Choose between the **London Eye** (see pp62–3) or **Westminster Abbey** (see pp68–9). Not far away is Trafalgar Square, where you can admire Nelson's Column before taking in the old masters at the **National Gallery** (see pp52–3).

AFTERNOON
Meander through St James's Park before enjoying afternoon tea at St James' Café. Peek through the gates at **Buckingham Palace** (see pp60–61), then hit swish St James's for dinner and cocktails.

Day ❹

MORNING
Start at the **British Museum** (see pp48–51), a two-million-year trove of human endeavour, then head down to Covent Garden for a leisurely stroll around the Apple Market and to marvel at the performances of the street acrobats.

AFTERNOON
St Paul's Cathedral (see pp76–9) is a short way by Tube. In the evening, return west to Leicester Square, where the bright lights of London's Theatreland await.

TOP 10 London Highlights

A city of infinite colour and variety, London is both richly historic, tracing its roots back over 2,000 years, and unceasingly modern, at the forefront of fashion, music and the arts. A selection of the best London has to offer is explored in the following chapter.

1 British Museum
The oldest national public museum in the world contains a rich collection of treasure and artifacts *(see pp48–51)*.

2 National Gallery and National Portrait Gallery
The nation's most important art collections are held here, including this 1581 miniature of Sir Francis Drake *(see pp52–5)*.

3 Natural History Museum
The enormous and varied collection here explores the history of life on earth *(see pp56–7)*.

4 Science Museum
A huge museum with fascinating interactive exhibits that explain and demonstrate the wonders of science *(see pp58–9)*.

5 Buckingham Palace
The official home of the queen, where the Changing the Guard takes place *(see pp60–61)*.

MARYLEBONE

BAKER STREET

TOTTENHAM COURT RD

OXFORD STREET

CHARING CROSS RD

SOHO

MAYFAIR

REGENT ST

PARK LANE

PICCADILLY CIRCUS

PICCADILLY

TRAFALGAR SQUARE

Hyde Park

Kensington Gardens

Green Park

St James's Park

KNIGHTSBRIDGE

PARLIAMENT SQUARE

KENSINGTON

BROMPTON RD

SLOANE STREET

GROSVENOR PL

WESTMINSTER

KNIGHTSBRIDGE

BUCKINGHAM PALACE ROAD

VAUXHALL BRIDGE RD

KING'S ROAD

CHELSEA

GROSVENOR ROAD

River Thames

6 London Eye
The world's tallest cantilevered observation wheel offers great views of the city *(see pp62–3)*.

7 Tate Modern and Tate Britain
London's two Tate galleries house collections of British and modern international art *(see pp64–7)*.

Westminster Abbey and Parliament Square 8
Since 1066, this royal abbey has hosted the coronations of all Britain's monarchs *(see pp68–71)*.

Tower of London 9
The Tower has been a royal palace, fortress and prison, and is the home of the Crown Jewels *(see pp72–5)*.

10 St Paul's Cathedral
Sir Christopher Wren's Baroque masterpiece still dominates the City skyline *(see pp76–9)*.

FINSBURY
GRAY'S INN RD
CLERKENWELL RD
OLD STREET
ALDERSGATE ST
CITY ROAD
LONDON WALL
BISHOPSGATE
COMMERCIAL ST
HOLBORN
KINGSWAY
FLEET STREET
CHEAPSIDE
CANNON ST
CITY
EASTCHEAP
VICTORIA EMBANKMENT
10
SOUTH BANK
River Thames
9
6
BLACKFRIARS RD
WATERLOO RD
HIGH ST
SOUTHWARK
TOWER BRIDGE RD
LONG LANE
GREAT DOVER ST
BOROUGH
LAMBETH RD
EMBANKMENT
LAMBETH
7

0 kilometres 1
0 miles 1

TOP 10 ⭐ British Museum

The world's oldest national public museum has over 8 million items spanning the history of the world's cultures, from the stone tools of early man to 21st-century artworks. The collection was started with the bequest of physician and antiquarian Sir Hans Sloane in 1753. In the 18th and 19th centuries, travellers and emissaries, such as Captain James Cook, Lord Curzon and Charles Townley, added treasures from around the world. The present building was completed in 1852. The central courtyard is used as a public space.

Parthenon Sculptures ①
This spectacular 5th-century BC frieze from Athens' Parthenon **(right)** was made under Pericles and shows a procession in honour of the goddess Athena. It was obtained in 1801 by Lord Elgin, ambassador of the Ottoman Empire.

② **Mummified Cat**
Cats and sacred cows were mummified in Ancient Egypt. This cat comes from Abydos and dates from the 1st century AD **(left)**. Many Egyptian deities took on animal shapes, as seen on wall paintings and other artifacts.

③ **Ram in a Thicket**
Decorated with shells, gold leaf, copper and lapis lazuli, this priceless ornament comes from Ur in Sumer, one of the world's earliest civilizations. Games and musical instruments are also displayed.

④ **Double-Headed Serpent Mosaic**
Carved in wood and covered with turquoise mosaic, this Aztec ornament was probably worn on the chest on ceremonial occasions.

⑤ **Rosetta Stone**
In 196 BC Egyptian priests wrote a decree about Ptolemy V on this granite tablet in Greek, in demotic and in Egyptian hieroglyphics. Found in 1799, it proved crucial in deciphering Egyptian pictorial writing.

⑥ **Portland Vase**
It is not known where and when this 1st-century blue and opaque glass vase was found. In 1778, it was purchased by Sir William Hamilton, Britain's ambassador to Naples, who sold it to the Duchess of Portland. It had to be reassembled after a visitor smashed it into 200 pieces in 1845.

⑦ **David Vases**
These blue and white porcelain altar vases dating from c. 1351 were made in Jingdezhen, China. They feature elephant handles in addition to various motifs.

8 Mildenhall Treasure

Some of the greatest early English treasures are these silver plates **(left)** from the 4th century, found at Mildenhall in Suffolk. Their decorations include sea nymphs, satyrs and Hercules.

Ramesses II 9

This is all that remains of the colossal granite statue of Egyptian pharaoh Ramesses II (c. 1279 BC) **(right)** from his memorial temple at Thebes. Its arrival in England in the 19th century is said to have inspired the poet Shelley to write the poem *Ozymandias*.

Museum Floorplan

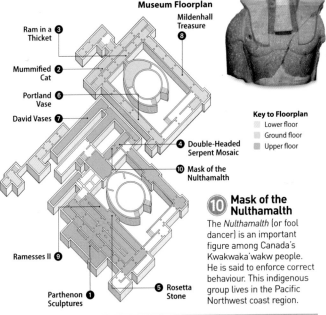

Mildenhall Treasure **8**

Ram in a Thicket **3**

Mummified Cat **2**

Portland Vase **6**

David Vases **7**

4 Double-Headed Serpent Mosaic

10 Mask of the Nulthamalth

Ramesses II **9**

Parthenon Sculptures **1**

5 Rosetta Stone

Key to Floorplan
- Lower floor
- Ground floor
- Upper floor

10 Mask of the Nulthamalth

The *Nulthamalth* (or fool dancer) is an important figure among Canada's Kwakwaka'wakw people. He is said to enforce correct behaviour. This indigenous group lives in the Pacific Northwest coast region.

NEED TO KNOW

MAP C2–C3 ■ Great Russell Street WC1 ■ 020 7323 8000 ■ www.british museum.org

Open 10am–5:30pm Sat–Thu, 10am–8:30pm Fri.

Adm free, except major temporary exhibitions

Free guided tours

Great Court: 10am–5:30pm Sat–Thu, 10am–8:30pm Fri

■ The Great Court's Reading Room is closed to the public.

■ There are two cafés, a pizzeria and the fine-dining Great Court Restaurant.

■ Picnic in the forecourt, by the main entrance.

■ Highlights tours (£14) introduce the collection.

■ The British Museum shop sells reproduction artifacts, books, jewellery and gifts.

Museum Guide

Free maps are available and guides are on sale at the information desks. Otherwise start to the left of the main entrance with the Assyrian, Egyptian, Greek and Roman galleries. The Asian collection provides a change from Classical artifacts, as do the early British, medieval and Renaissance galleries on the east side.

British Museum Collections

 Middle East
Some 6,000 years of history start with the spectacular carved reliefs depicting a variety of scenes from the Assyrian palace of Nineveh.

Ancient Egypt and Sudan
An extraordinary array of mummies and sarcophagi are among thousands of objects in one of the world's greatest collections.

Africa
The museum holds 350,000 objects from indigenous peoples around the world. The Africa gallery has an interesting collection of sculpture, textiles and graphic art.

Asia
Buddhist limestone reliefs, Chinese antiquities, Islamic pottery and a jaw-droppingly large cache of Japanese relics are displayed here.

Greece and Rome
There are several rooms covering the marvels of the Classical world (c.3000 BC to c. AD 400). The sculptures that once decorated the outside of the Parthenon are a particular highlight.

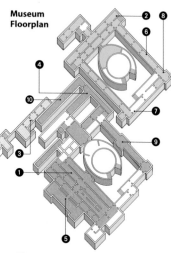
Museum Floorplan

Prehistory and Europe
Covering a long period from prehistoric cave dwellers to the modern day, this collection includes Lindow Man, the body found preserved in a peat bog of a man who died some time between 2 BC and AD 119, and fine decorative arts, including medieval jewellery and Renaissance clocks.

Money
The exhibit traces the history of money over 4,000 years - from shell currency to digital payment methods.

Islamic World
This stunning display of objects ranges from West Africa to Southeast Asia and covers the period from the 7th century to the present.

Enlightenment
This exhibition features the museum's 18th-century collections from around the world.

The Joseph Hotung Great Court Gallery
This small gallery is used for temporary exhibitions.

Ancient Greek vase

THE GREAT COURT

A magnificent glass-roofed addition encloses the heart of the British Museum. Opened in December 2000, the Great Court was designed by architect Sir Norman Foster. In the centre of the Court is the domed Reading Room, built in 1857. It once held one of the world's most important collections of books and manuscripts and was the workplace of some of London's greatest writers. It was used to host exhibitions from 2007 to 2013, after the Reading Room's collection was moved to a purpose-built building in St Pancras. The Great Court is the capital's largest covered square, containing shops, cafés and the British Museum's main ticket and information desk.

The Reading Room was restored to its original design.

The Great Court, at the centre of the museum, has a tesselated roof constructed of 3,312 unique panes of glass. It surrounds the Reading Room.

TOP 10
LIBRARY READERS

1 **Karl Marx**
(1818–83), German revolutionary

2 **Mahatma Gandhi**
(1869–1948), Indian leader

3 **Oscar Wilde**
(1854–1900), playwright and wit

4 **Virginia Woolf**
(1882–1941), Bloomsbury novelist

5 **W B Yeats**
(1865–1939), Irish poet and playwright

6 **Thomas Hardy**
(1840–1928), English novelist

7 **George Bernard Shaw**
(1856–1950), Irish playwright

8 **E M Forster**
(1879–1970), English novelist

9 **Rudyard Kipling**
(1865–1936), Poet, novelist and chronicler of the British Empire

10 **Leon Trotsky**
(1879–1940), Russian revolutionary

⭐ National Gallery

The National Gallery houses one of the world's greatest collections of European paintings. The collection was established in 1824, when a small group of paintings was gifted to the nation, and after rapid expansion it was moved to the present building in Trafalgar Square in 1838. The gallery is now home to over 2,300 paintings dating from the 13th to the 19th centuries. The Sainsbury Wing, built in 1991, showcases the gallery's outstanding collection of early Renaissance paintings and provides space for temporary blockbuster exhibitions.

1 The Virgin of the Rocks

This Renaissance masterpiece by Leonardo da Vinci (1452–1519) was originally painted as an altarpiece for a church in Milan. The Virgin and Child, with St John the Baptist and an angel, are depicted within a strange cavernous landscape.

5 The Rokeby Venus

Painted in Rome to replace a lost Venetian painting, *The Rokeby Venus* **(left)** is the only nude by Diego Velázquez (1599–1660), court painter to Spain's Philip IV. Venus, the goddess of love, is depicted here with her son, Cupid, who holds a mirror up for her to see her reflection and that of the viewer.

2 The Arnolfini Portrait

One of the most famous paintings from the extensive Flemish collection is this unusual portrait of an Italian banker and his wife in Bruges. Jan van Eyck (c.1385–1441) brought oil painting to a new and colourful height.

3 The Ambassadors

Symbols, such as the foreshortened skull foretelling death, abound in this 1533 painting by Hans Holbein (1497–1543).

The Wilton Diptych 4

A highlight of Gothic art, this exquisite English royal painting **(right)**, by an unknown artist, shows Richard II being recommended to the Virgin by saints John the Baptist, Edward and Edmund.

6 A Young Woman Standing at a Virginal

Dutch painter Jan Vermeer's (1632–75) works carry a sense of calm. Many of his interiors were painted in his home.

7 Samson and Delilah

This painting by Peter Paul Rubens (1577–1640) depicts the Old Testament legend and its theme of love and betrayal. Delilah caresses Samson while soldiers wait in the doorway to blind him.

The Sunflowers 8

Vincent Van Gogh (1853–90) painted this work **(right)** in Arles, France during a period of rare optimism while he was awaiting the arrival of his hero, the avant-garde painter Paul Gauguin.

9 Self Portrait at the Age of 63

Rembrandt's (1606–69) self-portrait, created in the last year of his life, is among his most poignant works. He painted many self-portraits during his lifetime, and two of these are on display at the National Gallery.

10 Bathers at La Grenouillière

Claude Monet (1840–1926), the original Impressionist, explored the effect of light on water at La Grenouillière, a popular bathing spot on the Seine close to Bougival to the west of Paris, where he worked alongside fellow painter Pierre-Auguste Renoir.

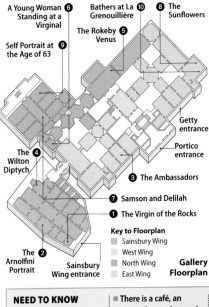

A Young Woman Standing at a Virginal **6**

Bathers at La Grenouillière **10**

8 The Sunflowers

The Rokeby Venus **5**

Self Portrait at the Age of 63 **9**

Getty entrance

Portico entrance

The Wilton Diptych **4**

3 The Ambassadors

7 Samson and Delilah

1 The Virgin of the Rocks

Key to Floorplan
- Sainsbury Wing
- West Wing
- North Wing
- East Wing

Gallery Floorplan

The Arnolfini Portrait **2**

Sainsbury Wing entrance

NEED TO KNOW

MAP C3 ▪ Trafalgar Square WC2 ▪ 020 7747 2885 ▪ www.nationalgallery.org.uk

Open 10am–6pm Sat–Fri (to 9pm Fri)

Adm free, except major temporary exhibitions

Free guided tours at 11:30am and 2:30pm daily (lasts one hour)

▪ There is a café, an espresso bar and a good fine-dining restaurant.

▪ The Sainsbury Wing has an excellent art bookshop.

▪ Audio tours are available and trails can be downloaded from the museum's website.

▪ Short lunchtime talks are held at 1pm Mon and Wed.

Gallery Guide

The gallery is divided into four areas. The Sainsbury Wing contains the Early Renaissance collection. The West Wing displays works from 1500 to 1600, the North Wing 1600–1700, and the East Wing 1700 to early 1900s. Although the main entrance is on Trafalgar Square, the Sainsbury Wing makes a more sensible starting point.

TOP 10 ★ National Portrait Gallery

Founded in 1856 and unrelated to the neighbouring National Gallery, this museum showcases Britain's most famous and historically important figures through a series of portraits. With both well- and lesser-known names and faces lining the walls, there are some fascinating paintings from Tudor times through to the present day. Monarchs are depicted, from Richard II (1367–1400) to Queen Elizabeth II, and the collection also holds a 1554 miniature, England's oldest self-portrait in oils. Displays change regularly so some of the paintings in this guide may not be on view.

Queen Elizabeth I
This anonymous portrait **(right)** is one of several of Elizabeth I, who presided over England's Renaissance (1533–1603). The Tudor rooms feature portraits of central figures of the period, from courtiers to dramatists.

2 Prince Charles Edward Stuart
This portrait of "Bonnie Prince Charlie", grandson of James II, was painted by Louis Gabriel Blanchett (1701–72) and was a splendid piece of propaganda for the Jacobite cause.

3 William Shakespeare
This is the only portrait of England's famous playwright known with certainty to have been painted during his lifetime (1564–1616) **(below)**.

4 The Whitehall Mural
The cartoon of Henry VIII and his father Henry VII by Hans Holbein (1537) was drawn for a large mural in the Palace of Whitehall. The mural was lost when the palace burned down in 1698.

5 George Gordon Byron, 6th Baron Byron
Made in 1813, this oil painting of Lord Byron (1788–1824) by Thomas Phillips (1770–1845) depicts the Romantic poet and champion of liberty dressed in Albanian costume. He died while supporting Greek insurgents in their fight against the Ottoman Empire.

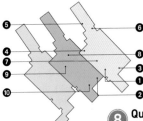

Key to Floorplan
- Ground floor
- First floor
- Second floor

Gallery Floorplan

6 Horatio Nelson

The 1800 portrait by Sir William Beechey (1753–1839) is considered to be a great likeness of the admiral, who died at the Battle of Trafalgar in 1805. Apart from Queen Victoria and the Duke of Wellington, Nelson was painted more than any other British figure in history.

7 Oliver Cromwell

Robert Walker's (1599–1658) oil painting shows Oliver Cromwell (1599–1658) posing in armour. The portrait is believed to date from 1649 – the year Charles I, whose death warrant Cromwell signed, was executed. Cromwell went on to become the Lord Protector of Great Britain.

8 Queen Victoria

Painted by Aaron Edwin Penley (1806–70), this pretty watercolour miniature **(below)** shows the young queen near the beginning of her reign. Her early devotion to her husband, Prince Albert, whom she married in the year of this picture, is shown by the bust of him to her left. Prince Albert's image can frequently be found in portraits of Queen Victoria made before and after his death.

9 Charles Darwin

This portrait of the scientist **(above)** was painted in 1883 by John Collier (1850–1934) and completed a year before Darwin's death. It is a replica of a portrait at the Linnaean Society and was donated to the gallery by Darwin's eldest son.

10 Mary Seacole

Painted by Albert Charles Challen (1847–81), this portrait is the only known oil painting of Mary Seacole, a Jamaican nurse who went to extraordinary lengths to care for the sick and wounded during the Crimean War.

NEED TO KNOW

MAP C3 ■ St Martin's Place WC2 ■ 020 7306 0055 ■ www.npg.org.uk

Open 10am–6pm daily (to 9pm Fri)

Adm (separate charge for some exhibitions)

■ The Portrait Restaurant on the top floor has great views across Trafalgar Square, down Whitehall to Parliament.

■ The bookshop stocks a huge range of fashion, costume, history and biography titles.

■ The ground-floor gift shop has good postcards.

■ A range of talks take place at lunchtimes, with regular evening events known as Friday Lates.

Gallery Guide

The National Portrait Gallery's three floors are arranged chronologically. Take the escalator to the second floor and start with the Tudor and Stuart galleries (1–8). Men and women of industry, science and art from the 18th and early 19th centuries are in rooms 9 to 20. The first floor mainly covers the Victorian period to the 20th century. The ground-floor galleries display contemporary portraiture and focus on temporary exhibitions.

TOP 10 ⭐ Natural History Museum

There are some 80 million specimens in the Natural History Museum's fascinating collections. Originally the repository for items brought home by Charles Darwin and Captain Cook's botanist, Joseph Banks, among others, the museum combines traditional displays with innovative, hands-on exhibits. It remains one of London's most popular museums and has a number of kid-pleasers, such as the impressive dinosaur collection and the life-sized model of a blue whale. A hot-house of research, it employs more than 300 scientists and librarians.

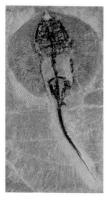

3 Treasures in the Cadogan Gallery

Treasures is an apt title for this extraordinary collection, from a rare first edition of Darwin's *On the Origin of Species* to the dinosaur teeth that led to the discovery that giant reptiles once walked the earth. The 23 exhibits on display here **(right)** were chosen for their scientific and historical importance and are true movers and shakers of natural history.

1 Fossils

Marine reptiles that existed at the time of the dinosaurs have survived as some remarkable fossils **(above)**, such as the pregnant female Ichthyosaur, found in a Dorset garden, which lived 187–178 million years ago.

4 Model Baby

A giant model of an unborn baby in the Human Biology galleries demonstrates sounds heard in the womb. Other hands-on exhibits test abilities and reactions and show how physical characteristics are inherited.

5 Images of Nature Gallery

This gallery showcases the museum's collection of historical and modern artworks, including prints from micro-CT scanners, watercolours and photographs. More than 110 exhibits span 350 years to the present day.

2 Hintze Hall

After a major renovation in mid-2017, the museum's cathedral-like hall **(right)** replaced "Dippy", the Diplodocus skeleton cast, with a giant blue whale skeleton. In alcoves along the sides of the hall are other stars of the museum, including an American mastodon.

6 Spirit Collection

Get a fascinating glimpse of the museum's vast collection of zoological specimens preserved in spirit, including creatures collected by Charles Darwin.

7 Darwin Centre

One of the centre's many attractions is the eight-storey Cocoon, a permanent exhibition where visitors can see insect specimens as well as world-leading scientists at work.

8 Blue Whale

The Mammal gallery houses this fascinating exhibit, where both modern mammals and their fossil relatives are dwarfed in comparison to the astounding life-sized model of a blue whale, the largest mammal on the planet.

9 Dinosaurs

T. Rex, one of the museum's life-like anim-atronic models, lurches and roars in this popular gallery. More traditional exhibits of fossilized skeletons are also on display. Taking pride of place in the Earth Hall is 6-m (19.5-ft) *Sophie*, **(above)** the most intact Stegosaurus fossilized skeleton ever found.

10 Attenborough Studio

On the ground floor of the Darwin Centre, the Attenborough Studio is a state-of-the-art audio-visual facility with 64 seats. The venue hosts events, films and talks covering all aspects of life on earth as well as scientific discovery.

Key to Floorplan
- Ground floor
- First floor
- Second floor

Museum Floorplan

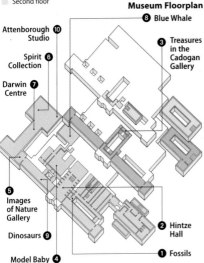

- ❽ Blue Whale
- Attenborough ❿ Studio
- Spirit ❻ Collection
- ❸ Treasures in the Cadogan Gallery
- Darwin ❼ Centre
- ❺ Images of Nature Gallery
- Dinosaurs ❾
- ❷ Hintze Hall
- Model Baby ❹
- ❶ Fossils

NEED TO KNOW

MAP A5 ■ Cromwell Road SW7 ■ 020 7942 5000 ■ www.nhm.ac.uk

Open 10am–5:50pm daily. Last admission 5:30pm

Closed 24–26 Dec

Adm free (admission charge for some special exhibitions)

■ There is a restaurant in the green zone, and several cafés and snack bars.

■ A number of different self-guided trails are available, and you can visit the outdoor Wildlife Garden. Details at the Central Hall information desk.

Museum Guide
The Natural History Museum is divided into four zones: the blue zone, which includes the dinosaur gallery and Images of Nature; the green zone, with the ecology and creepy-crawlies galleries; the orange zone, with a wildlife garden; and the red zone, incorporating the geological displays.

The Cromwell Road entrance leads to the Hintze Hall with its grand staircase.

An additional entrance on Exhibition Road leads to the red zone.

TOP 10 ★ Science Museum

Packed with hands-on exhibits, this museum explores the world of science through centuries of scientific and technological development. The collection showcases how Britain led the Industrial Revolution, with looms and steam engines, navigation and early flight. It also has displays on contemporary science, climate change and cutting-edge technologies, with many interactive exhibits in the hi-tech Wellcome Wing. The first floor of the museum is expected to have new medicine galleries.

5 Apollo 10 Command Module

The Apollo 10 Command Module, which went around the moon in May 1969, is on display, as is a replica of the Apollo 11 Lunar Lander **(left)**. Buzz Aldrin and Neil Armstrong stepped onto the moon from the original in July 1969 and became the first humans to set foot on the lunar surface.

6 Wonderlab: The Statoil Gallery

With its 50 hands-on exhibits, this interactive gallery captivates 5- to 15-year-olds, to whom it primarily caters. From the friction slide to the magnetic sculpture, learning about science has never been so much fun.

1 Exploring Space

Rockets, satellites, space probes and landers can all be explored, and you can learn about Sputnik, the world's first satellite, how we sent spacecrafts to other planets and walked on the moon.

2 Information Age

The Queen opened this fascinating gallery with her first tweet in October 2014. It is divided into six themes and covers 200 years of communication and modern information technology from the earliest telegraph messages to the internet and mobile phones.

3 The Secret Life of the Home

This gallery contains a wacky variety of household gadgets and gizmos, from washing machines and vacuum cleaners to burglar alarms.

4 Puffing Billy

Puffing Billy **(below)** is the world's oldest remaining steam locomotive. It was built in England in 1813 and used to transport coal. George Stephenson's famous 1829 *Rocket*, the first locomotive engine to pull passenger carriages, is also on display.

7 Who Am I?
The continually updated Who Am I? gallery presents the latest in brain science and genetics through interactive exhibits and object-rich displays.

8 Fly Zone
This zone offers three kinds of flight simulators. With the virtual reality Space Descent, experience a journey from the International Space Station to Earth.

10 IMAX 3D Cinema
The state-of-the-art cinema **(above)** shows mainly 3D films on a screen that is taller than four double-decker buses. An impressive six-channel surround-sound system will totally immerse you in the action.

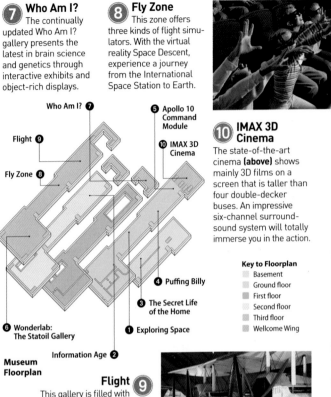

Who Am I? 7
Flight 9
Fly Zone 8

5 Apollo 10 Command Module
10 IMAX 3D Cinema

4 Puffing Billy
3 The Secret Life of the Home
1 Exploring Space
6 Wonderlab: The Statoil Gallery
Information Age 2

Museum Floorplan

Key to Floorplan
- Basement
- Ground floor
- First floor
- Second floor
- Third floor
- Wellcome Wing

Flight 9
This gallery is filled with extraordinary aircraft reflecting both UK and international achievements in aviation. Highlights include Amy Johnson's *Gipsy Moth* and the *Vickers Vimy* **(right)**, which first crossed the Atlantic in 1919.

NEED TO KNOW

MAP A5 ■ Exhibition Road SW7 ■ 020 7942 4000 ■ www.science museum.org.uk

Open 10am–6pm daily (last entry 5:15pm)

Closed 24–26 Dec

Adm free (separate charge for special exhibitions, simulator rides and IMAX cinema)

■ There is a restaurant, several cafés and a picnic area.

■ Printed maps with a guide provide details of exhibits.

■ The museum store is good for innovative gifts.

Museum Guide
The museum is spread over seven floors; however, the fourth and fifth floors are closed for renovation. Space exploration, steam engines and the IMAX cinema are on the ground floor. Information Age, the temporary exhibition area, Media Space and climate science are on the second floor. Flight and the interactive games and simulators can be found on the third floor along with Wonderlab. The Secret Life of the Home can be found in the basement.

🔟 ⭐ Buckingham Palace

London's most famous residence, and one of its best recognized landmarks, Buckingham Palace was built as a town house for the first Duke of Buckingham around 1705. In 1825, George IV commissioned John Nash to extend the house into a substantial palace. The first resident of the palace was Queen Victoria, from 1837. The extensive front of the building was refaced by Sir Aston Webb in 1914. The palace is now home to Queen Elizabeth II and the State Rooms are open to the public during summer. Many royal parks and gardens in London are also accessible to the public.

① The Balcony
On special occasions, the queen and other members of the Royal Family step onto the palace balcony to wave to the crowds below.

② Queen's Gallery
The gallery hosts a changing programme of exhibitions of the Royal Collection's masterpieces, including works by artists such as Jan Vermeer and Leonardo da Vinci.

③ Changing the Guard
The Palace guards, in their red tunics and tall bearskin hats **(below)**, are changed at 11am daily from May to July (and alternate days from August to April, weather permitting). The guards march to the palace from the Wellington Barracks.

Façade of Buckingham Palace

④ Grand Staircase
The Ambassadors' Entrance leads into the Grand Hall. From here the Grand Staircase, with gilded balustrades, rises to the first floor where the State Rooms are found.

⑤ Throne Room
This houses the thrones of Queen Elizabeth and Prince Philip used for the coronation. Designed by John Nash, the room has an ornamented ceiling and magnificent chandeliers.

⑥ Picture Gallery
One of the largest rooms in the palace, it has a barrel-vaulted glass ceiling and a number of paintings from the Royal Collection, including works by Rembrandt, Rubens and Van Dyck.

8 State Ballroom
Banquets for visiting heads of state are held here **(left)**. The annual event is the Diplomatic Reception in early December, attended by over 1,500 guests from about 130 countries.

7 Brougham
Every day a horse-drawn Brougham carriage sets out to collect and deliver royal packages between Buckingham Palace and St James's Palace.

PALACE LIFE

The official business of the monarchy takes place in Buckingham Palace, which employs over 800 staff. Several members of the royal family have offices in the palace, but due to ongoing restoration work, these have had to move to temporary premises. The work is due to finish in 2027. The most senior member of the Royal Household is the Lord Chamberlain. The Master of the Household and the Palace's domestic staff organize many functions every year, including Investitures for recipients of awards which are given by the Queen.

---

9 Royal Mews
The finest working stables in Britain care for horses that pull the royal coach on state occasions. The collection of coaches, motorcars and carriages includes the Gold State Coach, used at every coronation since 1821.

10 Palace Garden
The 16-hectare (39-acre) Palace garden is an oasis for wildlife and includes a 1-hectare (3-acre) lake. It can be visited on tours. There are at least three Royal Garden Parties each year, attended by over 30,000 people **(below)**.

NEED TO KNOW

MAP C4 ▪ Buckingham Palace SW1
▪ 020 7766 7300 ▪ royalcollection.org.uk
Under-5s free. Combined tickets available

State Rooms: end-Jul–Aug: 9:30am–7pm daily (last adm 5:15pm), Sep: 9:30am–6pm daily (last adm 4:15pm); Adm adults £24, students & over-60s £22, under-17s £13.50; family £61.50

Royal Mews: Apr–Oct: 10am–5pm daily (last adm 4:15pm), Feb, Mar & Nov: 10am–4pm daily (last adm 3:15pm); Adm adults £11, students and over-60s £10, under-17s £6.40, family £28.40

Queen's Gallery: 10am–5:30pm daily (last adm 4:15pm), Aug–Sep: opens 9:30am; Adm adults £12, students and over-60s £10.80, under-17s £6, family £30

📺 ⭐ London Eye

An amazing feat of engineering, the world's tallest cantilevered observation wheel offers fascinating views over the whole of London. Towering over the Thames opposite the Houses of Parliament, it was built to celebrate the millennium year, and has proved enormously popular. Its 32 enclosed capsules each hold up to 28 people and offer total visibility in all directions. A rotation on the London Eye takes 30 minutes and, on a clear day, you can see up to 40 km (25 miles) across the capital and the south of England.

2 Houses of Parliament

The London Eye rises high above the Houses of Parliament *(see p70)* on the far side of the Thames. From here you can look down on Big Ben (**left**) and see the Commons Terrace, where Members of Parliament and the House of Lords drink, dine and discuss policy by the river.

1 BT Tower

Built for the Post Office in 1961–4, this 190-m (620-ft) tower is now a TV, radio and tele-communications tower. It was given Grade II Listed Building status in 2003, meaning its defunct antennas needed special permission to be removed.

3 One Canada Square

With its distinctive pyramid roof, One Canada Square is located in the heart of Docklands, which is the East London business and finance centre. It stands in the middle of the Isle of Dogs.

The London Eye, South Bank

4 Wren Churches

The enormous dome of St Paul's Cathedral (**left**) *(see pp76–9)* stands out as the star of the City churches. Pricking the sky around it are the spires of some of Wren's other churches, including St Bride's, which has a tiered design that has inspired wedding cakes, and Wren's favourite, St James's on Piccadilly.

5 Alexandra Palace

The BBC transmitted the world's first high-definition public television broadcasting service from Alexandra Palace on 2 November 1936. There are exhibition halls and an ice rink here.

6 Crystal Palace

This TV and radio transmission mast, to the south of the city, is near the site of the 1851 Great Exhibition "Crystal Palace." It was moved here from Hyde Park in 1852 and burned down spectacularly in 1936.

7 The Shard
Designed by Renzo Piano, this 306-m (1,004-ft) glass spire **(left)** rises from London Bridge station and gives the city skyline a new defining point. The 95-storey building houses offices, restaurants and a hotel. There is an observation deck on the 72nd floor.

MILLENNIUM LEGACY

The London Eye was one of a number of nationwide projects designed to mark the millennium. The focus in London was on the enormous Millennium Dome, a spectacular structure built in Greenwich to house a national exhibition. Other projects were Tate Modern *(see pp64–5)* and Millennium Bridge, the Waterloo Millennium Pier, the Great Court at the British Museum *(see pp48–51)* and the opening up of Somerset House *(Strand)*.

8 Heathrow
To the west of the city, London's main airport is one of the busiest international airports in the world. The Thames acts as a kind of runway, as planes line up overhead to begin their descent.

NEED TO KNOW

MAP D4 ■ South Bank SE1
■ www.londoneye.com

Open Sep–Mar & May: 11am–6pm daily; Apr & Jun–Aug: 10am–8:30pm daily; closed 25 Dec and 2 weeks in Jan. Ticket office opens 9:30am

Adm adults £27, children £22, under-3s free; check website for discounts

Timed tickets on the hour and half-hour

■ There are cafés in County Hall and on the South Bank.

■ Tickets are available on the day but advance booking is advisable to avoid standing in long queues.

■ All capsules are fitted with interactive tablet guides.

9 Queen Elizabeth II Bridge
On a clear day you can just make out the lowest downstream crossing on the Thames, a huge suspension bridge at Dartford, some 32 km (20 miles) away. Traffic flows north in a tunnel under the river, south over the bridge.

10 Windsor Castle
Windsor Castle sits by the Thames to the west of London **(below)**. The largest occupied castle in the world, it is still a favourite residence of the royal family.

🔟⭐ Tate Modern

Affiliated with Tate Britain, Tate Modern is one of London's most exciting galleries and is housed in the Bankside power station. In 2016, the Blavatnik Building was added to this site. Large enough for huge installations, the galleries provide an airy space for the collection of international modern art. This includes works by Dalí, Picasso, Matisse, and Pollock, as well as pieces by many acclaimed contemporary artists. The displays are changed frequently.

② The Snail
This 1953 cutout is one of Henri Matisse's (1869–1954) final works, completed whilst he was bedridden. The paper spirals represent a snail's shell.

③ Black on Maroon
One of a series of large contemplative abstracts by the artist Mark Rothko (1903–70), the sombre and meditative *Black on Maroon* was painted in 1958 and later donated to the Tate.

① Three Dancers
Pablo Picasso (1881–1973) was noted for the different painting styles he mastered as he pushed the boundaries of modern art. The energetic, unsettling *Three Dancers* (1925) **(above)** followed the most serene stage of his work, and marked the beginning of a radical phase of distortion and emotional violence in his art.

④ Whaam!
Inspired by an image from *All American Men of War*, published by DC Comics in 1962, Roy Lichtenstein (1923–97) created *Whaam!* **(below)** in 1963. He was inspired by comics and advertisements, presenting powerful or emotive scenes in an impersonal and detached style.

⑤ Lobster Telephone
This iconic Surrealist work by Salvador Dalí (1904–1989) is made from steel, plaster, rubber, resin and paper. Created in 1936, this combination of objects with sexual overtones is one that Dalí returned to many times.

6 Summertime No. 9A

Jackson Pollock (1912–1956) was the pioneer of Action painting. The American created his first "drip" artwork in 1947, pouring paint onto huge canvases on the floor. Pollock embraced the element of chance while controlling the rhythm and flow, thickness and layering of the paint in such works. *Summertime No. 9A* dates from 1948.

9 Fish

Constantin Brancusi (1876–1957) created *Fish* **(right)** in 1926. Known for his ability to capture the qualities of his subjects in elementary, abstract forms, this sculpture presents a bronze "fish" on a polished metal disc balanced on a smooth, carved wooden base. The play of light on both the polished metal disc and the bronze adds a sense of movement.

The Tate Modern

10 Fountain

One of the most iconic works of 20th-century art on display, Marcel Duchamp's (1887–1968) much discussed *Fountain* is a urinal simply signed 'R. Mutt 1917'. This is a 1964 replica – the original, which consisted of a standard urinal, is lost. Made from glazed earthenware, it was painted to resemble the original porcelain. The ordinary object, presented largely unchanged but out of its usual context, is often used as an example to debate what constitutes a "work of art".

7 Composition B (No. II) with Red

The Dutch painter Piet Mondrian (1872–1914) gradually refined his art to a rigorous and pure abstract language of straight lines and squares of primary colours, an example of which is this painting, completed in 1935.

8 The Reckless Sleeper

Painted in 1928 by René Magritte (1898–1967), this work explores Surrealism and Freudian symbolism. A man sleeps in an alcove above a tablet embedded with everyday (but interpreted as Freudian) objects, as if dreamed by the sleeper.

NEED TO KNOW

MAP E3 ■ Bankside SE1 ■ 020 7887 8888 ■ www.tate.org.uk

Open 10am–6pm Sun–Thu, 10am–10pm Fri–Sat; closed 24–26 Dec

Adm for temporary exhibits

A Tate-to-Tate boat service from Bankside connects Tate Modern with Tate Britain (see p66–7)

■ The Turbine Hall has a wide selection of art and culture books.

■ Daily events are advertised in the main hall.

Gallery Guide

There are seven levels in the Boiler House, and eleven levels in the Blavatnik Building. The main entrance on Holland Street leads to the Turbine Hall on level 0, where the information and ticket offices, main shop and temporary installations are located. The other points of entry – River Entrance and Blavatnik Building Entrance – are on level 1.

The Start Display on level 2 of the Boiler House presents the main exhibitions, displayed on levels 2, 3 and 4 of both buildings and in The Tanks on level 0 of the Blavatnik Building.

Level 6 of the Boiler House and level 9 of the Blavatnik Building have restaurants, whereas level 10 is a viewing platform.

TOP 10 ⭐ Tate Britain

Opened in 1897 as the National Gallery of British Art, the magnificent collection at London's first Tate gallery ranges from 1500 to the present day. Its founder was Henry Tate (1819–99), who made his fortune from sugar. The collection contains works by major British painters, and was greatly added to by J M W Turner. Paintings are often moved to the Tate's other galleries, loaned out or removed for restoration. The works on these pages, therefore, may not always be on display.

1 Norham Castle, Sunrise

J M W Turner (1775–1851) was the great genius of English landscape painting. This 1845 work (above) typifies his use of abstraction and luminosity of colour.

2 A Bigger Splash

British artist David Hockney (b.1937) celebrates his love affair with California with this 1960 work depicting the state's climate through the use of colour and light.

3 Sunset: Carthorses Drinking at a Stream

Thomas Gainsborough's (1727–88) family groups in landscapes are among the finest "conversation pieces" in English art. This vivid scene of peasants going to market, 1760, shows his more pastoral and poetic side.

4 Elohim Creating Adam

Poet, mystic, illustrator and engraver William Blake (1757–1827) claimed to be guided by visions. *Elohim Creating Adam* is typical of his work. Illustrating the Book of Genesis, it shows Adam growing out of the earth ("Elohim" is the Hebrew name for God).

5 Ophelia

Detailed and accurate observation of nature was a key element of the Victorian Pre-Raphaelite painters, as in this tragic scene from Shakespeare's *Hamlet* (above) by John Everett Millais (1829–96), painted in 1852.

6 Flatford Mill

Painted near his home in Dedham Vale, and depicting a mill on the Stour, this (left) is one of the first landscapes that John Constable (1776–1837) painted outdoors rather than in his studio.

7 Girl with a Kitten

This 1947 portrait by Lucian Freud (1922–2011) shows the artist's first wife holding a kitten by its neck in a tense grip, seeming to half-strangle it without concern. His portraits are known for their psychological depth.

9 Carnation, Lily, Lily, Rose

John Singer Sargent (1856–1925) moved to London from Paris in 1885 and adopted Impressionist techniques. The title of this 1886 work **(right)** was taken from a popular song of the time.

10 Three Studies for Figures at the Base of a Crucifixion

A leading light of the Soho arts scene, Francis Bacon (1910–1992) was uncompromising in his view of life. When first shown, this triptych **(below)** caused an immediate sensation, shocking audiences with its savage imagery. It is now among his best-known works.

8 Recumbent Figure

Henry Moore (1898–1986) was a sculptor whose work is on public display around London. This 1938 work became a recurrent theme of Moore's prolific output.

NEED TO KNOW

MAP C5 ▪ Millbank SW1 ▪ 020 7887 8888 ▪ www.tate.org.uk

Open 10am–6pm daily; Closed 24–26 Dec

Adm for temporary exhibitions

Tate-to-Tate boat service between Tate Britain and Tate Modern every 40 minutes from Millbank Pier

▪ There is an excellent restaurant on the lower floor with a good wine list.

▪ Free guided tours daily, weekly talks and films shown monthly.

▪ The Tate's art bookshop is very comprehensive.

Gallery Guide

The permanent collection occupies most of the Main Floor. Starting in the north-west corner, it follows a broad chronological sweep from the 16th century to the present. Alongside the permanent collection are a smaller number of regularly changing displays focusing on individual artists, movements or topics. The Turner Collection – about 300 oil paintings and about 20,000 watercolours by J M W Turner – is displayed in the adjoining Clore Gallery.

⭐ Westminster Abbey

A glorious example of medieval architecture on a truly grand scale, this former Benedictine abbey church stands on the south side of Parliament Square *(see pp70–71)*. Founded in the 11th century by Edward the Confessor, it survived the Reformation and continued as a place of royal ceremonials. Queen Elizabeth II's coronation was held here in 1953 and Princess Diana's funeral in 1997. It was also the chosen venue for the wedding of Prince William to Catherine Middleton in April 2011.

1 St Edward's Chapel

The shrine of Edward the Confessor (1003–66), last of the Anglo-Saxon kings, lies at the heart of Westminster Abbey. He built London's first royal palace at Westminster, and founded the present abbey on the site.

2 Coronation Chair

This chair **(above)** was made in 1301 for Edward I. It is placed in front of the high-altar screen on the 13th-century mosaic pavement when used for coronations.

3 Nave

At 32 m (102 ft), this is among the tallest Gothic naves **(right)** in England and took 150 years to build. Designed by the great 14th-century architect Henry Yevele, it is supported externally by flying buttresses.

4 Poets' Corner

This corner of the transept contains memorials to literary giants, including Shakespeare and Dickens.

5 Lady Chapel

The spectacular fan vaulting **(below)** above the nave of this eastern addition to the church is late Perpendicular in style. Built for Henry VII (1457–1509), it includes two side aisles and five smaller chapels and is the home of the Order of the Bath *(see p72)*.

6 Tomb of Elizabeth I

England's great Protestant queen (1553–1603) is buried in a huge marble tomb complete with a recumbent effigy on one side of the Lady Chapel. The tomb of her Catholic rival and first cousin once removed, Mary Queen of Scots (beheaded in 1587), is on the other side of the chapel. Mary's remains were brought to the abbey by James I in 1612.

7 The Queen's Diamond Jubilee Galleries

These grand galleries in the Abbey's medieval triforium display treasures reflecting its history. The triforium offers arresting views to the Houses of Parliament and into the church. Access to the galleries is via the Weston Tower by a spiral staircase or lift.

ABBEY HISTORY

A Benedictine monastery was established by St Dunstan (AD 909–988) on what was the marshy Isle of Thorney. King Edward the Confessor re-endowed the monastery, and founded the present church in 1065. William the Conqueror was crowned here in 1066. Henry III's architect Henry of Reyns rebuilt much of the church in 1245. The nave was completed in 1376. The eastern end of the church was extended by Henry VII, who had the Lady Chapel built. Finally, in 1734–45, the twin towers on the west front were completed by Nicholas Hawksmoor.

8 Tomb of the Unknown Warrior

The body of an unknown soldier from the battlefields of World War I was buried here in 1920. His grave **(above)** represents all those who have lost their lives in war.

9 Chapter House

This octagonal building with a 13th-century tiled floor is one of the largest in England and is where the abbey's monks once gathered. The House of Commons met here between 1257 and 1542. Run by the abbey, it can also be reached via Dean's Yard.

10 Cloisters

The cloisters were located at the heart of the former Benedictine monastery and would have been the monastery's busiest area. On the east side are the only remaining parts of the Norman church, the Undercroft and the Pyx Chamber, where coinage was tested in medieval times.

Abbey Floorplan

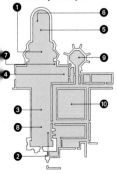

NEED TO KNOW

MAP C4 ▪ 20 Dean's Yard SW1 ▪ 020 7222 5152
▪ www.westminster-abbey.org ▪ Guided tours available

Adm adults £22; concessions £17; children 6–16 £9 (under-6s free); for family tickets see website

Abbey: 9:30am–3:30pm Mon–Fri, 4:30–6pm Wed, 9am–1pm Sat, Sun for worship only

Cellarium Café and Terrace: 8am–6pm Mon–Fri, 9am–5pm Sat, 10am–4pm Sun

Pyx Chamber and Chapter House: 10am–4:30pm Mon–Fri (till 4pm Sat)

▪ Hear the choir sing at 5pm weekdays except Wednesday, 3pm on Saturdays and at Sunday services.
▪ Listen to free organ recitals at 5:45pm every Sunday.

TOP 10 ⭐ Parliament Square

The spiritual and political heart of the city, the Palace of Westminster was built here a thousand years ago and has served as a royal household, seat of government and abbey. The square was planned as part of the rebuilding programme after a fire destroyed the palace in 1834. Usually known as the Houses of Parliament, the new Palace of Westminster stands opposite Westminster Abbey. On the north side of the square, Parliament Street leads to Whitehall and No.10 Downing Street.

1 Westminster Abbey
See pp68–9.

2 St Margaret's Church
Winston Churchill was among many eminent figures to marry in this 15th-century church **(below)**. William Caxton (c. 1422–92), who set up the first printing press in England, and the writer and explorer Sir Walter Raleigh are both buried here. Charles I is also remembered.

3 Big Ben
The huge Elizabeth Tower of the Palace of Westminster is known as Big Ben **(left)**. The name refers to the clock's 13.5-tonne bell, thought to be named after Sir Benjamin Hall, Chief Commissioner of Works in 1858. It will only chime on special occasions until 2021.

4 Houses of Parliament
A Gothic Revival building by Sir Charles Barry and Augustus Welby Pugin, built between 1840 and 1870, the Houses of Parliament **(right)** cover 3 hectares (8 acres) and have 1,100 rooms around 11 courtyards. The Commons Chamber is where Members of Parliament sit and debate policy.

5 Westminster Hall
This lofty hall is about all of the original palace that remained after the 1834 fire. For centuries the courts of law sat beneath its grand 14th-century hammer-beam roof.

6 Central Hall
This large assembly hall, built in Viennese Baroque style, was funded by a collection among the Methodist Church to celebrate the centenary of their founder, John Wesley (1703–91).

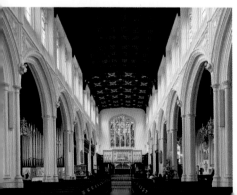

7 Jewel Tower

Built in 1365 to safeguard the treasure of Edward III, this is an isolated survivor of the 1834 fire. A museum about the history of the tower **(left)** is housed inside.

8 Winston Churchill Statue

This statue of the UK's wartime leader (1874–1965) is one of several in the square, including prime minister Benjamin Disraeli (1804–81) and Nelson Mandela (1918–2013).

PARLIAMENT

The 650 elected Members of Parliament sit in the House of Commons, where the Prime Minister and his or her government sits on the right-hand side of the Speaker, who ensures the House's rules are obeyed. The opposing "shadow" government sits on his left. The House of Lords seats around 800 members (most appointed by the Queen) who have limited powers. The Prime Minister attends a weekly audience with the Queen, who today has only a symbolic role.

9 Dean's Yard

Buildings around this square were once used by monks, however the Dissolution of the Monasteries in the 1530s closed their school here. A new Westminster School was founded by Elizabeth I and is still one of Britain's top public schools.

NEED TO KNOW

MAP C4 ▪ Parliament Square SW1
▪ www.parliament.uk

Tours can be arranged through MPs at www.parliament.uk

Tickets for tours on Saturdays and during recess are available online or call 020 7219 4114

▪ The Public Galleries at the Houses of Parliament have limited seating for visitors during debates. Check times online or call 020 7219 4272.

▪ The basement café in Central Hall is a good place for a snack.

▪ To avoid long queues for the Public Galleries, time your visit after 6pm on a Monday, Tuesday or Wednesday.

Plan of the Square

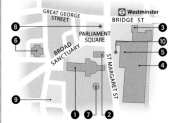

10 Statue of Oliver Cromwell

Oliver Cromwell (1599–1658) presided over England's only republic, which began after the Civil War. He was buried in Westminster Abbey, but after the monarchy was restored in 1660, his corpse was taken to Tyburn and hanged as a criminal.

🔟⭐ Tower of London

London's great riverside fortress is usually remembered as a place of imprisonment, but it has a much more varied past. Originally a moated fort, the White Tower was built for William I (the Conqueror) and begun around 1078. Enlarged by later monarchs – including Henry VIII, who famously sent two of his wives to their deaths on Tower Green – it became home to the city arsenal, the Crown Jewels, a menagerie and the Royal Mint.

③ The White Tower

The heart of the fortress is a sturdy keep, 30 m (90 ft) tall with walls 5 m (15 ft) thick. Constructed under William I, it was completed in 1097 and is the Tower's oldest surviving building. In 1240 it was whitewashed inside and out, hence its name.

① Yeoman Warders

The Tower's 37 Yeoman Warders **(above)** now include a female Warder. Former non-commissioned military officers with Long Service and Good Conduct Medals, they wear uniforms dating from Tudor times.

④ Imperial State Crown

This is the most dazzling of a dozen crowns in the Jewel House. It contains 2,868 diamonds, and the sapphire at its top is from the reign of Edward the Confessor (r.1042–66). The crown was made for the coronation of George VI in 1937.

The Tower of London

⑤ Chapel of St John the Evangelist

The finest Norman place of worship in London **(left)**, which remains much as it was when it was built, is on the upper floor of the White Tower. In 1399, in preparation for Henry IV's coronation procession, 40 noble knights held vigil here. They then took a purifying bath in an adjoining room and Henry made them the first Knights of the Order of the Bath. It is still used as a royal chapel today.

② The Bloody Tower

The displays here explore the dark history of the Bloody Tower, where murderous deeds, including the alleged killing of the little princes took place.

6 Ravens

The saying goes that when ravens leave the Tower the building and the monarchy will fall. There are seven ravens in residence, looked after by the Ravenmaster.

Plan of the Tower

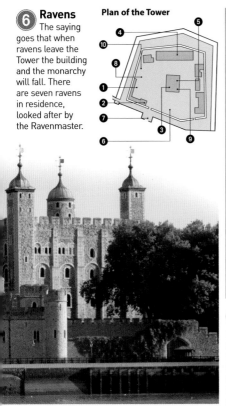

TOWER HISTORY

William I's White Tower was intended to defend London against attacks – and to be a visible sign to the native Anglo-Saxon population of the conquering Normans' power. Henry III (r.1216–72) built the inner wall with its 13 towers and brought the Crown Jewels here. The city arsenal was kept here, and under Henry VIII (r.1509–47) the Royal Armouries were improved. James I (r.1603–25) was the last monarch to stay in residence. All coinage in Great Britain was minted in the Tower's Outer Ward until 1810, when the Royal Mint was established on Tower Hill.

9 The Line of Kings

Drawn from the Royal Armouries' collection, this exhibition showcases the arms and armour of centuries of monarchs, displayed on and along-side sculpted horses.

7 Traitors' Gate

The oak and iron water gate in the outer wall (right) was used to bring many prisoners to the Tower, and became known as Traitors' Gate.

8 Beauchamp Tower

The walls here are engraved with graffiti made by real prisoners of the Tower, including Lady Jane Grey. The tower takes its name from Thomas Beauchamp, Earl of Warwick, who was imprisoned here between 1397 and 1399 by Richard II.

10 Tower Green

The place of execution for nobility, including Lady Jane Grey (1554) and two of Henry VIII's wives – Anne Boleyn (1536) and Katherine Howard (1542).

Tower Prisoners

1 Bishop of Durham

The first political prisoner to be held in the White Tower was Ralph de Flambard, Bishop of Durham. Locked up by Henry I in 1100, he was seen as responsible for the unpopular policies of Henry's predecessor, William II.

2 Henry VI
During the Wars of the Roses, between the rival families of York and Lancaster, Henry VI was kept in Wakefield Tower for five years, until restored to power in 1470.

3 The Little Princes
The alleged murder of Edward, 12, and Richard, 10, in 1483, gave the Bloody Tower its name. It is thought their uncle, Richard III, was responsible.

4 Sir Thomas More
Chancellor Thomas More's refusal to approve Henry VIII's marriage to Anne Boleyn led to his imprisonment in the lower Bell Tower. He was beheaded in 1535.

5 Henry VIII's Wives
Some of the Tower's most famous victims – such as the

Anne Boleyn

beheaded wives of Henry VIII, Anne Boleyn and Katherine Howard – are buried in the Chapel Royal of St Peter ad Vincula.

6 Lady Jane Grey
In 1554 Lady Jane Grey was queen for just nine days. Aged 16, she was held in the gaoler's house on Tower Green and later executed by order of Queen Mary I.

7 Catholic Martyrs
Under the reign of Elizabeth I (1558–1603), many Catholics were executed. Most, including Jesuits, were held in the Salt Tower.

Sir Thomas More

8 John Gerard
Jesuit priest Gerard escaped from the Cradle Tower with a fellow prisoner in 1597, using a rope strung over the moat by an accomplice.

9 Guy Fawkes
The most famous of the Catholic conspirators, Guy Fawkes tried to blow up King James I and Parliament in 1605. He is burned in effigy each year on 5 November.

10 Rudolf Hess
The Tower's last prisoner was Hitler's deputy. He was held in the Queen's House in 1941, after flying to the UK to ask for peace.

Sites of Imprisonment

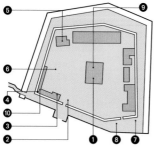

THE CROWN JEWELS

The lavish, bejewelled items that make up the sovereign's ceremonial regalia are all in the care of the Tower of London. The collection dates from 1661 when a new set was made to replace those destroyed by Cromwell following the execution of Charles I in 1649. St Edward's Crown was the first subsequent crown to be made of pure gold, and is the oldest of the ten crowns here. Other coronation jewels on display include a gold, jewel-studded orb, made in 1661, and a sceptre containing the 530-carat Cullinan 1, the biggest cut diamond in the world. The Sovereign's Ring, made for William IV, is sometimes called "the wedding ring of England".

TOP 10 JEWELS

1 Imperial State Crown
2 St Edward's Crown
3 Imperial Crown of India
4 Queen Victoria's Crown
5 Royal Sceptre
6 Jewelled State Sword
7 George V's Crown
8 The Sovereign's Ring
9 The Sovereign's Orb
10 The Sovereign's Sceptre

The Imperial State Crown is heavily encrusted with 2,868 diamonds, 17 sapphires, 11 emeralds, 4 rubies and 269 pearls. It was designed for the coronation of George VI in 1937.

Queen Elizabeth II wore the Imperial State Crown at her coronation on 2 June 1953.

TOP 10 ⭐ St Paul's Cathedral

This is the great masterpiece of Christopher Wren, who rebuilt the City's churches after the Great Fire of 1666. Completed in 1711, it was England's first purpose-built Protestant cathedral, but the exterior design shares similarities with St Peter's in Rome, most notably its ornate dome. One of its bells, Great Paul, was the largest in Europe until the 2012 Olympic bell was cast. The hour bell, Great Tom, strikes the hour and marks the death of royalty and senior church officials. The cathedral is renowned for its music, and draws its choristers from St Paul's Cathedral School.

3 Dome
One of the largest domes in the world **(left)**, it is 111 m (365 ft) high and weighs 65,000 tonnes. The Golden Gallery at the top, and the larger Stone Gallery, both have great views.

4 Whispering Gallery
Inside the dome is the famous Whispering Gallery **(right)**. Words whispered against the wall can be heard on the gallery's opposite side.

1 Quire
The beautiful stalls and organ case in the Quire are by Grinling Gibbons. Handel and Mendelssohn both played the organ, which dates from 1695.

5 St Paul's Watch Memorial
Set in the nave, this memorial honours those who saved St Paul's from destruction during the Blitz by fighting fires started by bombs dropped on and near it.

2 The Light of the World
This painting by the Pre-Raphaelite artist William Holman Hunt (1827–1910) shows Christ knocking on an overgrown door that opens from inside, meaning that God can enter our lives only if we invite Him in.

6 West Front and Towers
The imposing West Front **(right)** is dominated by two huge towers. The pineapples at their tops are symbols of peace and prosperity. The Great West Door is 9 m (29 ft) high and is used only for ceremonial occasions.

High Altar ⑦

The magnificent High Altar **(right)** is made from Italian marble, and the canopy, constructed in the 1950s after the cathedral was bombed during World War II, is based on one of Wren's sketches.

ST PAUL'S HISTORY

The first known church dedicated to St Paul was built on this site in AD 604. Made of wood, it burned down in 675 and a subsequent church was destroyed by Viking invaders in 962. The third church was built in stone. Following another fire in 1087, it was rebuilt under the Normans as a much larger cathedral, with stone walls and a wooden roof. This was completed in 1300. In 1666 Sir Christopher Wren's plans to restore the building had just been accepted when the Great Fire of London burned the old cathedral beyond repair.

⑧ Tijou Gates

The French master metal worker Jean Tijou designed these ornate wrought-iron gates in the South and North Quire, along with the Whispering Gallery balcony and other cathedral metalwork.

⑨ Mosaics

Colourful mosaic ceilings were installed in the Ambulatory and Quire in the 19th century. They are made with glass tesserae, angled so that they sparkle.

⑩ Moore's Mother and Child

This piece is one of a growing number of works of art that have been introduced into St Paul's since the 1960s. The sculptor, Henry Moore (1898–1986), is commemorated in the crypt.

Cathedral Floorplan

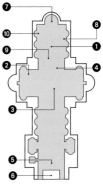

NEED TO KNOW

MAP E3 ■ Ludgate Hill EC4 ■ 020 7246 8350 ■ www.stpauls.co.uk

Adm adults £18; children 6–17 £8 (under-6s enter free); seniors and students 18 and over £16; family £44; for groups, check website. Services are free.

Cathedral: 8:30am–4:30pm Mon–Sat

Galleries: 9:30am–4:15pm Mon–Sat

■ Guided tours usually take place at 10am, 11am, 1pm, 2pm and are included in the admission. Reserve a place at the guiding desk.

■ Food and drink are served in Wren's Pantry.

■ You can hear the choir during the very popular choral evensong service (usually at 5pm daily).

■ Multimedia guides are also available and included in the price of admission.

St Paul's Monuments

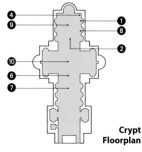

Crypt Floorplan

Detail, American roll of honour

1 Tomb of Christopher Wren

St Paul's architect Christopher Wren's (1632–1723) tomb inscription reads, "*Lector, si monumentum requiris, circumspice*" – "Reader, if you seek a monument, look around you".

2 Wellington's Tomb

The UK's great military leader and prime minister Arthur Wellesley, 1st Duke of Wellington (1769–1852), lies in the crypt. He also has a monument in the nave.

3 John Donne's Memorial

The metaphysical poet John Donne (1572–1631) was made Dean of St Paul's in 1621. His memorial is in the Dean's Aisle in the Ambulatory on the cathedral floor.

4 Turner's Tomb

The great landscape painter J M W Turner (1775–1851) is buried in the OBE chapel.

5 American Memorial

Behind the High Altar on the cathedral floor, the American Memorial Chapel's roll of honour lists the US servicemen killed while stationed in the UK in World War II.

6 Gallipoli Memorial

This memorial is dedicated to those who died in the 1915 Gallipoli campaign of World War I.

7 Churchill Memorial Gates

These gates commemorate Sir Winston Churchill (1874–1965), who during the 1940–41 Blitz said "at all costs, St Paul's must be saved".

8 The Worshipful Company of Masons Memorial

This City guild's plaque near Wren's tomb reads, "Remember the men who made shapely the stones of Saint Paul's Cathedral".

9 OBE Chapel

At the eastern end of the crypt is a chapel devoted to those appointed to the Order of the British Empire, an honour established in 1917, and the first to include women.

10 Nelson's Tomb

Preserved in brandy and brought home from the Battle of Trafalgar, sea hero Admiral Lord Nelson's (1758–1805) body lies in a black sarcophagus in the centre of the crypt.

Nelson's Tomb, St Paul's Cathedral

ST PAUL'S ROLE IN HISTORY

St Paul's, as the Cathedral for the Diocese of London, belongs to the parishes all across London, as well as to the nation. It is run by a Dean and Chapter of priests. One of the cathedral's main functions is as a place of national mourning and celebration. In the 19th century, 13,000 people filled the cathedral for the funeral of the Duke of Wellington. Queen Victoria's Jubilee was a spectacular occasion held on the steps of the cathedral. The Prince of Wales and Lady Diana Spencer chose to be married at St Paul's rather than the royal Westminster Abbey. The decision helped to portray the couple as the people's prince and princess.

TOP 10 MOMENTS IN ST PAUL'S HISTORY

1 Elizabeth II's Diamond Jubilee (2012)

2 Prince Charles and Lady Diana's wedding (1981)

3 Winston Churchill's funeral (1965)

4 Martin Luther King Jr preaches (1964)

5 Cathedral bombed (1940)

6 Queen Victoria's Diamond Jubilee (1897)

7 Duke of Wellington's funeral (1852)

8 Nelson's funeral (1806)

9 First service (1697)

10 Gunpowder Plotters executed in the churchyard (1606)

The wedding of Prince Charles and Lady Diana Spencer, 1981

The Duke of Wellington's funeral at St Paul's Cathedral

Top 10 London sights
see pp46–79

Top 10 Restaurants

1 **Aqua Shard**
Fine dining and views

2 **Barrafina**
Tapas

3 **Rules**
Classic British fare

4 **Ye Olde Cheshire Cheese**
Traditional pub

5 **Anchor & Hope**
Gastropub

6 **The Cinnamon Club**
Innovative Indian cuisine

7 **Joy King Lau**
Cantonese

8 **Wild Food Café**
Vegetarian

9 **Rock and Sole Plaice**
Fish and chips

10 **The Wolseley**
Famous brasserie

Top 10 Amsterdam

Begijnhof courtyard

Exploring Amsterdam

Amsterdam is a comparatively small city and good to explore on foot as almost all of the key attractions are close together. However, expect rain at any time, and much of the city centre is cobbled, which can be hard on the feet. Here are some ideas for two and four days of sightseeing.

Brouwersgracht, the "Brewers' Canal", provides a picturesque backdrop for a stroll or canal cruise.

Two Days in Amsterdam

Day ❶

MORNING

Start the morning at the **Anne Frank House** *(see pp112–3)* – having bought your online ticket in advance. Then pop along to the Westerkerk *(Prinsengracht 279)* before wandering part of the **Grachtengordel** *(see p91)*.

AFTERNOON

Enjoy the bustle of the Leidseplein as you continue on to the **Rijksmuseum** *(see pp92–5)* with its superb collection of paintings.

Day ❷

MORNING

Start in **Dam Square** *(see pp114–5)* and the Koninklijk Paleis, and then on to the Red Light District, **Oude Kerk** *(see pp108–9)* and **Ons' Lieve Heer op Solder** *(see pp100–101)*.

AFTERNOON

Allow at least an hour or two for the **Van Gogh Museum** *(see pp96–9)*. Alternatively, modern art lovers can visit the neighbouring Stedelijk Museum *(Museumplein 10)* – those with museum fatigue may prefer to explore the greenery of the Vondelpark instead.

Four Days in Amsterdam

Day ❶

MORNING

Begin the morning with a canal cruise from Stationsplein and then proceed to **Dam Square** *(see pp114–5)*, at the heart of the

Van Gogh Museum, a must-visit for art lovers; the world's largest collection of works by the tortured artist is on permanent display here.

EYE Film Institute

Het IJ

FERRY

Centraal Station

Stationsplein

Ons' Lieve Heer op Solder

Oude Kerk

Red Light District

Nieuwmarkt

OUDE ZIJDE

Key
— Two-day Itinerary
▬ Four-day Itinerary

PLANTAGE

Hortus Botanicus

Amstel

The Rijksmuseum's main building is a familiar Amsterdam landmark.

city, visiting the Koninklijk Paleis (Dam Square) and the Nieuwe Kerk (Dam Square).

AFTERNOON

Take lunch on the Nieuwmarkt before exploring the Red Light District, visiting both the **Oude Kerk** (see pp108–9) and the clandestine church **Ons' Lieve Heer op Solder** (see pp100–101).

Day ❷
MORNING

Head up to Brouwersgracht and then stroll through the Grachtengordel as the mood suits you. This is the prettiest part of Amsterdam and you can get a flavour for its history at the **Museum Van Loon** (see pp110–11).

AFTERNOON

Set the whole afternoon aside for the **Rijksmuseum** (see pp92–5) with its wonderous collection of Golden Age (Dutch) paintings. Take tea here too.

Day ❸
MORNING

Don't miss the much vaunted **Van Gogh Museum** (see pp96–9) or visit the Stedelijk Museum (Museumplein 10) of modern art next door. Afterwards, take a stroll through the Vondelpark.

AFTERNOON

Take the tram back to Centraal Station and then catch the ferry over the River IJ to the EYE Film Institute (IJpromenade 1), from where there are great views back over the city.

Day ❹
MORNING

Begin the day at the **Anne Frank House** (see pp112–3) and then drop by the Westerkerk (Prinsengracht 279), where Rembrandt was interred, before viewing the quiet charms of the **Begijnhof** (see pp102–3).

AFTERNOON

Spend the afternoon visiting the **Amsterdam Museum** (see pp104–7), which traces the city's history. Time permitting, round off the day at the city's botanical gardens, the Hortus Botanicus (Plantage Middenlaan 2a).

Top10 Amsterdam Highlights

Amsterdam has an appeal that is absolutely unique. It is a vibrant treasure trove of extraordinary artistic riches, and the living embodiment of 900 years of history. Elegant and serene, Amsterdam also has its seamy side, as much a part of its character as its famous network of canals. This small city packs a big punch.

1 Canals and Waterways

Amsterdam's canals – in particular, the ring of 17th-century canals known as the Grachtengordel – are its defining feature (see pp88–91).

Rijksmuseum 2

The national museum houses an unrivalled collection of 17th-century Dutch art. Star exhibits include Rembrandt's *The Night Watch* (see pp92–5).

3 Van Gogh Museum

The Van Gogh Museum houses the most comprehensive collection of the artist's work to be seen anywhere in the world – including some of his most famous paintings (see pp96–9).

Museum Ons' Lieve Heer op Solder 4

This fascinating 17th-century house in the Red Light District is a rare example of a perfectly preserved hidden Catholic church (see pp100–101).

5 Begijnhof

A haven of peace, the Begijnhof was built as a refuge for the Beguines, a lay Catholic sisterhood. Amsterdam's oldest house can be found here (see pp102–3).

6 Amsterdam Museum

Housed in the old city orphanage, this vibrant collection traces the city's history from the 12th century (see pp104–7).

0 metres 500
0 yards 500

7 Oude Kerk

This great Gothic basilica retains a number of its treasures, despite being stripped of its paintings and statuary during the Iconoclasm (see pp108–9).

8 Museum Van Loon

The Van Loon family residence on the Keizersgracht has been lovingly restored in the style of the mid-18th century (see pp110–11).

9 Anne Frank House

The hiding place of Anne Frank and her family, before they were discovered, arrested and sent to their deaths, is today a deeply moving museum (see pp112–3).

10 Dam Square

Where it began: Amsterdam's main square is on the site of the dam on the Amstel, around which the city grew (see pp114–5).

TOP 10 ⭐ Canals and Waterways

With their pretty bridges (1,703 in all), idiosyncratic gabled houses and relaxed waterside cafés, Amsterdam's 75 km (47 miles) of canals are perfect for a leisurely stroll. They are a constant reminder that the Netherlands is the world's flattest country, portions of which have been reclaimed from the sea with the aid of dykes, canals, tidal barriers, and man-made land. Before exploring the canals on foot, take a boat tour for a fascinating overview. In 2010 the 17th-century canal ring was added to the UNESCO World Heritage List.

① Herengracht
Stateliest canal of the Grachtengordel (see p91), the elegant Herengracht **(above)** is famous for its Golden Bend – a grand stretch of mansions built for the richest merchants. A more beautiful stretch lies between Huidenstraat and Leidsestraat, best viewed from the east side.

③ Reguliersgracht
Much loved for its pretty canal houses and humpback bridges, Reguliersgracht was cut in 1664. Look out for Nos. 57, 59 and 63.

④ Entrepotdok
An imposing stretch of former dockland has been restored to provide offices and apartments, with outdoor cafés overlooking colourful houseboats.

Vier Heemskinderen bridge

⑥ Leidsegracht
This canal was cut in 1664 as a barge route to Leiden. Today it is one of the city's most exclusive addresses.

⑤ Prinsengracht
The outermost canal of the Grachten-gordel, designed for warehouses and artisans' housing, has a breezy, laid-back air. It is peppered with cafés, art galleries and houseboats. Cycle its 3-km (2-mile) length, or explore short stretches on foot **(right)**.

② Keizersgracht
A central canal of the Grachtengordel **(above)** has fine stretches between Brouwersgracht and Raadhuisstraat, and again between Runstraat and Leidsestraat.

Map of the canals

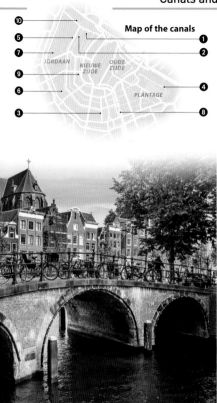

JORDAAN NIEUWE ZIJDE OUDE ZIJDE

PLANTAGE

HOW AMSTERDAM'S HOUSES ARE BUILT

Each house is built on wooden piles sunk into the marshy, porous subsoil. It wasn't until the 17th century, when the piles could be sunk deep enough to reach the hard layer of sand that lies at 13 m (42 ft), that any real stability was achieved. Some reach even further, to a second layer of sand at 18 m (58 ft). If piles come into contact with air, they rot, so today, concrete is used instead of wood.

⑧ Amstel River

Before the construction of the Grachtengordel, the river Amstel was the city's *raison d'être*. It is still used by barges to transport goods to the city's port.

⑨ Singel

The innermost ring of the Grachtengordel, the Singel was originally a moat circling the city during the Middle Ages. In the Golden Age it was lined with canal houses.

⑦ Bloemgracht

Crossed by cast-iron bridges, this is known locally as "the Herengracht of the Jordaan", because of its elaborately gabled houses.

NEED TO KNOW

■ Three perfect canal-side cafés are Papeneiland, at Prinsengracht 2, Van Puffelen, where you can sit on a barge in summer *(Prinsengracht 375-377)*, and Café de Sluyswacht *(Jodenbreestraat 1)*.

■ If you are short on time, at least take a stroll to the Huis op de Drie Grachten (House on Three Canals), step-gabled on all three of its canal-facing sides, at Oudezijds Voorburgwal 249. Afterwards, visit Het Grachtenhuis for a fascinating exhibition on the creation of Amsterdam's canal ring *(Herengracht 386)*.

⑩ Brouwersgracht

The happy-go-lucky feel of the "Brewers' Canal" **(above)** makes a pleasant contrast to the sophisticated elegance of the Grachtengordel.

Unexpected Sights on a Canal Tour

The exterior of the Dutch National Bank building

1 The Dutch National Bank

The vaults of the Dutch National Bank are sunk some 15 m (48 ft) below ground level. In the event of an alarm, they have been designed to allow the waters of the Singelgracht to flood into them.

2 The Prison Bridge

 The Torensluis – the widest bridge in the city – spans the Singel on the site of a 17th-century tower. A lock-up jail, sometimes open to the public, was built into its foundations.

3 The Cat Boat

 Hundreds of feline waifs and strays are given refuge in De Poezenboot (The Cat Boat), moored on the Singel.

4 The Drunken Tsar

In 1716, Peter the Great got drunk at his friend Christoffel Brants' house at Keizersgracht 317, and kept the mayor waiting at a civic reception. That night, he stayed at the house of the Russian ambassador, Herengracht 527, where Napoleon stayed in 1811.

5 The Narrowest House

 Singel 7: the smallest house in Amsterdam? No, it's the back door of a wedge-shaped house.

6 Blue Angel

 Cast your eye upwards to the beautiful Blue Angel statue perched on the former Levensverzekering Maatschappij - Noord-Braband building, at the corner of Singel and Haarlemmerstraat.

7 The Most Crooked Café

Teetering Café de Sluyswacht, built in 1695, makes an alarming sight as you glide by along the Oudeschans.

8 The Wrapped-Up House

Look carefully at Victoria Hotel, near the station, and you will see two tiny 17th-century houses in the monumental 19th-century façade. A little old lady, so the story goes, refused to sell up, so the hotel had to wrap itself around the houses.

9 Museumhaven, Oosterdok

The jetty leading up to the elevated hood of Nemo Science Museum is lined with vintage boats and barges dating from the 19th century.

10 The Tower of Tears

Originally part of the medieval city wall, this 15th-century tower has the saddest of names: Schreierstoren, from where weeping women waved farewell to their seafaring men.

THE GRACHTENGORDEL

Declared a UNESCO World Heritage Site in 2010, Amsterdam's magnificent semicircle of four canals – the Singel, Herengracht, Keizersgracht, and Prinsengracht – is the city's defining characteristic. Lined by elegant gabled houses, and connected by intimate cross-streets, the three outer canals were devised in the early 17th century to cope with the rapid rise in population. Previously a moat, the Singel was now considered a part of the ring, as houses were built on it during this period. Built in two stages, this costly plan was purely aesthetic – the land along the banks was sold in single, long plots that were taxed on width; the wealthy bought two together.

Amsterdam had its unlikely beginnings some 400 years earlier, when a fishing settlement grew up on the marshy banks of the river Amstel. (It was dammed in 1222 – hence the name, a contraction of Amstelledamme.) As the town expanded, canals were cut to drain more land and provide transport channels; the outer canals were fortified. A glance at a map shows the limits of the medieval town, bounded by the curved Singel, with the rest of the Grachtengordel fanning out beyond.

Magere Brug, literally "skinny bridge", was built over the River Amstel in 1934.

TOP 10 BRIDGES

1 **Magere Brug** (Amstel)
2 **Python Bridge**
3 **Jan Schaefer Bridge**
4 **Nieuwe Amstelbrug** (Amstel)
5 **Berlagebrug** (Amstel)
6 **Torensluis** (Singel)
7 **St Antoniesluis** (Zwanenburgwal)
8 **Seven (humpback) bridges** (Reguliersgracht)
9 **White wooden drawbridges** (Western Islands)
10 **Sleutelbrug** (Oudezijds Voorburgwal)

The Grachtengordel looks its best bathed in dusk light.

TOP 10 ⭐ Rijksmuseum

The magnificent national museum of the Netherlands possesses nearly one million Dutch works of art, only a fraction of which is on display. It was established by King Louis Napoleon in 1808 in the Royal Palace on the Dam, moving to its present location near the Vondelpark in 1885. The main building, designed by P J H Cuypers, underwent extensive renovation for ten years, reopening in 2013.

The Kitchen Maid ①
The sense of realism in this painting (c.1658) by Jan Vermeer (1632–75) is conveyed by his mastery of light, colour and perspective. Seen slightly from below against a bare wall, the simple, sturdy girl seems almost tangible – quiet and still, but for the milk flowing from her jug **(right)**.

② FK23 Bantam
Designed by Frits Koolhoven in 1917, this aeroplane is an icon of the Dutch contribution to aviation, with a fuselage with wooden frames, wooden propeller and wicker pilot's chair.

④ Temple Guard
This depiction of temple guard Naraen Kongo (Ungyo) dates from between 1300 and 1400 and is made from wood with traces of polychromy **(left)**.

⑥ Our Lady of Sorrows
This unique Flemish terracotta bust (c.1500–1510) is a lifelike depiction of Mary in mourning: the Mater Dolorosa.

⑤ Two Toilet Caskets
Created by the celebrated Parisian furniture maker André-Charles Boulle (c.1688), these paired toilet caskets are a fine example of the artist's work, representing the Baroque styles of tortoiseshell and gilded bronze.

⑦ Windmill on a Polder Waterway
Paul Joseph Constantin Gabriel's (1828–1903) balanced composition **(left)** is heavily influenced by Impressionist ideas, with its use of quick brushstrokes. It was acquired by the Rijksmuseum in 1889 and was considered modern for the time.

③ The Night Watch
Rembrandt's *The Militia Company of Captain Frans Banning Cocq* (1642) – otherwise known as *The Night Watch* – is the museum's prized possession, given pride of place in its own gallery.

The Jewish Bride (8)

In creating one of the most tender portraits ever painted (**right**; 1667), Rembrandt – in an unusually free style – depicts a couple in the guise of biblical characters Isaac and Rebecca.

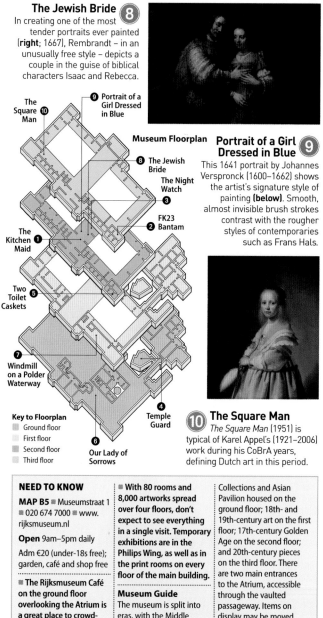

Museum Floorplan

The Square Man (10)

Portrait of a Girl Dressed in Blue (9)

(8) The Jewish Bride

The Night Watch (3)

FK23 Bantam (2)

The Kitchen Maid (1)

Two Toilet Caskets (5)

Windmill on a Polder Waterway (7)

Temple Guard (4)

Our Lady of Sorrows (6)

Key to Floorplan
- Ground floor
- First floor
- Second floor
- Third floor

Portrait of a Girl Dressed in Blue (9)

This 1641 portrait by Johannes Verspronck (1600–1662) shows the artist's signature style of painting (**below**). Smooth, almost invisible brush strokes contrast with the rougher styles of contemporaries such as Frans Hals.

The Square Man (10)

The Square Man (1951) is typical of Karel Appel's (1921–2006) work during his CoBrA years, defining Dutch art in this period.

NEED TO KNOW

MAP B5 ■ Museumstraat 1 ■ 020 674 7000 ■ www. rijksmuseum.nl

Open 9am–5pm daily

Adm €20 (under-18s free); garden, café and shop free

■ The Rijksmuseum Café on the ground floor overlooking the Atrium is a great place to crowd-watch and rest weary feet.

■ With 80 rooms and 8,000 artworks spread over four floors, don't expect to see everything in a single visit. Temporary exhibitions are in the Philips Wing, as well as in the print rooms on every floor of the main building.

Museum Guide

The museum is split into eras, with the Middle Ages, Renaissance, Special Collections and Asian Pavilion housed on the ground floor; 18th- and 19th-century art on the first floor; 17th-century Golden Age on the second floor; and 20th-century pieces on the third floor. There are two main entrances to the Atrium, accessible through the vaulted passageway. Items on display may be moved around the museum.

Rijksmuseum Features

1 The Building
The architect P J H Cuypers attracted strong criticism from the Protestant community, who took exception to the building's Neo-Gothic roofs and ornately decorated façade. King William III refused to set foot inside.

2 The Gardens
A little-known, immaculate haven, these are studded with statues and architectural curiosities.

3 Atrium
The entrance and heart of the museum, the two courtyards of the Atrium – now restored to their original 1885 condition – are linked by an underground passageway.

4 Terrazzo Floor
Covered in 1920 and hacked away in the late 20th century, Cuypers' original terrazzo floor has been restored to its former glory. Hundreds of thousands of small marble stones make up this floor, which is rich in symbolism.

5 Library
The library is only open to researchers of art history, but museum visitors can have a look from a gallery on the second floor to view its impressive interior and book collection.

6 Asian Pavilion
A quiet, meditative place, this is a wonderful retreat from the swarming masses. Elsewhere, Dutch art proliferates; the Asian Pavilion offers an insight into a different culture, with works spanning 4,000 years from 2000 BC.

Museum Floorplan

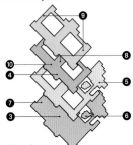

Key to Floorplan
◻ Ground floor
◻ First floor
◻ Second floor
◻ Third floor

7 Special Collection
The Special Collection ranges from amusing to bizarre, with rooms full of boxes, animals, Meissen porcelain, miniature silver, an armoury, and even the hair of Jacoba of Bavaria, the 15th-century Countess of Holland and Zeeland.

8 The Golden Age
Renowned the world over for its 17th-century collection, the Rijksmuseum draws many visitors to see paintings by Dutch masters such as Rembrandt, Jan Vermeer, Jan Steen and Frans Hals.

9 Modern Art
Two loft-like spaces on the third floor house art from the 20th century: one 1900–1950; the other 1950–2000.

10 Great Hall
The second-floor Great Hall has been reconstructed to how it looked in Cuypers' day, with elaborate, beautiful late 19th-century decoration.

Seated Guanyin, Asian Pavilion

REMBRANDT AND THE NIGHT WATCH

Self-Portrait, Rembrandt

Popular belief holds that Rembrandt's greatest painting, *The Night Watch* (1642), was responsible for his change in fortune from rich man to pauper. In fact, it was more a case of poor personal financial management than of public dissatisfaction with the artist, although it's very likely that the militiamen who commissioned the portrait would have been dismayed at the result. *The Night Watch* differs radically from other contemporary portraits of companies of civic guards, in which they are depicted seated, serious and soberly dressed. Rembrandt, by contrast, shows a tumultuous scene – the captain issuing orders to his lieutenant, the men taking up arms ready to march. This huge painting was originally even larger, but it was drastically cut down in 1715, when it was moved to the town hall, and tragically the other pieces of the masterpiece were lost. In 1975, the painting was slashed, but was meticulously repaired.

TOP 10 EVENTS IN REMBRANDT'S LIFE

1 Born in Leiden (1606)

2 Studies with Pieter Lastman (1624)

3 Receives first important commission and marries Saskia van Uylenburgh (1634)

4 Reputation grows; buys large house in Amsterdam (1639) – now the Museum Het Rembrandthuis

5 Titus, his only child to survive into adulthood, is born (1641)

6 Saskia dies; *The Night Watch* is completed (1642)

7 Hendrickje Stoffels moves in (1649)

8 Applies for bankruptcy (1656)

9 Titus and Hendrickje acquire the rights to his work (1660)

10 Death of Titus (1668); in October the following year, Rembrandt dies

The Night Watch by Rembrandt, was arguably the 17th-century Dutch master's greatest-ever work.

TOP 10 ⭐ Van Gogh Museum

The most comprehensive collection in the world of Vincent Van Gogh's work was amassed by his art dealer brother Theo, and is housed in this museum. It includes more than 200 of his paintings, over 500 drawings and hundreds of letters, as well as works by his contemporaries – though not all are on display. The display in Gerrit Rietveld's stunning 1973 building works thematically through Van Gogh's life, exploring his struggles and development as an artist and how he influenced, and was influenced by, other artists.

1 The Bedroom
The mastery of this painting (1888) lies in the simplicity of the subject and the subtly alternating blocks of colour (right). Van Gogh was so happy with the result he made two copies.

2 Almond Blossom
Van Gogh made this picture of white almond blossom against a blue sky for his new nephew, born in January 1890 and named after him.

3 The Reaper
While undergoing treatment in Saint-Rémy, Van Gogh found solace painting people who worked the land. He painted three versions of *The Reaper* (1889).

5 A Pair of Shoes
Van Gogh gives character to a pair of worn boots in one of the first paintings after his move to Paris (1886). The dark palette harks back to his Nuenen work.

6 Fishing Boats on the Beach at Les Saintes-Maries-de-la-Mer
A trip to the sea in 1888 produced these colourful, stylized boats. Look closely and you will see grains of sand, blown onto the canvas and fixed there forever as the paint dried.

7 The Potato Eaters
The culmination of his years in Nuenen, this was Van Gogh's first major composition (1885). He wanted to portray the peasants realistically, not to glamorize them, but the painting was not the critical success he had hoped for.

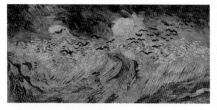

4 Wheatfield with Crows
One of the panoramic landscapes that Van Gogh painted in 1890, during the last days of his life, this famous picture with its dead-end track and menacing, crow-filled sky, perhaps reveals his tortured state of mind (above).

Sunflowers 8

This vibrant painting (1889) was intended to be one of a series of still lifes to fill the "Yellow House" at Arles. Van Gogh chose sunflowers because he was expecting Paul Gauguin, and knew his friend liked them. The predominant yellows and oranges contrast with strokes of brilliant mauve and red **(right)**.

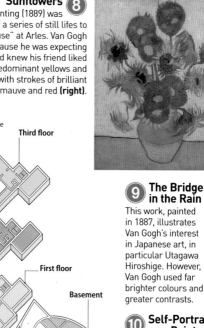

Key to Floorplan

- Temporary exhibitions
- Self-portraits and timeline
- Van Gogh 1883–1889
- Van Gogh close-up
- Van Gogh 1889–1890

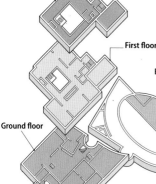

Third floor

Second floor

First floor

Basement

Ground floor

Museum Floorplan

9 The Bridge in the Rain

This work, painted in 1887, illustrates Van Gogh's interest in Japanese art, in particular Utagawa Hiroshige. However, Van Gogh used far brighter colours and greater contrasts.

10 Self-Portrait as a Painter

The last and most accomplished in a series of self-portraits painted in 1887, shortly before he left Paris, reveals Van Gogh's distinctive inter-pretation of Pointillism. He chose himself as the subject since he could seldom afford models.

NEED TO KNOW

MAP B6 ∎ Museumplein 6 ∎ 020 570 5200 ∎ www. vangoghmuseum.nl/en

Open Jan–Feb & Nov–21 Dec: 9am–5pm daily (to 9pm Fri); Mar–Jun & Sep-Oct: 9am–6pm daily (to 9pm Fri); Jul–Aug & 22 Dec–31 Dec: 9am–7pm daily (to 9pm Fri & Sat)

Adm €19 (under-18s free) Audio tours €5; group tours (up to 15 people) €85, by appointment only

∎ The museum has a useful self-service café, which is situated on the ground floor.

∎ To avoid the crowds, buy tickets on the museum's website. The best times for viewing the gallery are early morning or after 3pm. Last admission is 30 minutes before closing.

Museum Guide

Exhibits are displayed on all floors and present the complete story of the artist, his vision, his ideas and ambitions, his influences and the various myths surrounding him. The works are set in the context of other artists of the time. Many of the pivotal paintings form the focus of a theme. Check the latest floorplan at the museum as exhibits are moved around regularly.

Van Gogh Museum: Other Artists

View of Prins Hendrikkade, **Monet**

1 View of Prins Hendrikkade and the Kromme Waal in Amsterdam

Claude Monet painted this cityscape in the winter of 1874 from a boat on the IJ river. Rapid brush strokes loosely recreate the light and feel of the city.

2 Young Peasant Girl with a Hoe

Jules Breton (1827–1906) was an idol of Van Gogh. In rural scenes like this one (1882), he places an idealized figure of a peasant girl in a realistic setting.

3 Exhausted Maenads after the Dance

In this Lawrence Alma-Tadema (1836–1912) painting of 1874, three devotees *(maenads)* of the wine god, Bacchus, have fallen asleep.

4 Portrait of Bernard's Grandmother

Van Gogh swapped one of his self-portraits, *Self-Portrait with a Straw Hat,* for this painting (1887) by Émile Bernard (1868–1941), while in Paris.

5 Young Woman at a Table, "Poudre de Riz"

This early painting by Toulouse-Lautrec (1864–1901), who became a friend of Van Gogh, is probably of his mistress, Suzanne Valadon.

6 Portrait of Guus Preitinger, the Artist's Wife

The vivid use of colour in Kees van Dongen's (1877–1968) wild, lush portrait of his wife (1911) is characteristic of Fauvism.

7 Self-Portrait with a Portrait of Bernard, "Les Misérables"

In his powerful self-portrait (1888), Paul Gauguin (1848–1903) identified himself with the hero of Victor Hugo's *Les Misérables*, Jean Valjean.

8 Saint Geneviève as a Child in Prayer

An oil study (1876) by Puvis de Chavannes (1824–98) for the huge murals he painted at the Panthéon in Paris on the theme of St Geneviève's childhood.

Saint Geneviève as a Child in Prayer, **de Chavannes**

9 "Grand Paysan"

Jules Dalou (1838–1902) shared Van Gogh's preoccupation with peasants, whom he saw as heroic labourers. He devised this life-size sculpture in 1889.

10 Two Women Embracing

Van Gogh's influence on the Dutch artist Jan Sluijters (1881–1957) is obvious in the brushwork and colour of this painting of 1906.

THE LIFE OF VINCENT VAN GOGH

Self-Portrait,
Van Gogh

Born on 30 March 1853 in Zundert, Vincent Van Gogh was the eldest son of a pastor and his wife. Aged 16, he joined his uncle's business, Goupil & Co., art dealers. Seven years later, displaying increasingly erratic behaviour, he was dismissed. After a couple of false starts as a teacher and an evangelist, in 1880 he decided to be a painter. From 1883 to 1885, he lived with his parents in Nuenen, but in 1886 he went to Paris to study in Fernand Cormon's studio. He lived with his brother Theo, met renowned artists and changed his style. In 1888, he moved to Arles where he dreamed of establishing an artists' colony with Paul Gauguin. Soon after Gauguin arrived, the friends had a fierce argument and, during a psychotic attack, Van Gogh cut off a piece of his own left ear lobe. He enrolled as a voluntary patient in a clinic in Saint-Rémy in 1889. The following year, he left for the rural village Auvers-sur-Oise, where his state of mind deteriorated and he shot himself in the chest on 27 July 1890. He died, with Theo at his bedside, two days later.

TOP 10
19TH-CENTURY
ARTISTS

1 Vincent Van Gogh
(1853–1890)

2 Claude Monet
(1840–1926)

3 Pierre-Auguste
Renoir (1841–1919)

4 Paul Cézanne
(1839–1906)

5 Auguste Rodin
(1840–1917)

6 Edouard Manet
(1832–83)

7 Edgar Degas
(1834–1917)

8 J M W Turner
(1775–1851)

9 Eugène Delacroix
(1798–1863)

10 Jean-Baptiste
Camille Corot
(1796–1875)

The Yellow House
(1888) was the abode Van Gogh had hoped to share with Gauguin.

™10 ⭐ Museum Ons' Lieve Heer op Solder

Contrasting sharply with its surroundings in the Red Light District, this 17th-century house has, concealed in its upper floors, a church. It is a rare, perfectly preserved example of the many clandestine churches built after the Alteration. Local Catholics worshipped here from 1663 to 1887. Its little-changed interiors transport you back to the Dutch Golden Age. The museum was restored and expanded to include another building in 2011, which now forms the main entrance, and houses a café and exhibition space.

1 The Hidden Church
At the top of the stairs, the *huiskerk* (house church), Ons' Lieve Heer op Solder (Our Lord in the Attic), is a charming sight **(right)**. In c.1735, it was remodelled in Baroque style with the addition of two tiers of galleries, suspended from the roof by cast-iron rods, to provide extra seating.

2 The Confessional
In 1739, this living room in the middle of the three houses became the church's confessional. One of the two wooden confessional boxes still remains **(left)**.

3 The Maria Chapel and Peat Room
This chapel comprises a small altar dedicated to the Virgin Mary. The statue is one of the few original objects belonging to the 17th-century church.

5 The Sael
Adhering to strict rules of proportion and symmetry, the family's *sael* (formal parlour) is a superb example of the Dutch Classical style fashionable in the 17th century. It is this room the family would have used to receive guests.

6 Canal Room
This 17th-century living room overlooks the canal to the front, and is where residents would spend most of their time during the day. It is decorated with authentic furnishings from the era, including a replica stove.

4 The Priest's Room
Formerly the servants' quarters, the Priest's Room is in a corner on a bend in the stairs. It's a tiny, enclosed bedroom with a box bed, simply furnished as it would have been for the priest, who lived in the house **(above)**.

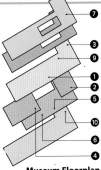

Key to Floorplan
- Ground floor
- First floor
- Second floor
- Third floor
- Fourth floor
- Fifth floor

Museum Floorplan

7 The Rear Houses

The rear houses were gradually taken over by the church, but there are still signs of their original use as family rooms.

THE ALTERATION

The revolt of the (Calvinist) Northern Netherlands against the (Catholic) Spanish Habsburgs began in 1568, but it was not until 1578, when Amsterdam joined William of Orange in a peaceful revolution known as the Alteration, that Calvinists seized power and the city became the Protestant capital of an infant Dutch Republic. The Catholics couldn't worship in public, but Dutch tolerance ensured that they were able to continue in private.

NEED TO KNOW

MAP D2 ▪ Oudezijds Voorburgwal 38
▪ 020 624 6604
▪ www.opsolder.nl

Open 10am–6pm Mon–Sat, 1–6pm Sun, public hols; closed 27 Apr

Adm €12.50, children 5–18 €6

▪ The audio tour is free, and for an extra €1 there is a Ladybird in the Attic tour for kids.

▪ No wheelchair access. A virtual tour in the annexe can be arranged.

▪ There's a museum shop and café.

▪ Sunday Mass is on 1st Sunday of the month.

8 The Building

The spout-gabled canal house was built in 1661 for Jan Hartman, a Catholic merchant. He combined its attic with the attics of two smaller houses behind to create the hidden church, which was extended in c.1735.

9 The Folding Pulpit

The ingenious pulpit was designed to fold away under the left column of the altar when not in use. The painting above the altar is *The Baptism of Christ* by Jacob de Wit (1695–1754).

10 The Kitchen

Once part of the sacristan's secret living quarters, the charming 17th-century kitchen **(left)** has original Delft wall tiles, an open hearth, stone sink and black-and-white floor.

🔟 ⭐ Begijnhof

This bewitching sanctuary of elegant houses around a tranquil green was founded in 1346 for the members of a lay Catholic sisterhood, the Beguines, the last of whom died in 1971. Although no original buildings survive, nor the early design of the courtyard surrounded by water, there is a fascinating 15th-century wooden house, a lovely church of the same period and an appealing hidden chapel. Visitors are asked to respect the privacy of the current residents.

③ 17th- and 18th-Century Houses

After several devastating fires, most of the existing houses were built in the 17th and 18th centuries **(right)**. They are typically tall and narrow, with large sash windows and spout or neck gables. The sisterhood owned them, so if a Beguine left or died, outsiders could not claim her house. Today, they provide homes for 100 or so single women.

① Engelse Kerk

Before the Alteration (see p101), the Beguines worshipped in this pretty 15th-century church **(above)**. Confiscated in 1578, it was let to a group of English and Scottish Presbyterians in 1607, who renamed it the "English Church".

② The Beguine in the Gutter

To make amends for her family's conversion to Protestantism, Cornelia Arents requested in her will not to be buried in the church, but in the gutter outside. Legend has it that her coffin was left inside the church on 2 May 1654, but the following day it was found outside, where she was eventually buried.

④ Het Houten Huis

No. 34, Het Houten Huis, is one of the oldest houses in Amsterdam **(below)**, and one of only two wood-fronted houses in the city. It predates the 1521 ban on the construction of wooden houses, introduced to reduce the risk of fire.

Plan of Begijnhof

❼ ❽ ❾❷ ❸

NIEUWEZIJDS VOORBURGWAL

GEDEMPTE BEGIJNENSLOOT

SPUI

❹ ❿ ❺ ❻ ❶

⑤ Spui Entrance

Members of the public use the arched entrance from Gedempte Begijnensloot, but be sure to peep discreetly into the pretty vaulted and tiled passageway leading to Spui.

6 Statue of a Beguine

The statue by Engelse Kerk shows a Beguine dressed in a traditional *falie* (headdress) and long garment of undyed cloth.

9 Wall Plaque on No. 19

The story depicted on this handsome plaque illustrates the return from Egypt to Israel of Jesus, Mary and Joseph after the death of Herod.

7 Begijnhof Chapel

The city's first hidden chapel **(below)** was created in 1665, when the Beguines converted two ordinary houses into a little church *see (pp100–101)*. The Miracle of Amsterdam is commemorated here.

10 Courtyard with Wall Plaques

Set into the wall of the courtyard behind Het Houten Huis is a collection of wall plaques from demolished houses. In keeping with the religious nature of the Beguines, each one tells a biblical story.

8 Mother Superior's House

The grandest house, No. 26, belonged to the Mother Superior. In the 20th century, the last of the Beguines lived together here.

THE WELFARE SYSTEM

Charity lies at the heart of Amsterdam's long tradition of caring for the poor and needy, which goes back to the Middle Ages. In the 14th century, primary responsibility for social welfare passed from the church to the city authorities. They distributed food to the poor, and set up institutions to care for orphans, the sick and the insane. In the 17th century, a number of wealthy merchants funded *hofjes* (almshouses) that provided subsidized mass housing for the city's needy.

NEED TO KNOW

MAP C3 ▪ Spui (entrance on Gedempte Begijnensloot) ▪ 020 622 1918 ▪ www.begijnhof amsterdam.nl

Open 9am–5pm daily

Begijnhof Chapel: open 1–6:30pm Mon, 9am–5pm Tue–Fri, 9am–6pm Sat–Sun

▪ Café Luxembourg and traditional Café Hoppe are just round the corner in Spui (at Nos. 18 and 24 respectively).

▪ Services are held in Dutch (daily) and French (Sundays) in the Roman Catholic Begijnhof Chapel. Services in English are held in the Protestant Engelse Kerk (Sundays).

▪ Enjoy a concert at the Engelse Kerk.

▪ Pick up an information booklet from Het Houten Huis.

🔟 ⭐ Amsterdam Museum

The Amsterdam Museum houses a collection of artifacts, archaeological finds, clothes, jewellery, maps, paintings and sculptures that chart Amsterdam's metamorphosis over the centuries. The building was originally a convent, and in 1580 it became the city orphanage. Extensions were added by Hendrick and Pieter de Keyser before Jacob van Campen's magnificent rebuilding of 1634. The orphans moved out in 1960; in 1975 the museum moved in.

1 Terrestrial and Celestial Globes

A pair of costly globes lent prestige to any self-respecting 17th-century intellectual. Joan Willemsz Blaeu must have made this unique pair after 1644 because they show the Australian coast, just discovered by Abel Tasman.

2 Turbo Shell

This exquisite mother-of-pearl *Turbo marmoratus* is covered in tiny engraved animals (above). It dates from c.1650 and was probably brought from the Orient by the Dutch East India Company (VOC).

3 Dam Square with the New Town Hall under Construction

This 1656 snapshot of the Dam by Johannes Lingelbach (1622–74) (above) exudes energy.

4 Ceremonial Keys to the City

Two gold and silver keys, made by Diederik Lodewijk Bennewitz, were presented by the mayor to Emperor Napoleon on his first and only visit in October 1811.

5 De Witkar

Take a virtual drive in "De Witkar" (The White Car). Luud Schimmelpennink's idea, conceived around 1970, was one of the first car-share projects in the world. The electric cars are unlocked with a magnetic key.

6 Wedding Rings of Amsterdam's First Married Gay Couple

The Netherlands was the first country in the world to legalize same-sex marriage, with the first ceremony of four couples taking place in 2001. These rings were worn by one of those couples.

7 Bird's-Eye View of Amsterdam

Cornelis Anthonisz's 1538 map of Amsterdam (the oldest extant) shows the Dam, Oude Kerk and Nieuwe Kerk (left).

Civic Guardsmen of the Company of Captain Albert Coenraetsz Burgh and Lieutenant Pieter Evertsz Hulft ⑧

This 1625 oil painting **(right)** by Werner Jacobsz van den Valckert (c.1580–1627) shows merchant and dyer Albert Burgh keeping watch over Amsterdam's harbour.

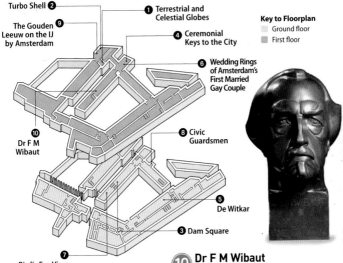

- ❷ Turbo Shell
- ❾ The Gouden Leeuw on the IJ by Amsterdam
- ❶ Terrestrial and Celestial Globes
- ❹ Ceremonial Keys to the City
- ❻ Wedding Rings of Amsterdam's First Married Gay Couple
- ❿ Dr F M Wibaut
- ❽ Civic Guardsmen
- ❺ De Witkar
- ❸ Dam Square
- ❼ Bird's-Eye View of Amsterdam

Museum Floorplan

Key to Floorplan
- Ground floor
- First floor

⑨ The Gouden Leeuw on the IJ by Amsterdam

Willem van de Velde's (1633–1707) painting (1686) shows the Gouden Leeuw with a view of Amsterdam.

⑩ Dr F M Wibaut

This bronze head **(above)** was made in 1934 by Tjipke Visser (1876–1955), favourite sculptor of the Social Democratic Workers' Party (SDAP). The subject was Floor Wibaut, SDAP Councillor for housing in the 1920s, who dedicated himself to building new apartments for the working class.

Amsterdam Museum Rooms

Regents' Chamber, decorated as it was in the 17th century

1 Regents' Chamber
The orphanage governors met in this 17th-century room, maintained in the original Old Holland style.

2 Amsterdam Gallery
This glassed-over gallery displays Amsterdam group portraits – from famous Dutch footballers to the city's 17th-century militia.

3 Temporary Exhibition Space
Once used to house a girls' refectory and needlework rooms, it is now used for temporary exhibitions.

4 Room 0.5: Turbulent Times
Displays from the late 16th century include the Civic Guard's Italian-made armour, and silver that escaped melting down for "crisis coins" in 1578.

5 Room 0.3: The Dam
The bustling heart of the city was a popular subject in 17th-century paintings like Lingelbach's *Dam Square with the New Town Hall under Construction.*

6 Amsterdam DNA
This 3D exhibition takes visitors on a 45-minute historical tour of Amsterdam, telling the multifaceted story of the city.

7 World – City
A permanent exhibition which focuses on the relationship between Amsterdam and the world, and tells the stories behind the many different nationalities who have made the city their home.

8 The Little Orphanage
The history of the building is brought to life in this sensory exhibition which explores the old orphanage – children will particularly enjoy the interactive displays.

9 Where Orphans Played
The lockers in the Boys' Courtyard now contain personal objects of the orphans who lived here.

10 David and Goliath
Constructed around 1650, these large wooden statues once stood in a pleasure garden as part of a biblical tableau.

Museum Floorplan

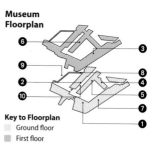

Key to Floorplan
Ground floor
First floor

THE GOLDEN AGE

The economic boom of the 17th century laid the foundations for the flowering of the arts in Amsterdam. Plans were made to surround the city with a triple ring of canals lined with fine houses, a project which required the work of many architects. The most powerful city in the Dutch Republic recognized the importance of the arts, and rewarded its artists well – and with the supremacy of the Protestants came the freedom to paint secular subjects. To show their wealth and status, rich patrons commissioned portraits of themselves and their families. The artists' best clients, however, were the municipal bodies such as the guilds, who commissioned group portraits as well as decorative pieces of silver and glass. Painters began to focus their energies on a single area of painting – whether historical, portraiture, interiors, genre, still lifes, urban scenes, landscapes or seascapes – and this specialization greatly enhanced the quality of their workmanship.

The Silver Marriage Cup features a hinged bowl above the woman's head and one formed by her full skirt. Once the wedding was in full swing, the bride and groom would down both together.

TOP 10
HIGHLIGHTS OF THE GOLDEN AGE

1 *The Night Watch* by Rembrandt (1642, Rijksmuseum) *(see p95)*

2 **The Grachtengordel,** designed by Hendrick Staets (begun in 1613) *(see p91)*

3 **Ons' Lieve Heer op Solder** (1663) *(see pp100–101)*

4 **Westerkerk** by Hendrick de Keyser (1631) *(Prinsengracht 279)*

5 **Huis met de Hoofden,** built by Hendrick de Keyser and his son Pieter (1622) *(Keizersgracht 123)*

6 **Claes Claeszhofje** (1616)

7 **Silver Marriage Cup** by Gerrit Valck (1634)

8 **Café Hoppe** (c.1670)

9 **Delftware** (second half 17th century)

10 **Burgerzaal,** Koninklijk Paleis *(Dam Square)*

Dutch Battle Ships **by Ludolf Backhuysen**

🔟 ⭐ Oude Kerk

The city's oldest monument and first parish church stands on the site of an early 13th-century wooden chapel that was destroyed by fire. Rebuilt as a small stone hall church in the 14th century, over the years it expanded into a mighty Gothic basilica, now in the heart of the Red Light District. The interior boasts some exquisite stained glass, rare ceiling paintings, and a world-famous organ, and regularly hosts art exhibitions, performances and debates. It is dedicated to St Nicholas, patron saint of the city.

3 Stained Glass of the Burgemeesters
The colourful stained-glass windows flanking the chancel depict the arms of the city burgomasters from 1578 to 1807 **(left)**. One was designed by De Angeli in 1758; the other by Pieter Jansz in 1654.

1 Spire
From the graceful late-Gothic spire, built by Joost Bilhamer in 1565, there are splendid views over the Oude Zijde. The tower contains a 47-bell carillon, a 17th-century addition that rings out every Saturday afternoon.

4 Great Organ
With its eight pairs of bellows, magnificent oak-encased pipework, marbled wood statues and gilded carving, the great organ is a glorious sight. Built by Christian Vater in 1724 and renovated by Johann Caspar Müller 14 years later, it is known as the Vater-Müller organ.

2 Ceiling
The massive wooden vaulted ceiling **(below)** is claimed to be the largest in Western Europe. It was only during restoration work in 1955 that the beautiful 15th-century paintings were revealed.

Oude Kerk

5 Red Door into the Old Sacristy
Rembrandt famously passed through this door to announce his marriage. "Marry in haste, repent at leisure" is inscribed above it.

6 Little Organ
Attractively painted shutters form the original casing built in 1658 – however, the pipework was replaced in 1965. It is tuned as it would have been before 1700, so early Baroque music can now be part of the organist's repertoire.

Church Floorplan

7 Maria Kapel

The most stunning stained glass is in the three windows of the Lady Chapel. All date from the 16th century; two show scenes from the Virgin's life, above the customary picture of the family who donated the window.

THE ICONOCLASM OF 1566

In the 1566 Iconoclasm, or *Beeldenstorm* – precursor to the Alteration of 1578 when the city became Protestant – the Calvinists looted Catholic churches and destroyed their treasures, among them the Oude Kerk's pictures, altars and statues. Only the ceiling paintings and stained glass were spared, as they were out of reach. The Calvinists also disapproved of the beggars and pedlars who gathered in the church, and threw them out, ending its role as a city meeting place.

8 Saskia's Grave

Among the great and the good buried here is Saskia van Uylenburgh, Rembrandt's first wife, who died in 1642. Her grave is number 29K in the Weitkopers Kapel.

NEED TO KNOW

MAP D2 ▪ Oudekerksplein 23 ▪ 020 625 8284 ▪ www.oudekerk.nl

Open 10am–6pm Mon–Sat, 1–5:30pm Sun; closed 27 Apr, 25 Dec

Adm €12; students €7; under-13s free (separate charge for exhibitions)

Guided tours by appointment; www.westertorenamsterdam.nl.

▪ For food and peoplewatching, head for Nieuwmarkt; In de Waag (Nieuwmarkt 4) is recommended.

▪ Go to the Dutch Reformed Church service at 11am Sunday, or a concert or contemporary art exhibition.

▪ Don't miss the votive ships hanging from the choir ceiling of Oude Kerk.

9 Decorated Pillars

Pre-1578 relics, these pillars **(above)** once supported niches for statues of the Apostles destroyed in the Iconoclasm, and were painted to look like brocade, since the real thing was unsuited to the church's humidity.

10 Misericords

The 15th-century misericords helped choristers take the weight off their feet. Their charming carvings illustrate traditional Dutch proverbs.

TOP10 ⭐ Museum Van Loon

Step back into the 18th century at this delightful canal house on Keizersgracht, which has been the property of the prestigious Van Loon family (co-founders of the Dutch East India Company, later bankers and royal courtiers) since 1884. In 1973, the family, who still reside here, opened it to the public, having painstakingly restored it to its appearance in the 1750s, when it was owned by Dr Abraham van Hagen and his heiress wife, Catharina Trip. It is beautifully furnished with Van Loon family possessions throughout.

1 The Building
In 1672, Jeremias van Raey built two large houses on Keizersgracht **(above)**. One he occupied, the other – No. 672, now the Museum Van Loon – he rented to Rembrandt's most famous pupil, Ferdinand Bol.

The Garden Room

2 The Staircase
The balustrade was installed by Dr Van Hagen, who had his and his wife's names incorporated into the ornate brass work **(right)**. When the canals ceased to freeze over regularly, the 18th-century sledge in the hall became a plant stand.

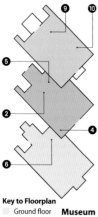

Key to Floorplan
Ground floor
First floor
Second floor

Museum Floorplan

3 The Coach House
The restored coach house has the family's original coach and livery on display. Temporary exhibitions are held here.

4 The Dining Service
Rare 18th-century Dutch porcelain and 19th-century Limoges ware grace the dining room.

7 The Garden

Laid out according to a plan of the property from 1700, the peaceful, sculptural garden ends in the false Neo-Classical façade of the coach house (left). This original amalgamation of canal house, coach house and garden can be seen nowhere else.

8 The Family Portraits

Portraits of the family (below) are displayed throughout the house.

9 The Painted Room

Painted wall hangings such as the ones in this room, featuring ruins, Classical buildings and human figures, were very popular in the 1700s.

5 The Wedding Portrait

Golden Age painter Jan Molenaer's first major commission in Amsterdam portrays the whole family. It's a second marriage: the bride holds her stepson's hand in acceptance, while the fallen chair symbolizes the groom's deceased brother.

The Kitchen 6

Cosy and inviting, the basement kitchen has been restored to look as it did in a photograph from 1900 (right).

NEED TO KNOW

MAP D5
- Keizersgracht 672
- 020 624 5255 ■ www.museumvanloon.nl

Open 10am–5pm daily; closed 1 Jan, 27 Apr, 25 Dec

Adm €10; concessions €8

Guided tours on request.

■ There is a small café in the coach house that serves coffee, tea and wonderful apple cake.

■ Serene and elegant, the Museum Van Loon makes a perfect visit for adults, but it's not so well suited to children. There is no wheelchair access.

Museum Guide
Visitors are welcomed as guests in a private house and encouraged to wander around freely. Temporary exhibitions of modern art and sculpture are displayed in the house, garden and the coach house. The museum also participates in the open Garden Days in June.

---

10 The Romantic Double Portrait

Painted by J F A Tischbein in 1791, this intimate, relaxed portrait of these Van Loon ancestors is typical of the Age of Enlightenment, conveying love and happiness as well as duty.

TOP 10 ⭐ Anne Frank House

This deeply moving museum tells a tragic story. When, in 1942, the Nazis began to round up Jews in Amsterdam, the Frank and Van Pels families went into hiding. For 25 months, they hid in a secret annexe in the Anne Frank House. In August 1944, they were arrested and deported. Only Otto survived. The diary of his daughter Anne, who died in Bergen-Belsen concentration camp in February 1945 at the age of 15, has made her one of the most inspiring figures of the 20th century. The ever-popular museum attracts more than a million visitors each year.

① The Warehouse

Otto Frank's business made pectin for jam, and spice and herb mixtures. The annexe was over his warehouse **(below)**; the families had to keep quiet for fear that the workers would hear them.

② The Offices

Upstairs are the offices of Otto Frank and the staff who helped to hide him and his family, along with Otto's business partner, Hermann van Pels, and his wife and son. In Anne's diary, the Van Pels became the Van Daans.

③ The Moveable Bookcase

To hide the entrance to the annexe, one of the helpers made a swinging bookcase **(right)**. As Anne wrote, "no one could ever suspect that there could be so many rooms hidden behind..."

④ Anne's Room

Film-star pin-ups still adorn the wall of Anne's room **(right)**. After her sister Margot moved in with her parents, Anne had to share this space with a new member of the group, a dentist called Fritz Pfeffer – in Anne's first estimation, "a very nice man".

⑤ The Secret Annexe

The claustrophobic rooms in which the eight lived have been left unfurnished, as they were when cleared of possessions by the Germans after their arrest. On one wall, pencil marks record the growth of Anne and Margot.

⑥ Peter's Room

The small refuge of Peter van Pels **(right)** was the room behind the attic. Anne often spent time here talking with Peter.

⑦ The Front Attic

In a moving display in the front attic, visitors learn the fate of each member of the group after they were betrayed to the Nazis. Tragically, Anne and Margot Frank died shortly before Bergen-Belsen concentration camp was liberated.

8 The Diary Room
As well as the now famous diary **(above)**, Anne wrote short stories and ideas for novels. As time went on, she began to edit her original diary with a book called *The Secret Annexe* in mind.

ANNE FRANK'S DIARY

On the day the family were taken away, Miep Gies, who had helped conceal them, found Anne's diary. With the words "Here is your daughter Anne's legacy to you", she handed it to Otto Frank on his return from Auschwitz. He prepared a transcript, and the diary was published to great acclaim in the Netherlands in 1947, and in Britain and the United States in 1952. It has since been published in more than 70 languages.

Key to Floorplan
- Ground floor
- First floor
- Second floor
- Third floor
- Attic

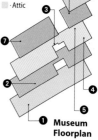

1 Museum Floorplan

8 9 10 in separate building

9 Otto Frank Exhibit
An interview with Otto Frank from 1967 and documents from his personal collection are on show. A notebook of entries made after Otto's return from Auschwitz is most poignant.

10 The Exhibition Room
The multimedia exhibition space screens. *Reflections on Anne Frank*, a film in which 22 writers, actors, museum visitors and those who knew her talk about what she meant to them.

NEED TO KNOW

MAP B2 ■ Westermarkt 20 ■ 020 556 7105 ■ www.annefrank.org

Open Nov–Mar: 9am–7pm daily; Apr–Oct: 9am–10pm daily; closed Yom Kippur (Check website for other exceptions)

Adm €10; children 10–17 €5; under-10s free

A 360-degree virtual reality tour is available for the disabled.

■ There is a pleasant, airy café with a great view of the Westerkerk.

■ Note that tickets must be booked in advance online for a specific date and time. Tickets cannot be bought on the door.

■ Take care around the house as the stairs are steep and narrow.

■ The visit is a moving experience, so plan something contemplative afterwards: climb the Westerkerk spire, or walk to the Western Islands.

📌10 ⭐ Dam Square

The very heart of Amsterdam, Dam Square – or "the Dam", as the locals call it – marks the site of the original 13th-century dam on the Amstel river. By the 17th century, with the town hall here and the Exchange nearby, the Dam had become the focus of Amsterdam's political and commercial life. Today an architectural parade spanning six centuries includes the glorious Nieuwe Kerk and the Koninklijk Paleis. The passage of years may have eroded some of the square's grandeur, but none of its colour or vitality.

1 Madame Tussauds Amsterdam
Displays at this outpost of the London waxworks range from the fascinating to the bizarre. Special effects, including animatronics, bring to life scenes from Holland's past **(above)**.

5 Koninklijk Paleis
Built as the town hall, Jacob van Campen's unsmiling Classical edifice symbolizes the worldly power of 17th-century Amsterdam. The Royal Palace is still used by the Dutch Royal House for state occasions, but is otherwise open to visitors to discover its rich history and interior.

2 Street Performances and Events
Busking, mime acts, funfairs, book fairs, exhibitions, concerts – such things have gone on in the Dam **(right)** since J Cabalt introduced his puppet show in 1900.

3 Damrak
Damrak was once the medieval city's busiest canal, with ships sailing up to be unloaded at the Dam. In 1672, the canal was partially filled in, and Damrak became the vibrant shopping strip it is today **(below)**.

4 Nationaal Monument
This 22-m- (70-ft-) tall obelisk commemorates the Dutch killed in World War II. Embedded in the wall behind are urns containing soil from the Dutch provinces and overseas colonies.

6 De Bijenkorf
De Bijenkorf (which literally translates as "the beehive") is Amsterdam's most famous high-end department store. It boasts a vast perfumery, designer fashion boutiques and much more.

7 Kalverstraat
Music shops jostle with both tacky and trendy clothes stores at the Dam end of this pedestrian shopping street.

8 Rokin
The Rokin had its heyday in the 19th century, when its broad sweep was a promenade for the well-to-do.

INSIDE THE KONINKLIJK PALEIS

The ponderous exterior belies the magnificent interior – especially the dramatic Burgerzaal (Citizen's Hall). See fine sculptures by Artus Quellien and Rombout Verhulst, ceilings and friezes by Rembrandt's pupils, and Empire furniture owned by Louis Napoleon. The Vierschaar (Tribunal) is a macabre room, still intact, where judges once pronounced the death sentence.

10 Nieuwe Kerk
Now a venue for exhibitions, the Nieuwe Kerk **(left)** has hosted royal events since 1814. Treasures include a Jacob van Campen organ case and an elaborately carved pulpit by Albert Vinckenbrinck.

Plan of Dam Square

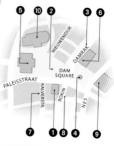

9 Grand Hotel Krasnapolsky
Adolf Wilhelm Krasnapolsky, an emigré Polish tailor with ambition, rented the down-at-heel Nieuwe Poolsche Koffiehuis in the 1870s, swiftly transforming it into a fashionable hotel **(left)**.

NEED TO KNOW

Madame Tussauds Amsterdam: **MAP C2**; 020 522 1010; open 10am–9:30pm daily, closed 27 April; Adm €24.50, children 5–15 €20.50, under-5s free, €5 discount when booked online; www.madame tussauds.nl

Koninklijk Paleis: **MAP C2**; 020 522 6161; open 10am–5pm daily (except state functions); Adm €10, seniors/students €9, under-18s free; www.paleisamsterdam.nl

Nieuwe Kerk: **MAP C2**; 020 638 6909; open during exhibitions:

10am–5pm daily; Adm; www.nieuwekerk.nl

■ Eat at the cafés in de Bijenkorf or the Nieuwe Kerk – the latter's terrace overlooks the Dam.

■ Go to one of the concerts or exhibitions held at the Nieuwe Kerk.

Top 10 Amsterdam sights
see pp86–115

Top 10 Restaurants

1. **Supperclub**
   Lively eatery
2. **Mamouche**
   Moroccan and French fusion
3. **Bazar**
   Middle Eastern
4. **De Jaren**
   Canal-side café
5. **Royal Cafe De Kroon**
   Dutch and International
6. **De Engelbewaarder**
   Good value fare
7. **Rozemboom**
   Homely Dutch fare and pancakes
8. **Tujuh Maret**
   Indonesian
9. **1e Klas**
   Traditional café
10. **Belhamel**
    French and Dutch

Top 10 Barcelona

The soaring, tree-like columns
of the Sagrada Família's nave

Exploring Barcelona

You'll be utterly spoiled for choice for things to see and do in Barcelona, which is packed with historical buildings, parks, museums and beaches. Whether you're coming for a weekend, or want to get to know the city better, these two- and four-day itineraries will help you make the most of your visit.

Two Days in Barcelona

Day ❶
MORNING
Stroll along Barcelona's most celebrated avenue, **La Rambla** *(see pp128–9)*, then dive into the warren of medieval streets that makes up the Barri Gòtic and visit **Barcelona Cathedral** *(see pp130–31)*.

AFTERNOON
Continue your exploration of Barcelona's historic heart with a wander around the Born neighbourhood. Visit the **Museu Picasso** *(see pp140–41)*, then see if you can get tickets for an evening performance at the lavish *Modernista* **Palau de la Música Catalana** *(see pp142–3)*.

Day ❷
MORNING
Spend the morning marvelling at Gaudí's incredible **Sagrada Família** *(see pp124–7)*, but make sure you've booked tickets online in advance to avoid the long queues.

AFTERNOON
Ride the funicular up the green hill of Montjuïc to the **Fundació Joan Miró** *(see pp138–9)*, a stunning modern building that is home to a spectacular collection of Miró's work.

Four Days in Barcelona

Day ❶
MORNING
Make the day's first stop the playful, whimsical **Parc Güell** *(see pp134–5)*, a UNESCO World Heritage Site.

AFTERNOON
Head south to the city's most iconic building, the **Sagrada Família** *(see pp124–7)*, then take in the **Museu**

The vibrant Mercat de la Boqueria is one of Europe's largest markets for fresh produce, cheese and meat.

Picasso *(see pp140–41)*, set in a complex of five interconnected Gothic palaces. Book tickets online in advance to avoid queues at these attractions.

Day ❷
MORNING
Take a stroll along **La Rambla** *(see pp128–9)*, ducking into the Mercat de la Boqueria *(La Rambla)* to admire the dizzying range of produce. Then meander through the medieval lanes of the Barri Gòtic to find **Barcelona Cathedral** *(see pp130–31)*.

AFTERNOON
Take in the smart boutiques of the elegant Passeig de Gràcia, then visit one of Gaudí's most remarkable buildings, **La Pedrera** *(see pp136–7)*. In summer, you can book in advance for jazz on its undulating rooftop.

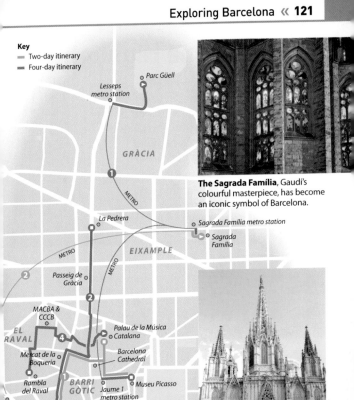

Key
— Two-day itinerary
— Four-day itinerary

Parc Güell

Lesseps metro station

GRÀCIA

❶

METRO

La Pedrera

METRO

Sagrada Família metro station

Sagrada Família

EIXAMPLE

❷

Passeig de Gràcia

METRO

❷

MACBA & CCCB

EL RAVAL

❹

Palau de la Música Catalana

Barcelona Cathedral

Mercat de la Boqueria

Rambla del Raval

BARRI GÒTIC

❶

Jaume 1 metro station

Museu Picasso

Paral·lel metro station

La Rambla

| 0 metres | 500 |
| 0 yards | 500 |

The Sagrada Família, Gaudí's colourful masterpiece, has become an iconic symbol of Barcelona.

Barcelona's 13th-century cathedral has a magnificent façade and a quiet cloister.

Day ❸
MORNING
Relax in one of the many gardens on Montjuïc, perhaps the Jardins Laribel or the Jardins de Miramar, before visiting the **Fundació Joan Miró** (see pp138–9), one of the world's largest Miró collections.

AFTERNOON
You'd need more than an afternoon to see every gallery at the **Museu Nacional d'Art de Catalunya** (see pp132–3), but the Romanesque and Gothic collections are a must. In the evening, enjoy the light show at the Font Màgica (Plaça de Carles Buïgas).

Day ❹
MORNING
Take a tour of the **Palau de la Música Catalana** (see pp142–3), a breath-taking Modernista masterpiece with an eye-popping auditorium.

AFTERNOON
Check out the contemporary art at the **Museu d'Art Contemporani (MACBA) and Centre de Cultura Contemporània (CCCB)** (see pp144–5), then relax over a coffee on the nearby Rambla del Raval.

TOP 10 Barcelona Highlights

Blessed with desirable geographical genes, this sparkling Mediterranean jewel has it all, from beautiful *Modernista* buildings, atmospheric medieval streets and enchanting squares to beaches, treasure-filled museums and a thriving port area.

Sagrada Família ①

Gaudí's otherworldly *pièce de résistance* is the enduring symbol of the city and its *Modernista* legacy. Of the 18 planned spires, 12 jut into the sky *(see pp124–7)*.

② La Rambla

Barcelona's centrepiece, this thriving pedestrian thoroughfare cuts a wide swathe through the old town, from Plaça de Catalunya to the glittering Mediterranean Sea *(see pp128–9)*.

③ Barcelona Cathedral

Dominating the heart of the old town is this magnificent Gothic cathedral, with a soaring, elaborate façade and a graceful, sun-dappled cloister containing palm trees and white geese *(see pp130–31)*.

Museu Nacional d'Art de Catalunya ④

The stately Palau Nacional is home to the Museu Nacional d'Art de Catalunya (MNAC). Its extensive collections boast some of the world's finest Romanesque art, rescued from churches around Catalonia during the 1920s *(see pp132–3)*.

⑤ Parc Güell

With its whimsical dragon, fairy-tale pavilions and sinuous bench offering dramatic city views, this magical hillside park is indubitably the work of Gaudí *(see pp134–5)*.

6 La Pedrera

Unmistakably Gaudí, this *Modernista* marvel seems to grow from the very pavement itself. Its curving façade is fluid and alive, and mosaic chimneys keep watch over the rooftop like shrewd-eyed knights *(see pp136–7)*.

7 Fundació Joan Miró

An incomparable blend of art and architecture, this museum showcases the work of Joan Miró, one of Catalonia's greatest 20th-century artists. Paintings, sculptures, drawings and textiles represent 60 prolific years *(see pp138–9)*.

8 Museu Picasso

Housed in a medieval palace complex, this museum charts Picasso's rise to fame with an extensive collection of his early works, including numerous masterful portraits that he painted at the age of 13 *(see pp140–41)*.

0 metres 500
0 yards 500

9 Palau de la Música Catalana

No mere concert hall, the aptly-named Palace of Catalan Music is one of the finest, and most exemplary, *Modernista* buildings in Barcelona *(see pp142–3)*.

10 Museu d'Art Contemporani and Centre de Cultura Contemporània

The city's gleaming contemporary art museum and its cutting-edge cultural centre have sparked an urban revival in the El Raval area *(see pp144–5)*.

🔟⭐ Sagrada Família

Nothing prepares you for the impact of the Sagrada Família. A *tour de force* of the imagination, Antoni Gaudí's church has provoked endless controversy. It also offers visitors the unique chance to watch a wonder of the world in the making. Over the last 90 years, at incalculable cost, sculptors and architects have continued to build Gaudí's dream. Now financed by over a million visitors each year, it is hoped the project will be complete by 2026, the 100th anniversary of Gaudí's death.

① Spiral Staircases

These helicoidal stone stairways **(above)**, which wind up the bell towers, look like snail shells.

② Nave

The immense central body of the church **(below)**, now complete, is made up of leaning, tree-like columns with branches that are inspired by a banana tree spreading out across the ceiling; the overall effect is that of a beautiful stone forest.

③ Nativity Façade

Gaudí's love of nature is visible in this façade **(above)**. Up to 100 plant and animal species are sculpted in stone, and the two main columns are supported by turtles.

④ Apse

Adorned with serpents, four large snails and lizards, this was the first section to be completed by Gaudí. Here, the stained glass graduates in tones beautifully.

5 Hanging Model

This contraption is testimony to Gaudí's ingenuity. He made the 3D device – using multiple chains and tiny weighted sacks of lead pellets – as a model for the arches and vaulted ceilings of the Colonia Güell crypt. No one in the history of architecture had ever designed a building like this.

6 Spires

Gaudí's plan originally detailed a total of 18 spires. For a close-up look at the mosaic tiling and gargoyles on the existing spires, take the lift up inside the bell tower for views that are equally spectacular.

7 Rosario's Claustro

In the only cloister to be finished by Gaudí, the imagery is thought to be inspired by the anarchist riots that began in 1909. The Devil's temptation of man is represented by the sculpture of a serpent wound around a rebel.

Church Floorplan

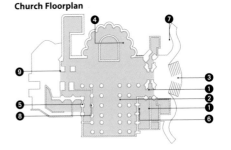

8 Crypt Museum

Gaudí now lies in the crypt (below), and his tomb is visible from the museum. Using audio-visual exhibits, the museum provides information about the construction of the church. The highlight is the maquette workshop, producing scale models for the ongoing work.

9 Passion Façade

Created between 1954 and 2002, this Josep Subirachs façade represents the sacrifice and pain of Jesus. The difference between the Gothic feel of Subirachs' style and the intricacy of Gaudí's work has been controversial.

10 Unfinished Business

The church buzzes with activity: sculptors dangle from spires, stonemasons carve huge slabs of stone and cranes and scaffolding litter the site. Observing the construction in progress allows visitors to grasp the monumental scale of the project.

NEED TO KNOW

MAP F3 ■ Entrances: C/Marina (for groups only) and C/Sardenya ■ 93 207 30 31 ■ www.sagrada familia.org

Open 9am–6pm daily (to 7pm Mar & Oct, 8pm Apr–Sep)

Adm €15 (€22 with audio guide); €24 for combined ticket with Casa-Museu Gaudí, including audio guide; €29 including lift access to one tower.

Advance online booking is recommended.

Check website for full details of guided tours.

■ Sit in a terrace bar on Av Gaudí and drink in the view of Gaudí's masterpiece illuminated at night.

■ For the best photos, get here before 8am: the light on the Nativity Façade is excellent and the tour buses haven't yet arrived.

■ In the cryptogram on the Passion Façade, the numbers add up to the age of Christ at his death.

Church Guide
The main entrance is on C/Marina, in front of the Nativity Façade, along with gift shops. There is a lift in each façade (stairs are not open to the public). The museum is near the entrance on C/Sardenya. 12 of the 18 planned towers are built and are open to the public, but these are not accessible for those with disabilities.

Key Sagrada Família Dates

1882
The first stone of the Sagrada Família is officially laid, with architect Francesc del Villar heading the project. Villar soon resigns after disagreements with the church's religious founders.

2 1883
The young, up-and-coming Antoni Gaudí is commissioned as the principal architect. He goes on to devote the next 40 years of his life to the project: by the end he even lives on the premises.

3 1889
The church crypt is completed, ringed by a series of chapels, one of which is later to house Gaudí's tomb.

1904
The final touches are made to the Nativity Façade, which depicts Jesus, Mary and Joseph amid a chorus of angels.

1925
The first of the 18 planned bell towers, measuring 100 m (328 ft) in height, is finished.

6 1926
On 10 June, Gaudí is killed by a tram while crossing the street near his beloved church. No one recognizes the city's most famous architect.

Sculpture, Passion Façade

7 1936
The military uprising and the advent of the Spanish Civil War bring construction of the Sagrada Família to a halt for some 20 years. During this period, Gaudí's studio and the crypt in the Sagrada Família are burned by revolutionaries, who despise the Catholic Church for siding with the nationalists.

8 1987–1990
Sculptor and painter Josep Maria Subirachs (b.1927) takes to living in the Sagrada Família, just as his famous predecessor did. Subirachs completes the statuary of the Passion Façade. His angular, severe and striking sculptures draw both criticism and praise.

9 2000
On 31 December, the nave is at long last declared complete.

10 2010–2026
The central nave of the church is complete, and in November 2010 Pope Benedict XVI consecrated it as a basilica. The Sagrada Família is to be completed by 2026. The construction, as Gaudí intended, relies on donations. With so many visitors pouring in daily, work is gaining momentum. The Lion of Judah, among other things, was added to the Passion Façade in 2018, marking its completion.

Stained-glass windows in the apse

ANTONI GAUDÍ

Gaudí (1852–1926)

A flag bearer for the *Modernista* movement of the late 19th century, Antoni Gaudí is Barcelona's most famous architect. A strong Catalan nationalist and a devout Catholic, he led an almost monastic existence, consumed by his architectural vision and living in virtual poverty for most of his life. In 2003 the Vatican opened the beatification process for Gaudí, which is the first step towards declaring his sainthood. Gaudí's extraordinary legacy dominates the architectural map of Barcelona. His name itself comes from the Catalan verb *gaudir*, meaning "to enjoy", and an enormous sense of exuberance and playfulness pervades his work. As was characteristic of *Modernisme*, nature prevails, not only in the decorative motifs, but also in the very structure of Gaudí's buildings. His highly innovative style is also characterized by intricate wrought-iron gates and balconies and *trencadís* tiling.

TOP 10
GAUDÍ SIGHTS IN BARCELONA

1 **Sagrada Família**
2 **La Pedrera** (1910)
see pp136–7
3 **Parc Güell** (1900)
see pp134–5
4 **Casa Batlló** (1905)
5 **Palau Güell** (1890)
6 **Torre Bellesguard** (1875)
7 **Finca Güell** (1887)
8 **Casa Calvet** (1899)
9 **Colegio Teresiano** (1890)
10 **Casa Vicens** (1885)

Casa Batlló's many chimneys are adorned with tiled designs. These usually unremarkable parts of a building became Gaudí's whimsical trademark.

TOP 10 ⭐ La Rambla

There may be no better place in the country to indulge in the Spanish ritual of the *paseo* (stroll) than on this wide pedestrian street. Throughout the day and into the night, La Rambla is a lively hub of exuberant activity. Human statues stand motionless among the passers-by; buskers croon crowd-pleasing classics; caricaturists deftly sketch faces; bustling stalls sell bright bouquets and souvenirs; and round-the-clock kiosks sell everything from *The Financial Times* to eclectic souvenirs and handmade crafts.

Gran Teatre del Liceu 1

The city's grand opera house **(right)**, founded in 1847, brought Catalan opera stars such as Montserrat Caballé to the world. Twice gutted by fire, it has been fully restored.

Crowds on La Rambla

2 Mercat de la Boqueria

A cacophonous shrine to food, this cavernous market has it all, from stacks of fruit to suckling pigs and fresh lobsters.

Flower Stalls 3

La Rambla is teeming with life and things to distract the eye, but the true Rambla old-timers are the flower stalls flanking the pedestrian walkway, many run by the same families for decades.

4 Monument a Colom

Pointing resolutely out to sea, this 1888 bronze statue of Christopher Columbus **(left)** commemorates his return to Spain after discovering the Americas. A lift whisks visitors to the top of the column for sensational views.

Font de Canaletes 5

Ensure that you come back to the city by sipping water from this 19th-century fountain **(right)**, inscribed with the legend that those who drink from it "will fall in love with Barcelona and always return".

6 Miró Mosaic

On the walkway on La Rambla is a colourful pavement mosaic by Catalan artist Joan Miró. His signature abstract shapes and primary colours unfold at your feet.

Map of La Rambla

7 Palau de la Virreina

This Neo-Classical palace was built by the viceroy of Peru in 1778. Today, the Palace of the Viceroy's Wife is home to the Centre de la Imatge, run by the city council, and hosts art exhibitions and cultural events.

NEED TO KNOW

Mercat de La Boqueria: **MAP D5**; La Rambla 91; open 8am–8:30pm Mon–Sat; www.boqueria.info

Palau de la Virreina: **MAP D5**; La Rambla 99; open noon–8pm Tue–Sun; Tiquets Rambles: open Mon–Fri 10am–8:30pm; 93 316 1000; ajuntament.barcelona.cat/ lavirreina/en;

Gran Teatre del Liceu: **MAP D5**; La Rambla 51–59; www.liceubarcelona.cat

Arts Santa Mònica: **MAP D5**; La Rambla 7; open 11am–9pm Tue–Sat, 11am–5pm Sun; www.artssantamonica.cat

■ Kick back at the Cafè de l'Òpera at No. 74 and soak up the Rambla ambience with a cool *granissat* (crushed ice drink) in hand.

■ La Rambla is rife with pickpockets – be careful with your belongings.

8 Bruno Quadras Building

Once an umbrella factory, this playful late 19th-century building **(above)** is festooned with umbrellas.

9 Arts Santa Mònica

Once the haunt of rosary beads and prayers, this former 17th-century monastery was reborn in the 1980s, thanks to government funding, as a contemporary art centre. Exhibitions here range from large-scale video installations to photography. The space may be turned into a Museum of Architecture.

10 Església de Betlem

From a time when the Catholic Church was rolling in pesetas (and power), this hulking 17th-century church is a seminal reminder of when La Rambla was more religious than risqué.

🔟⭐ Barcelona Cathedral

From its Gothic cloister and Baroque chapels to its splendid 19th-century façade, the cathedral, dating from 1298, is an amalgam of architectural styles, each one paying homage to a period in Spain's religious history. Records show that an early Christian baptistry was established here in the 6th century, later replaced by a Romanesque basilica in the 11th century, which gave way to the current Gothic cathedral. This living monument still functions as the Barri Gòtic's spiritual hub.

1 Main Façade
The 19th-century façade **(below)** has the entrance, flanked by twin towers, *Modernista* stained-glass windows and 100 carved angels. The restoration process took eight years and was completed in 2011.

2 Choirstalls
The lavish choir-stalls (1340), crowned with wooden spires, are decorated with colourful coats of arms by artist Joan de Borgonya.

4 Nave and Organ
The immense nave **(above)** is supported by soaring Gothic buttresses, which arch over 16 chapels. The 16th-century organ looming over the interior fills the space with music during services.

3 Cloister
Graced with a fountain, palm trees and roaming geese, the cloister dates back to the 14th century. The mossy fountain is presided over by a small iron statue of Sant Jordi – St George.

Crypt of Santa Eulàlia 5
In the centre of the crypt lies the graceful 1327 alabaster sarcophagus **(right)** of Santa Eulàlia, Barcelona's first patron saint. Reliefs depict her martyrdom.

6 Capella de Sant Benet
Honouring Sant Benet, the patron saint of Europe, this chapel displays the 15th-century altarpiece *Transfiguration of the Lord* by Catalan artist Bernat Martorell (active 1427; died 1452).

7 Capella de Santa Llúcia
This lovely Romanesque chapel is dedicated to Santa Llúcia, the patron saint of eyes and vision. On her saint's day (13 December), the blind come to pray at her chapel.

Cathedral Floorplan

8 Capella del Santíssim Sacrament i Crist de Lepant
This 15th-century chapel features the Crist de Lepant (right) which, legend has it, guided the Christian fleet in its 16th-century battle against the Ottoman Turks.

9 Pia Almoina and Gaudí Exhibition Centre
The 11th-century Pia Almoina, once a rest house for pilgrims and the poor, houses the Gaudí Exhibition Centre where a collection of objects by Antoni Gaudí can be found.

10 Casa de l'Ardiaca
Originally built in the 12th century, the Archdeacon's House is located near what was once the Bishop's Gate in the city's Roman walls. Expanded over the centuries, it now includes a lovely leafy patio with a fountain.

NEED TO KNOW

Cathedral: **MAP D5**; Pl de la Seu; 93 342 82 62; open 12:30–7:45pm Mon–Fri, to 5:30pm Sat, 2–5:30pm Sun; adm choir and rooftops (via lift) €3 each, for cathedral floor and cloister €7 donation (see website for timings); www.catedralbcn.org

Casa de l'Ardiaca: **MAP D5**; C/Santa Llúcia 1; open 9am–8:45pm Mon–Fri (to 1pm Sat); Jul–Aug: 9am–7:30pm Mon–Fri

Gaudí Exhibition Centre: **MAP D5**; Av de la Catedral 4; open Apr–Oct: 10am–8pm daily; Nov–Mar: 10am–6pm daily; adm €15

■ Dress modestly to visit the cathedral (covered shoulders; no shorts).

■ Choral/organ concerts are usually held monthly; enquire at the Pia Almoina.

■ Watch *sardanes* – Catalonia's regional dance – in Plaça de la Seu (6pm Sat, noon Sun).

Cathedral Guide
The main entrance is the main portal on Plaça de la Seu. As you enter, to the left lie a series of chapels, the organ and lifts up to the roof. The Gaudí Exhibition Centre is to the left of the main entrance; Casa de l'Ardiaca is to the right.

TOP 10 ⭐ Museu Nacional d'Art de Catalunya

Holding one of the most important medieval art collections in the world, the Museu Nacional d'Art de Catalunya (MNAC) is housed in the majestic Palau Nacional, built in 1929. The highlight is the Romanesque art section, consisting of the painted interiors of Pyrenean churches dating from the 11th and 12th centuries. Other collections include works by Catalan artists from the early 19th century to the present day.

1 The Madonna of the Councillors

Commissioned by the city council in 1443, this work by Lluís Dalmau (1400–61) is rich in political symbolism, with the councillors, saints and martyrs kneeling before an enthroned Virgin.

2 Murals: Santa Maria de Taüll

The well-preserved interior of Santa Maria de Taüll (c.1123) gives an idea of how colourful the Romanesque churches must have been. There are scenes from Jesus's early life, with John the Baptist and the Wise Men.

3 Cambó Bequest

Catalan politician Francesc Cambó (1876–1974) left his huge art collection to Catalonia; two large galleries contain works from the 16th to early 19th centuries, including Tiepolo's 1756 *The Minuet* **(above)**.

4 Thyssen-Bornemisza Collection

A small but fine selection from Baron Thyssen-Bornemisza's vast collection. Among the magnificent paintings are Fra Angelico's (1395–1455) sublime *Madonna of Humility* (1433–5) and a charmingly domestic *Madonna and Child* by Rubens (1577–1640) **(left)**.

5 Frescoes: Sant Climent de Taüll

The interior of Sant Climent de Taüll **(below)** is a melange of French, Byzantine and Italian influences. The apse is dominated by *Christ in Majesty* and the symbols of the four Evangelists and the Virgin, with the Apostles beneath.

7 Woman with Hat and Fur Collar

Picasso's extraordinary depiction of his lover Maria-Thérèse Walter shows him moving beyond Cubism and Surrealism into a new personal language, soon to be known simply as the "Picasso style".

6 Ramon Casas and Pere Romeu on a Tandem

This painting (above) depicts the painter Casas (1866–1932) and his friend Romeu, with whom he began the Barri Gòtic tavern Els Quatre Gats.

8 Crucifix of Batlló Majesty

This splendid mid-12th-century wooden carving depicts Christ on the cross with open eyes and no signs of suffering, as he has defeated death.

9 Confidant from the Batlló House

Among the fine *Modernista* furnishings are some exquisite pieces by Antoni Gaudí, including an undulating wooden chair designed to encourage confidences between friends.

10 Numismatics

The public numismatic collection at the MNAC dates back to the 6th century BC and features medals, coins (above) (including those from the Greek colony of Empuries, which had its own mint from the 5th century BC) and early paper money as well as 15th-century Italian bills.

Gallery Floorplan

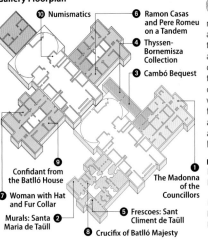

- ⑩ Numismatics
- ⑥ Ramon Casas and Pere Romeu on a Tandem
- ④ Thyssen-Bornemisza Collection
- ③ Cambó Bequest
- ⑨ Confidant from the Batlló House
- ⑦ Woman with Hat and Fur Collar
- ② Murals: Santa Maria de Taüll
- ① The Madonna of the Councillors
- ⑤ Frescoes: Sant Climent de Taüll
- ⑧ Crucifix of Batlló Majesty

Key to Floorplan

- ▢ Romanesque Art Gallery
- ▢ Modern Art; Drawings, Prints and Posters
- ▢ Gothic Art Gallery
- ▢ Renaissance and Baroque Art
- ▢ Library

NEED TO KNOW

MAP A5 ■ Palau Nacional, Parc de Montjuïc ■ www.museunacional.cat/en

Open 10am–6pm Tue–Sat (to 8pm May–Sep), 10am–3pm Sun; timings for roof terrace vary, check website.

Adm €12 (valid for 2 days in a month; €14 with audio guide); free on Sat from 3pm and first Sun of the month; free for under-16s & over-65s; roof terrace €2

Free guided tours first Sun of the month (except Aug; Catalan noon, Spanish 12:15pm), by appointment

■ The Oval Room has a great café. There's also an elegant restaurant in the Throne Room (first floor).

Gallery Guide

The Cambó Bequest, with works by Zurbarán and Goya, and the Thyssen-Bornemisza Collection, with works from the Gothic to the Rococo, are on the ground floor, as are the Romanesque works. On the first floor are the modern art galleries and the photography and numismatics collections.

🔟⭐ Parc Güell

Built between 1900 and 1914, Parc Güell was conceived as an English-style garden city, which were becoming popular in the early 20th century. Gaudí's patron, Eusebi Güell, envisaged elegant, artistic villas, gardens and public spaces. However, the project failed. The space was sold to the city and, in 1926, reopened as a public park where Gaudí had let his imagination run riot on the pavilions, stairways, the main square with its sinuous tiled bench and the tiled columns of the marketplace.

Casa del Guarda ④

The porter's lodge, one of two fairy-tale pavilions that guard the park entrance **(right)**, is now an outpost of MUHBA, the Barcelona History Museum *(Plaça del Rei)*. It contains an exhibition dedicated to the history of Parc Güell.

① **Sala Hipòstila**

Jujol was one of Gaudí's most gifted collaborators, responsible for decorating the 84 columns **(above)** of the park's marketplace, creating vivid ceiling mosaics from shards of broken tiles.

② **Tiled Bench**

An enormous bench, which functions as a balustrade, ripples around the edge of Plaça de la Natura. Artists ranging from Miró to Dalí were inspired by its beautiful abstract designs created from colourful broken tiles.

③ **Jardins d'Àustria**

These beautifully manicured gardens are modern, laid out in the 1970s on what was originally destined to be a plot for a mansion. They are especially lovely in the spring.

⑤ **L'Escalinata del Drac**

A fountain runs along the length of this impressive, lavishly tiled staircase, which is topped with whimsical creatures. The most famous of these is the enormous multicoloured dragon, which has become the symbol of Barcelona.

⑥ **Viaducts**

Gaudí created three viaducts **(below)** to serve as carriageways through Parc Güell. Set into the steep slopes, and supported by archways and columns in the shape of waves or trees, they appear to emerge organically from the hill.

⑦ **Plaça de la Natura**

The park's main square offers panoramic views across the city, and is fringed by a remarkable tiled bench. The square was originally called the Greek Theatre and was intended for open-air shows, with the audience watching from the surrounding terraces.

8 Pòrtic de la Bugadera

One of the park's many pathways, this is known as the Portico of the Laundress after the woman bearing a basket of washing on her head **(left)**, which is carved into an arch.

Map of Parc Güell

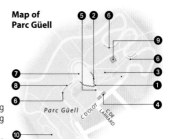

Parc Güell

UNFULFILLED IDEAS

Sadly, many of Gaudí's ideas for Parc Güell were never realized, owing to the economic failure of Eusebi Güell's garden city. Among the most daring of these ideas was his design for an enormous entrance gate, which he intended to be swung open by a pair of gigantic mechanical gazelles.

---

10 Turó de les Tres Creus

Three crosses crown the very top of the hill, marking the spot where Gaudí and Güell, both intensely religious men, intended to build Parc Güell's chapel. The climb to the top is well worth it in order to enjoy the spectacular city views.

9 Casa-Museu Gaudí

One of only two houses to be built in Parc Güell, this became Gaudí's home and contains original furnishings and memorabilia. It is located outside the Monumental Zone.

NEED TO KNOW

MAP E1 ■ C/d'Olot s/n ■ 90 220 03 02 (park); 93 256 21 22 (Casa del Guarda) ■ www.parkguell.cat

Open daily Jan–Mar: 8:30am–6:15pm; Apr: 8am–8:30pm; Jun–Aug: 8am–9:30pm; Sep & Oct: 8am–8:30pm; Nov & Dec: 8:30am–6:15pm; last entry 1 hr before closing

Adm to Monumental Zone €7 if bought online, €8.50

at entrance or from ticket machines; free under-6s, €5.25–6 under-12s; the rest of the park is free of charge; Casa del Guarda included with park ticket; separate ticket required for Casa-Museu Gaudí, adm €5.50.

Buy tickets online, from the automatic ticket machines at the park entrance or at the Vallcarca and Lesseps metro stations; admission is timed and you cannot

enter outside the time printed on the ticket.

■ It is a good idea to bring a picnic with you. While there is a restaurant in the park, it is expensive and always crowded.

■ A combined ticket for the Sagrada Família and Casa-Museu Gaudí is also available.

■ The park has a gift shop as well as a bookshop.

TOP 10 ⭐ La Pedrera

Completed in 1912, this fantastic, undulating apartment block with its out-of-this-world roof is one of the most emblematic of all Gaudí's works. Casa Milà, also known as La Pedrera ("the stone quarry"), was Gaudí's last great civic work before he dedicated himself to the Sagrada Família. What makes it so magical is that every detail bears the hallmark of Gaudí's visionary genius. Now restored to its former glory, La Pedrera contains the Espai Gaudí, an exhibition hall, courtyards, a roof terrace and the Pedrera Apartment.

1 Façade and Balconies
Defying the laws of gravity, La Pedrera's irreverent curved walls are held in place by undulating horizontal beams attached to invisible girders. Intricate wrought-iron balconies (below) are an example of the artisan skill so integral to *Modernisme*.

4 Roof
The strikingly surreal rooftop sculpture park has chimneys resembling medieval warriors and huge ventilator ducts twisted into bizarre organic forms (below), not to mention superb views over the Eixample.

La Pedrera's distinctive roof

2 Espai Gaudí
A series of drawings, photos, maquettes and multimedia displays help visitors grasp Gaudí's architectural wizardry. The museum is housed in the breathtaking vaulted attic, with its 270 catenary brick arches forming atmospheric skeletal corridors.

6 Temporary Exhibition Hall
This gallery space, run by the Catalunya-La Pedrera Foundation, holds regular free art exhibitions. It has shown works by Salvador Dalí, Francis Bacon, Marc Chagall and others. The ceiling looks as if it has been coated with whisked egg whites.

3 Interior Courtyard: Carrer Provença
A brigade of guides take the multitude of visitors through here each day. A closer inspection of this first courtyard reveals its beautiful mosaics and multicoloured wall paintings lining a swirling, fairy-tale staircase.

5 Gates
The mastery in imagining the huge wrought-iron gates (right) reveals the influence of Gaudí's predecessors – four generations of artisan metal workers. The use of iron is integral to many of Gaudí's edifices.

7 La Pedrera Apartment

This *Modernista* flat **(left)** with period furnishings is a reconstruction of a typical Barcelona bourgeois flat of the late 19th century. It provides an engaging contrast between the sedate middle-class conservatism of the era and the undeniable wackiness of the outer building itself.

8 Interior Courtyard: Passeig de Gràcia

Like the first courtyard, this too has a grand, ornate staircase **(below)**. This one is decorated with a stunning floral ceiling painting.

9 Auditorium

The auditorium, located in the former coach house, hosts regular events such as jazz and contemporary concerts. The adjacent garden offers visitors a glimpse of greenery.

NEED TO KNOW

MAP D3 ▪ Pg de Gràcia 92 ▪ 90 220 21 38 ▪ www.lapedrera.com/en

Open 9am–8:30pm daily (to 6:30pm Nov–Feb, 8:30pm at Christmas time); times for evening guided tours and temporary exhibits vary

Adm €22, premium tickets €29 (audio guides in several languages included); advance booking online advised

▪ Check the website for information on current activities and temporary exhibitions.

▪ Explore La Pedrera with nocturnal and early morning tours, or opt for a combined guided tour where you can experience the sight day and night.

▪ Tickets for the popular night-time sound and light show can be booked online for €34 (a glass of cava and snacks are included).

Sight Guide
The Espai Gaudí, the Pedrera Apartment, the Passeig de Gràcia and Carrer Provença Courtyards, the Exhibition Room and the roof are open to visitors. A lift goes up to the apartment, Espai Gaudí and the roof. The courtyards, staircases, café and shop are accessible from the entrance on the corner of Pg de Gràcia and C/Provença.

10 La Pedrera Shop and Café

A wide range of Gaudí-related memorabilia includes replicas of the warrior chimneys in ceramic and bronze.

🔟 ⭐ Fundació Joan Miró

Founded in 1975 by Joan Miró himself, who wanted it to be a contemporary arts centre, this is now a superb tribute to a man whose legacy as an artist and a Catalan is visible across the city. The museum holds more than 14,000 of Miró's paintings, sketches and sculptures, tracing his evolution from an innovative Surrealist in the 1920s to one of the world's most challenging modern artists in the 1960s.

① Tapis de la Fundació

This immense, richly coloured tapestry **(below)** represents the culmination of Miró's work with textiles, which began during the 1970s. The work framed the characteristic colour palette of Miró's output.

The façade of Fundació Joan Miró

Pages Catala al Car de Lluna ②

The figurative painting *Catalan Peasant by Moonlight* **(right)** dates from the late 1960s and highlights two of Miró's favourite themes: the earth and the night. The figure of the peasant, a very simple collage of colour, is barely decipherable, as the crescent moon merges with his sickle and the night sky takes on the rich green tones of the earth.

③ L'Estel Matinal

This is one of 23 paintings known as the Constellation Series. The *Morning Star's* intro-spective quality reflects Miró's state of mind at the outbreak of World War II, when he was hiding in Normandy. Spindly shapes of birds, women, heavenly bodies, lines and planes of colour are suspended in an undefined space.

④ Home i Dona Davant un Munt d'Excrement

Tortured and misshapen semi-abstract figures try to embrace against a black sky. Miró's pessi-mism at the time of *Man and Woman in Front of a Pile of Excrement* would soon be confirmed by the outbreak of the Civil War.

9 Terrace Garden

More of Miró's sculptures are randomly scattered on a spacious terrace **(left)**, from which you can appreciate the Rationalist architecture of Josep Lluís Sert's geometric building. The 3-m (10-ft) tall *Caress of a Bird* (1967) dominates the terrace.

5 Font de Mercuri

Alexander Calder donated the *Mercury Fountain* to the Fundació as a mark of his friendship with Miró. The work was an anti-fascist tribute, conceived in memory of the attack on the town of Almadén.

6 Espai 13

This space showcases the experimental work of new artists from around the world. The exhibitions, based on a single theme each year, are usually radical and often use new technologies.

10 Sculpture Room

This room **(below)** focuses on Miró's sculptures from the 1940s to the 1950s, when he experimented with ceramic, bronze and, later, painted media and found objects. Notable works include *Sun Bird* and *Moon Bird* (both 1946–9).

7 Sèrie Barcelona

The Fundació holds the only complete set of prints of this series of 50 black-and-white lithographs. This important collection is only occasionally on display.

8 Visiting Exhibitions

Over the years, a number of temporary exhibitions, which are usually held in the Fundació's west wing, have included retrospectives of high-profile artists such as Mark Rothko, Andy Warhol, René Magritte and Fernand Léger.

TOP 10 ⭐ Museu Picasso

Pay homage to the 20th century's most acclaimed artist at this treasure-filled museum. Highlighting Pablo Picasso's (1881–1973) formative years, the museum boasts the world's largest collection of his early works. At the tender age of 10, Picasso was already revealing remarkable artistic tendencies. In 1895 he moved to Barcelona where he blossomed as an artist. From precocious sketches and powerful family portraits to Blue- and Rose-period works, the museum offers visitors the rare chance to discover the artist as he was discovering himself.

1 Home amb boina

This portrait reveals brush strokes – and a subject matter – that are far beyond a 13-year-old child. No puppies or cats for the young Picasso; instead, he painted the portraits of the oldest men in the village. He signed this work P Ruiz, because at this time he was still using his father's last name.

4 L'Espera (Margot) and La Nana

Picasso's *Margot* is an evocative painting portraying a call girl as she waits for her next customer, while *La Nana* **(left)** captures the defiant expression and stance of a heavily rouged dwarf dancer.

5 El Foll

The Madman is a fine example of Picasso's Blue period. This artistic phase, which lasted from 1901 to 1904, was characterized by melancholic themes and monochromatic, sombre colours.

2 Autoretrat amb perruca

At 14, Picasso painted *Self-portrait with Wig*, a whimsical depiction of how he might have looked during the time of his artistic hero, Velázquez.

3 Ciència i Caritat

One of Picasso's first publicly exhibited paintings was *Science and Charity*. Picasso's father posed as the doctor.

6 Menu de Els Quatre Gats

Picasso's premier Barcelona exhibition was held in 1900 at the Barri Gòtic café and centre of *Modernisme*, Els Quatre Gats. The artist's first commission was the pen-and-ink drawing of himself and a group of artist friends **(left)**, which graced the menu cover of this bohemian hang-out.

8 Arlequí
A lifting of spirits led to Picasso's Neo-Classical period, typified by paintings like *Arlequí* or *The Harlequin* **(left)**, which celebrated the light-hearted liberty of circus performers.

7 Las Meninas Series
Picasso's reverence for Velázquez culminated in this remarkable series of paintings **(below)**, based on the Velázquez painting *Las Meninas*.

9 Home assegnt
Works such as *Seated Man* **(above)** confirmed Picasso's status as the greatest Analytic Cubist painter of the 20th century.

10 Cavall banyegat
The anguished horse in this painting later appears in Picasso's large mural *Guernica*, which reveals the horrors of war. This work gives viewers the chance to observe the process that went into the creation of one of Picasso's most famous paintings.

NEED TO KNOW

MAP E5 ■ C/Montcada 15–23 ■ www.museu picasso.bcn.cat

Open 9am–7pm Tue–Sun, to 9:30pm Thu

Adm €12; temporary exhibitions €6.50; combined ticket €14 (book both in advance). Free first Sunday of the month (permanent collections) and 6–9:30pm every Thursday

Guided tours in English are available at 3pm on Wednesday, 7pm on Thursday and 11am on Sunday; €6 plus price of ticket

■ The Museu Picasso is housed in a Gothic palace complex, replete with leafy courtyards, all of which can be explored.

■ The café has outdoor tables in summer and offers a changing menu of daily lunch specials.

Gallery Guide
The museum is housed in five interconnected medieval palaces. The permanent collection is arranged chronologically on the first and second floors of the first three palaces. The last two host temporary exhibitions on the first and second floors.

TOP 10 ⭐ Palau de la Música Catalana

Barcelona's *Modernista* movement reached its aesthetic peak in Lluís Domènech i Montaner's magnificent 1908 concert hall. The lavish façade is ringed by mosaic pillars, and each part of the foyer in Domènech's "garden of music", from banisters to pillars, has a floral motif. The concert hall, whose height is the same as its breadth, is a celebration of natural forms, capped by a stained-glass dome that floods the space with sunlight.

1 Stained-Glass Ceiling
Topping the concert hall is a breathtaking stained-glass inverted dome ceiling **(below)**. By day, sunlight streams through the fiery red and orange stained glass, illuminating the hall.

4 Stained-Glass Windows
Blurring the boundaries between the outdoors and the interior, the architect encircled this concert hall with vast stained-glass windows decorated with floral designs that let in sunlight and reveal the changing time of day.

2 Rehearsal Hall of the Orfeó Català
This semicircular, acoustically sound rehearsal room is a smaller version of the massive concert hall one floor above. At its centre is an inlaid foundation stone that commemorates the construction of the Palau.

5 Horse Sculptures
Charging from the ceiling are sculptor Eusebi Aranu's winged horses, infusing the concert hall with movement and verve. Also depicted is a representation of Wagner's chariot ride of the Valkyries, led by galloping horses that leap towards the stage.

6 Façade
The towering façade **(above)** reveals *Modernista* delights on every level. An elaborate mosaic represents the Orfeó Català choral society, founded in 1891.

Stage 3
The semicircular stage **(right)** swarms with activity – even when no one's performing. Eighteen mosaic and terracotta muses spring from the backdrop, playing everything from the harp to the castanets.

7 Foyer and Bar
Modernista architects worked with ceramic, stone, wood, marble and glass, all of which Domènech used liberally, most notably in the opulent foyer and bar.

8 Busts
A bust of Catalan composer Josep Anselm Clavé (1824–74) marks the Palau's commitment to Catalan music. Facing him across the concert hall, a stern, unruly-haired Beethoven **(above)** represents the hall's classical and international repertoire.

9 Lluís Millet Hall
Named after Catalan composer Lluís Millet, this immaculately preserved lounge boasts gorgeous stained-glass windows. On the main balcony outside are rows of stunning mosaic pillars, each with a different design.

Concert and Dance Series 10
Over 500 concerts and dance shows are staged each year, and seeing a show here is a thrilling experience **(right)**. For symphonic concerts, keep an eye out for the Palau 100 Series; for choral concerts, look out for the Orfeó Català series.

NEED TO KNOW

MAP E4 ■ Sant Pere Més Alt ■ 90 247 54 85 ■ www.palaumusica.cat

Guided tours daily, every 30 mins 10am–3:30pm (Easter & Jul: to 6pm; Aug: 9am–8pm); advance booking recommended; mini recital available

Adm €20 (check website for discounts); free for under-10s

■ Have a pre-concert drink at the *Modernista* stained-glass bar just beyond the foyer.

■ There are special concerts for children preceded by kid-friendly guided tours throughout the year.

■ Buy tickets online, or from the box office at C/Palau de la Música 4–6, 90 247 54 85, open 9:30am–9pm Mon–Sat, 9:30am–3pm Sun & two hours before every performance.

ORFEÓ CATALÀ
The famous choral group Orfeó Català, for whom the concert hall was originally built, performs here regularly and holds a concert on 26 December every year. Book in advance.

TOP10 ⭐ Museu d'Art Contemporani and Centre de Cultura Contemporània

Barcelona's sleek contemporary art museum stands in bold contrast to its surroundings. The Museu d'Art Contemporani (MACBA), together with the Centre de Cultura Contemporània (CCCB) nearby, has provided a focal point for the city since 1995 and has played an integral part in the rejuvenation of El Raval. MACBA's permanent collection includes big-name Spanish and international artists, while the CCCB serves as a cutting-edge exploration of contemporary culture.

Façade ①

American architect Richard Meier's stark, white, geometrical façade (right) makes a startling impression against the backdrop of this dilapidated working-class neighbourhood. Hundreds of panes of glass reflect the skateboarders who gather here daily.

② Visiting Artist's Space

The *raison d'être* of MACBA is this flexible area showing the best in contemporary art. Past exhibitions have included Zush and acclaimed painter Dieter Roth.

③ Revolving Permanent Collection

The permanent collection comprises over 2,000 – mostly European – modern artworks, 10 per cent of which are on show at any one time. All major contemporary artistic trends are represented. This 1974 work (below) by Eduardo Arranz Bravo is titled *Homea*.

④ Interior Corridors

Space and light are omnipresent in the bare white walkways that hover between floors (left). Look through the glass panels onto the Plaça dels Àngels for myriad images before you even enter the gallery spaces.

8 A Sudden Awakening
One of the only pieces of art on permanent display is Antoni Tàpies' (1923–2012) deconstructed bed (1992–3), with its bedding flung across the wall in disarray **(left)**. Its presence to the right of the main entrance underlines Tàpies' importance in the world of Catalan modern art.

5 Capella MACBA
One of the few surviving Renaissance chapels in Barcelona has been converted for use as MACBA's temporary exhibition space. It is located in a former convent across the Plaça dels Àngels.

9 Thinking and Reading Spaces
Pleasant and unusual features of MACBA are the white leather sofas between the galleries. Usually next to a shelf of relevant books and a set of headphones, these quiet spaces provide the perfect resting spot to contemplate – and learn more about – the art.

10 Temporary Exhibitions/ CCCB
Exhibitions at the CCCB tend to be more theme-based than artist-specific. It hosts the World Press Photo exhibition in spring and numerous literary festivals throughout the year. Home to avant-garde art exhibits, the CCCB is always at the forefront of the latest cultural trends.

El Pati de les Dones/CCCB 6
This courtyard **(right)** off Carrer Montalegre forms part of the neighbouring CCCB. An ultramodern prismatic screen acts as a mirror reflecting the medieval courtyard, giving visitors a magical juxta-position of different architectural styles.

7 Plaça Joan Coromines
The contrast between the modern MACBA, the University building, the Tuscan-style CCCB and the 19th-century mock-Romanesque church make this square one of the city's most enchanting. It is home to the terrace restaurants of MACBA and CCCB.

NEED TO KNOW

MACBA: **MAP D4**; Pl dels Àngels; 93 412 08 10; open 11am–8pm Mon, Wed & Fri, 10am–9pm Thu, 10am–7:30pm Sat, 10am–3pm Sun; adm €10 (all exhibitions and Experience MACBA); free for under-14s and over-65s; www.macba.cat/en

CCCB: **MAP D4**; C/ Montalegre 5; 93 306 41 00; open 11am–8pm Tue–Sun; adm €6 for 1 show, €8 for 2 shows; concessions €4 for 1 show, €6 for 2 shows; free for under-12s; free every Sunday 3–8pm; guided tours in English Jul & Aug: 11:30am Tuesday, 5:30pm Wednesday; www.cccb.org/en

■ Pause at the nearby Plaça dels Àngels café (C/Ferlandina), which offers nouvelle/Catalan food to a hip crowd, or at CCCB's C3 Bar.

■ MACBA offers tours in sign language as well as adapted tours for the visually impaired.

Galleries Guide
Although they share the Plaça Joan Coromines, MACBA and CCCB have separate entrances. Both multilevel galleries have flexible display spaces. MACBA has rest areas dotted among the galleries on all floors, allowing you to take breaks as you explore.

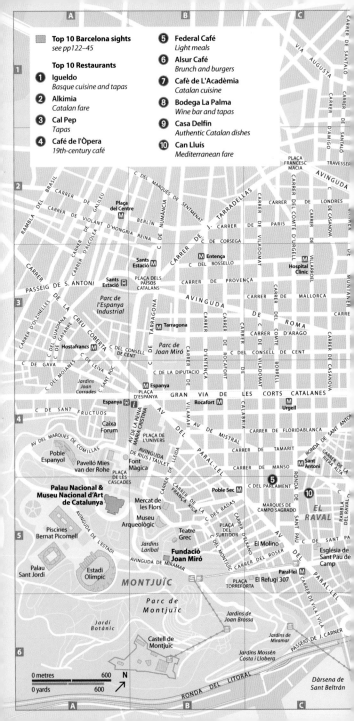

Top 10 Barcelona sights
see pp122–45

Top 10 Restaurants

1 **Igueldo**
Basque cuisine and tapas

2 **Alkimia**
Catalan fare

3 **Cal Pep**
Tapas

4 **Café de l'Òpera**
19th-century café

5 **Federal Café**
Light meals

6 **Alsur Café**
Brunch and burgers

7 **Cafè de L'Acadèmia**
Catalan cuisine

8 **Bodega La Palma**
Wine bar and tapas

9 **Casa Delfín**
Authentic Catalan dishes

10 **Can Lluís**
Mediterranean fare

Top 10 Lisbon

Interior at Palácio Nacional de Queluz

Exploring Lisbon

It's great fun travelling around Lisbon, especially by tram or bus, which will take you to most of the city's historical buildings, parks and museums. Whether you're coming for a weekend, or want to get to know the city better, these two- and four-day itineraries will help you to make the most of your visit.

Mosteiro dos Jerónimos features an elaborate façade.

| 0 metres | 1000 |
| 0 yards | 1000 |

The views from the Castelo de São Jorge are some of Lisbon's finest.

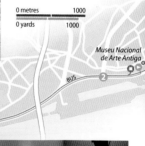

Key
— Two-day itinerary
— Four-day itinerary

Two Days in Lisbon

Day ❶
MORNING
From the Baixa district, take the famous tram 28 to the **Sé Catedral** (see pp158–9). After exploring its ancient interior, continue to the hilltop **Castelo de São Jorge** (see pp154–5), a Moorish castle offering fantastic views over the city.

AFTERNOON
Head north to the **Museu Calouste Gulbenkian** (see pp170–71). Housed in a modern cultural centre in attractive grounds, the museum displays an astonishing array of art – from ancient times to the 20th century.

Museu Nacional de Arte Antiga displays an exquisite collection of Portuguese art.

Day ❷
MORNING
Head west along the riverfront to the **Museu Nacional de Arte Antiga** (see pp160–61). Set in a former palace, the museum contains paintings, furniture and other works of decorative art, much of it from Portugal's colonial days.

AFTERNOON
Travel west to the riverside suburb of Belém. Close to the stunning **Mosteiro dos Jerónimos** (see pp156–7) stands the **Torre de Belém** (see pp164–5), built in the ornate Manueline style.

AFTERNOON
From Belém,
walk back along
the river to Lisbon's
docks. From here, it's
a short bus ride to the
**Museu Nacional de Arte
Antiga** *(see pp160–61)*, which
contains sumptuous furniture
and historic works of art.

Four Days in Lisbon

Day ❶
MORNING
The best place to get an idea of
Lisbon's layout is from the hilltop
Castelo de São Jorge *(see pp154–5)*.
The ruined walls offer amazing views.
From here, it's downhill to the **Sé
Catedral** *(see pp158–9)*, one of the
city's oldest structures. Take time to
explore the warren of streets below.
AFTERNOON
Take a bus east to the **Museu
Nacional do Azulejo** *(see pp166–7)* to
appreciate the amazing diversity
of ceramic tiles *(azulejos)* that you'll
see on many of the city's buildings.
The museum is located inside the
exquisite Madre de Deus convent.

Day ❷
MORNING
Take tram 15 to the riverside suburb
of Belém, packed with museums
and monuments. Highlights include
the **Mosteiro dos Jerónimos** *(see
pp156–7)*, and the nearby **Torre de
Belém** *(see pp164–5)*, built to defend
the Tejo estuary.

Day ❸
MORNING
Take the metro to **Museu Calouste
Gulbenkian** *(see pp170–71)*, which
houses an internationally acclaimed
collection of artworks spanning
4,000 years of art history. Then head
to the sloping Parque Eduardo VII for
fine views over the city.
AFTERNOON
Travel northeast on the metro to the
Parque das Nações *(see pp162–3)*,
a district built for Lisbon's Expo 98.
It offers a cable car, a science
museum, riverside walks and one
of Europe's largest oceanariums.

Day ❹
MORNING
Take a train from the city to the
Palácio Nacional de Queluz *(see
pp168–9)*, where the gardens and
interiors show the lavish lifestyle
enjoyed by the Portuguese royals.
AFTERNOON
Continue on the train to the village
of **Sintra** *(see pp172–3)*, a summer
hideaway for artists, monarchs and
the wealthy. Much of it is designated
a UNESCO World Heritage Site; its
highlights include the Palácio Nacional
da Pena and Castelo dos Mouros.

TOP 10 Lisbon Highlights

Lisbon is a city of immediate charms, and of a deeper beauty that must be sought out. One of the oldest cities in Europe, it is steeped in history, but not closed in on itself. Lisbon's youthful, modern side includes one of the liveliest and most diverse nightlife scenes in Europe.

1 Castelo de São Jorge
Crowning the hill where Lisbon's original settlers lived, this evocatively restored medieval castle boasts fabulous views *(see pp154–5)*.

Mosteiro dos Jerónimos **2**
The Manueline is Portugal's own architectural style. Some of its greatest expressions can be seen in this glorious monastery *(see pp156–7)*.

3 The Sé
Lisbon's cathedral was built in the middle of the 12th century, just after the Christian reconquest. It is a fortress-like structure with stonework that glows amber as the sun sets *(see pp158–9)*.

4 Museu Nacional de Arte Antiga
Housed in a grand 17th-century palace, Portugal's national gallery displays a treasure trove of art, and places the country in historical context through its exhibits *(see pp160–61)*.

5 Parque das Nações
Flanked by the Vasco da Gama Bridge, the site of Lisbon's sea-themed Expo 98 has been transformed into a dynamic leisure, business and residential area *(see pp162–3)*.

6 Torre de Belém

The defensive tower at Belém is one of Lisbon's emblems, and among the most perfectly proportioned examples of the Manueline style *(see pp164–5)*.

7 Museu Nacional do Azulejo

This museum is devoted to the quintessential Portuguese decorative element – the tile. It is also set in a stunning convent *(see pp166–7)*.

8 Palácio Nacional de Queluz

A Rococo feast, this summer palace just outside Lisbon was briefly the royal family's permanent residence. It exudes an air of ordered pleasure *(see pp168–9)*.

9 Museu Calouste Gulbenkian

A museum of international calibre, the Gulbenkian is a small and pleasant universe of art history *(see pp170–71)*.

10 Sintra

Sintra is a powerful magnet, but it is wise to do as Lord Byron did, and absorb the city first before moving on to Sintra – the better to appreciate the contrast *(see pp172–3)*.

🔟 ⭐ Castelo de São Jorge

This hilltop castle is traditionally regarded as the site of Lisbon's founding settlement. Archaeological finds dated to the 7th century BC support this theory, although the oldest castle remains are from the Moorish era. Portugal's first king, Afonso Henriques, captured the Moorish citadel in 1147 and his successors added the Alcáçovas palace, which remained the royal residence until 1511. Following centuries of neglect, the castle was imaginatively restored in 1938, providing the city with one of its most attractive viewpoints.

1 **Porta de São Jorge**

This grand gate leads onto the final steep climb up to the castle grounds. In a wall niche to the left is a figure of St George. His local connection may derive from the role played by English troops in the conquest of Moorish Lisbon.

2 **Casa do Leão**

This restaurant, in one of Lisbon's most exclusive locations, serves traditional Portuguese and international food. Although the interior is very impressive (it was part of the 13th-century Alcáçovas palace), try to sit outside if you can – the views are superb.

The restored battlements at Castelo de São Jorge

3 **Castle Museum**

On the site of the Alcáçovas palace, the museum **(left)** contains a collection of artifacts excavated from the hilltop, such as Iron Age cooking pots and 15th-century tiles.

4 **Torre de Ulisses**

In one of the inner battlement towers, a camera obscura attached to a periscope projects images of the city. The castle has a history of distant gazing: Lisbon's first observatory was set up there in c.1788.

5 Torre de São Lourenço

Connected to the castle by a long series of steps **(left)**, this tower once formed part of the outer fortifications. Today, it offers another angle from which to view the castle.

6 Santa Cruz Neighbourhood

The tiny neighbourhood of Santa Cruz do Castelo, within the old citadel, is one of the most picturesque parts of Lisbon. It is home to ageing residents, younger investors and luxury hotels.

MYTHICAL MARTYR

The myth of Martim Moniz, a soldier who is said to have given his life as a doorstopper in 1147 – allowing Afonso Henriques and his crusaders to enter the castle – has a durable grip on the Lisbon imagination. The gate where his unverified deed took place bears his name, as does a square below the castle.

7 Inner Battlements

The reconstruction of the inner castle is one of the great achievements of the 1938 restoration. With 11 towers and a dividing inner wall, the restored castle closely matches the layout and size of the original.

8 Archaeological Site

This site features traces of the most significant periods in Lisbon's history, including settlements from the Iron Age.

10 Esplanade

The esplanade **(above)** on top of the outer fortifications is one of the main rewards of a climb up to the castle. Dotted with archaeological remains and shaded by pines, it follows the castle's western perimeter, offering views of the river and lower city.

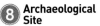

Plan of the Castle

FLORES DE S. CRUZ
S. CRUZ DO CASTELO
RECOLHIMENTO

NEED TO KNOW

MAP F3 ▪ Porta de São Jorge, Rua de Santa Cruz do Castelo ▪ 218 800 620 ▪ www.castelodesaojorge.pt

Main castle complex: 9am–9pm (6pm Nov–Feb) daily

Torre de Ulisses camera obscura: 10am–5pm daily (depending on visibility)

Castle museum: 9am–9pm daily (6pm Nov–Feb); adm €10; over-65s €8.50; concessions €5; under-12s free

▪ The west-facing esplanade is best in the late afternoon, when the sun is low.

▪ The bar at Chapitô (Costa do Castelo 7) is a good place to relax after a visit to the castle.

9 Statue of Afonso Henriques

This bronze statue of Portugal's first king **(right)** was added to the esplanade in 1947. It is a copy of an 1887 work by Soares dos Reis (the original is in Guimarães).

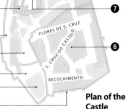

TOP 10 ★ Mosteiro dos Jerónimos

Few of Lisbon's monuments are overly grand, and while this historic monastery is imposing, its proportions remain accessible. Begun in the early 16th century by Diogo de Boytac and finished by João de Castilho and Jerónimo de Ruão, Jerónimos symbolizes Portugal's territorial expansion and expresses a uniquely national style. It's also a monument to Portuguese identity, housing tombs of men who helped make the country great, including navigator Vasco da Gama, Dom Sebastião and poet Luís de Camões.

1 South Portal
Restraint might not be the word for this towering sculpture of an entrance **(left)**, but look closely and you'll see that none of its parts is overpoweringly large. The figures include Henry the Navigator.

Nave 2
Many visitors find the well-lit nave **(right)** the most striking feature of Jerónimos, with its soaring carved pillars supporting a beautiful fan-vaulted ceiling.

NEED TO KNOW

MAP A4 ■ Praça do Império, Belém ■ 213 620 034 ■ www.mosteiro jeronimos.gov.pt

Open 10am–6:30pm (5:30pm Oct–Apr) Tue–Sun. Closed 1 Jan, Easter Sun, 1 May, 13 Jun, 25 Dec

Adm €10; concessions €5; under-12s free

■ This is one of the most visited sites in Lisbon. Think twice before going at weekends, or mid-mornings or mid-afternoons (the latter two are favoured by tour groups). Hit it at lunchtime, or just before it closes, when the stone turns honey-coloured.

■ After your visit, grab a bite to eat at nearby Cais de Belém *(Rua Vieira Portuense 64)*, and dine overlooking Jardim de Belém.

3 West Portal
The surrounds of this portal (now the main entrance) were sculpted by Nicolau Chanterène, and show the Manueline love of fantastical Renaissance decoration.

4 Cloister
The unique two-storey cloister is a lesson in Manueline tracery and lavish ornament **(above)**. Fernando Pessoa, the renowned poet, is buried in the cloister.

⑤ Refectory

The long, narrow refectory features fabulous vaulting and rope-like Manueline mouldings. The panel on the north wall **(left)** depicts the biblical story of the feeding of the 5,000.

STONE SURPRISES

Spend some time studying the carvings on the pillars in the nave and you will come across exotic plants and animals, along with exquisite human faces, and a few mythical figures. What better way to remind posterity that all this beauty was hewn by human hands, belonging to individuals who might occasionally let their imaginations roam free while carving.

⑧ Main Chapel

The current main chapel, dating from 1572, has a gridlike Mannerist layout. Look out for the tombs of Dom Manuel I and his wife Dona Maria (on the left) and Dom João III and his wife Dona Catarina (on the right).

⑨ Extension

Major restoration and extension works in the 19th century added the long Neo-Manueline west wing, which now houses the Museu de Arqueologia and part of the Museu de Marinha *(Praça do Império)*. A distinctive domed bell tower was built to replace the previous pointed roof.

⑥ Tombs of Dom Sebastião and Cardinal D. Henrique

As you pass under the stellar vault of the crossing, look to each side to see the grand tombs of Cardinal D. Henrique and the young king Dom Sebastião.

⑦ Chapterhouse

Completed only in the 19th century, the attractive chapterhouse was never used as such. It houses the tomb of Alexandre Herculano, a celebrated 19th-century historian who also served as the first mayor of Belém.

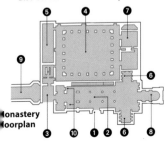

Monastery floorplan

⑩ Tombs of Vasco da Gama and Luís de Camões

In the Lower Choir – facing the aisles under the gallery – are the tombs of Vasco da Gama **(above)** and Luís de Camões, transferred here in 1898.

🔟⭐ The Sé

Lisbon's cathedral was built shortly after Afonso Henriques had taken Lisbon from the Moors in 1147, and stands on a site once occupied by the city's main mosque. Today's crenellated Romanesque building is a much-restored reconstruction, rebuilt in various architectural styles following earthquake damage. It is also an archaeological site, with new finds made regularly beneath the cloister – originally excavated to reinforce the building's foundations.

4 Treasury
The first-floor Treasury is a museum of religious art, with some important holdings. It lost its greatest treasure, the relics of St Vincent, in the 1755 earthquake.

6 Cloister
The Gothic cloister, reached through one of the chapels, was an early addition to the cathedral. Some of its decoration anticipates the Manueline style. It is closed for restoration until late 2020.

1 Rose Window
Reconstructed using parts of the original, the rose window (above) softens the façade's rather severe aspect, but unfortunately lets in only a limited amount of light.

2 Bell Towers
These stocky towers – defining features of the Sé – recall those of Coimbra's earlier cathedral, built by the same master builder, Frei Roberto. A taller third tower collapsed during the 1755 earthquake.

3 St Anthony's Font
Tradition has it that Fernando Martins Bulhões (later St Anthony) was baptized in this font, which now features a tile panel of the saint preaching to the fishes. He is also said to have attended the cathedral school.

5 Gothic Ambulatory Chapels
The Chapel of São Cosme and São Damião is one of nine along the ambulatory. Look out for the tombs of nobleman Lopo Fernandes Pacheco (below) and his wife, Maria Villalobos.

7 Romanesque Nave

Little remains of the original cathedral beyond the renovated nave **(above)**. It leads to a chancel enclosed by an ambulatory, a 14th-century addition.

Cathedral Floorplan

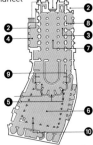

The distinctive bell towers of the Sé

8 Capela de Bartolomeu Joanes

This Gothic chapel, sponsored by a wealthy Lisbon merchant in 1324, contains the founder's tomb and a 15th-century Renaissance retable, painted by Cristóvão de Figueiredo, Garcia Fernandes and Diogo de Contreiras.

FINDS FROM LISBON'S PAST

Archaeologically, the Sé is a work in progress – just like the castle (see pp154–5) and many other parts of central Lisbon. All this digging means that an increasing number of ancient remains are being uncovered. Public information can lag behind archaeological breakthroughs, but make a point of asking – you may be treated to a glimpse of the latest discovery.

9 13th-century Iron Railing

One of the ambulatory chapels is closed off by a 13th-century iron railing, the only one of its kind to survive in Portugal.

10 Archaeological Finds

Remains left by Moors, Visigoths, Romans and Phoenicians have been found in the excavation of the cloister **(above)**.

NEED TO KNOW

MAP F3 ▪ Largo de Sé
▪ 218 866 752
Church: 9am–7pm daily
Cloister and Treasury:
10am–6:30pm Mon–Sat
Adm €2.50; concessions
€1.25

▪ The Sé is a very dark church, and much of interest in the chapels is literally obscured. Head for the lighter cloister, and try to go in the afternoon, when the low light enters the façade's rose window.

▪ A great place for a relaxed drink in the neighbourhood is the charming Pois, Café (*Rua São João da Praça 93–95*), where the Austrian owners are helping to keep Alfama cosmopolitan.

TOP 10 ⭐ Museu Nacional de Arte Antiga

Lisbon's Museu Nacional de Arte Antiga (MNAA) is Portugal's national gallery, a treasure trove of historically illuminating art. Housed in a 17th-century palace overlooking the river and port area, the museum was inaugurated in 1884. Today it contains a vast selection of European art dating from the 14th to the 19th centuries, and includes the most complete collection of Portuguese works in the world.

1 The Panels of St Vincent
A key Portuguese painting, this polyptych of around 1470 (probably by Nuno Gonçalves) portrays rich and poor in fascinating detail.

2 Martyrdom of St Sebastian
Painted by Gregório Lopes (1490–1550) around 1536, this work was a part of a group of paintings set to be placed on the altars of the Rotunda of the Convento de Cristo.

4 Portuguese and Chinese Ceramics
The museum's 7,500-piece collection of ceramics illustrates the interplay of international trade influences. From the 16th century, Portuguese faïence displays traces of Ming, while Chinese porcelain includes Portuguese coats of arms and other similar motifs.

5 Indo-Portuguese Furniture
The most interesting of the museum's furniture collections is probably the group of Indo-Portuguese pieces. The *contadores* (left) are many-drawered chests that combine orderliness with decorative abandon.

3 Chapel of St Albert
The chapel of the former Carmelite convent of Santo Alberto (currently closed for renovation) is decorated with *azulejos*.

NEED TO KNOW

MAP D4 ■ Rua das Janelas Verdes ■ 213 912 800
■ www.museudearteantiga.pt

Open 10am–6pm Tue–Sun. Closed 1 Jan, Easter Sun, 1 May, 13 Jun, 25 Dec

Adm €6; concessions €3; under-12s free

■ There is a lot to see here, so study the layout and decide what to concentrate on. For 15 minutes with Nuno Gonçalves or Hiëronymus Bosch, it may be worth giving the world's largest collection of 18th-century French silverware a miss.

■ An alternative to the museum restaurant for lunch or dinner is the nearby rooftop bar Le Chat, which offers breathtaking views, live music and good cocktails (www.lechatlisboa.com).

6 Namban Screens

After encountering Portuguese travellers in the 16th century, Japan's artists portrayed them as *namban-jin*, or "southern barbarians". These screens **(below)** depict the arrival of Portuguese ships in the port of Nagasaki.

8 St Jerome

This unusual portrait transcends the conventions of religious art. Painted in 1521 by Albrecht Dürer (1471–1528) – who used a 93-year-old man from Antwerp as his model – it is a powerful portrayal of wisdom and old age.

LA NUIT DES MUSÉES

If you are in Lisbon in May, visit this museum at night to enjoy a programme of concerts and other events – not least the guided midnight tours. Part of a Europe-wide French initiative to make museum visits more than occasional Sunday afternoon outings, La Nuit des Musées gives access to the museum's treasures in a quite different context.

9 The Temptations of St Anthony

Hiëronymus Bosch's (1450–1516) three-panelled feast of fear and fantasy **(below)**, painted around 1500, is one of the gallery's great treasures – and one of the world's greatest paintings.

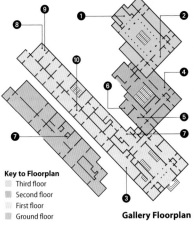

Key to Floorplan

- Third floor
- Second floor
- First floor
- Ground floor

Gallery Floorplan

7 Garden, Restaurant and Shop

The museum's restaurant has lovely views of the garden and the river. There is a well-stocked gift shop on the first floor.

10 Conversation

Pieter de Hooch (1629–84) was a genre painter whose treatment of light was perhaps more complex than that of his contemporary Vermeer. This work shows his key qualities as an artist.

TOP 10 ⭐ Parque das Nações

Built on the site of Lisbon's Expo 98 world exposition, held to mark the 500th anniversary of Vasco da Gama's epic voyage to India, the "Park of Nations" is a modern, self-contained riverside district east of the centre. It showcases contemporary Portuguese architecture, in stark contrast to the Manueline extravaganzas of historic Lisbon and Belém. A bustling amusement park and trade-fair centre by day, by night the park becomes a lively concert and events venue.

1 Cable Car
Running most of the length of the Parque, the cable car **(above)** gives an overview of the area and views of the river and Vasco da Gama bridge. If the breeze is up, the cars may swing from side to side.

2 Torre Vasco da Gama
At 145 m (476 ft), this is Lisbon's tallest building, albeit removed from the rest of the urban skyline. The viewing gallery at the top is now an upmarket restaurant.

3 Nautical Centre
The Doca dos Olivais nautical centre rents out equipment for various water sports and related activities.

4 Oceanário
The world's second-largest aquarium **(above)** has hundreds of aquatic species organized by habitat and viewed on two levels. The vast central tank has species large and small, but it's the cute sea otters in a side tank that get the most attention.

5 Restaurants
There are over 40 waterfront restaurants, many with outdoor seating. Popular for weekend lunches, they also form part of the Parque's nightlife scene.

6 Casino
A newer addition to the Parque, in the former Future Pavilion, the casino caters to all gamblers, offering slot machines, poker, roulette and blackjack.

7 Shops

Most shops are in the Vasco da Gama centre **(left)**, but there are also electronics and home interiors showrooms elsewhere in the Parque. Crowds flock to see the latest offers when the FIL trade-fair area puts on a consumer show.

CARD ADVANTAGES

The Lisboa Card ranges in price from €19 (valid for 24 hours) to €40 (72 hours). It provides free transport on the entire network (including the lifts and the train from Rossio to Sintra) and free entry to 29 places of interest. The card covers one adult, plus two children under the age of five. You can buy it online at www.askmelisboa.com.

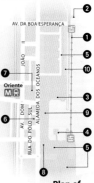

Plan of the park

NEED TO KNOW

MAP F5 ■ www. portaldasnacoes.pt

Oceanário: 218 917 000; open 10am–8pm daily (to 7pm in winter); adm €15; concessions €10; under-4s free; www.oceanario.pt

Knowledge Pavilion – Ciência Viva: 218 917 100; open 10am–6pm Tue–Fri, 11am–7pm Sat & Sun; adm €9; under-18s €7; over-65s €6; children 3–11 €6; under-3s free (family ticket available); www. pavconhe cimento.pt

Casino: www.casino-lisboa.pt

■ Summer afternoons here are hotter and more humid than in most of the city. The lawn next to the Oceanário and the riverfront benches are good spots for a rest.

8 Knowledge Pavilion – Ciência Viva

This large, child-friendly science museum is full of interactive multimedia exhibits, simulations, experiments and activities for various age groups, using cutting-edge technology.

9 Portugal Pavilion

With its concrete canopy suspended like a sail above the forecourt, the Portugal Pavilion **(below)** was once going to house the Council of Ministers. The space is currently used for special events and temporary exhibitions.

10 Gardens

Many of the rather anaemic-looking gardens planted for Expo 98 have grown into healthy patches of urban greenery, effectively softening the concrete and steel, particularly along the waterfront.

🔟 ⭐ Torre de Belém

The defensive tower at Belém is a jewel of the Manueline architectural style, combining Moorish, Renaissance and Gothic elements in a dazzling whole. It was built in 1514–20 by Francisco de Arruda, probably to a design by Diogo de Boytac. At that time, the tower stood on an island in the river Tejo, about 200 m (650 ft) from the northern bank, commanding the approach to Lisbon. The land between the tower and the Jerónimos monastery has since been reclaimed.

1 **Battlements**
The merlons of most of the tower's battlements are decorated with the cross of the Order of Christ, carved to look like features on a shield. The smaller merlons at the rear and on top of the tower are crowned with pyramid-shaped spikes.

2 **Watchtowers**
You can't miss the Moorish-influenced watchtowers **(below)**. Their domes are seated on Manueline rope-like circles and rise to a pile of small spheres reminiscent of the tops of chess pieces.

Dazzling carved exterior of the Torre de Belém

3 **Exhibitions**
The tower's former dungeon, now quite bright, is often used for temporary exhibitions, as well as for a permanent information display for visitors and a gift shop.

4 **Virgin and Child Sculpture**
A statue of Our Lady of Safe Homecoming stands by the light well that was used to lower cannons into the dungeon. She evokes the intrepid explorers of Portugal's past, but also everyday sailors – and the concerned longing for absent husbands and sons known in Portugal as *saudade*.

5 **Governor's Room**
Now empty, this room was used by the tower's first governor, Gaspar de Paiva. After it became obsolete, lighthouse keepers and customs officials worked here. The room's acoustics amplify even the slightest whisper.

6 **Rhinoceros Detail**
Each of the sentry boxes is supported by a naturalistically carved stone. The rhinoceros on the northwestern box is the most famous, thought to be the first European carving of this animal. Time has now rounded its features.

7 Renaissance Loggia

An arcaded loggia overlooks the main deck – comparisons to a ship are unavoidable here. The loggia breaks with the military style of most of the building and adds a theatrical element, while the railing and tracery of the balustrade **(left)** are pure Manueline. Balconies on each side of the tower echo the loggia's style.

8 Manueline Twists

Ropes and knots were the main theme for the Manueline masons here. The tracery of some of the balustrades features the near-organic shapes that would be developed in later Manueline buildings.

9 Dungeon

From the tower's vaulted bottom level **(below)** – also used as a dungeon – 17 cannon once covered the approaches to Lisbon.

10 Armillary Spheres

The armillary spheres carved above the loggia were instruments for showing the motion of the stars around the earth. They became a symbol of Portugal, and still feature on the national flag.

HOLY NAMESAKE

Belém means Bethlehem – and the name is taken from a chapel dedicated to St Mary of Bethlehem, built in the mid-15th century near the river's edge, in what was then Restelo. This chapel subsequently gave way to the grand Jerónimos church and monastery; the church is still known as Santa Maria de Belém. The name Restelo, for its part, now applies to the area above and behind Belém, a leafy district of fine residences and embassy buildings.

NEED TO KNOW

MAP A5 ■ Avda Brasília ■ 213 620 034 ■ www. torrebelem.gov.pt

Open 10am–5:30pm Tue–Sun (last adm 5pm; May–Sep: to 6:30pm; last adm 5pm). Closed 1 Jan, Easter Sun, 1 May, 13 Jun, 25 Dec

Adm €6; senior citizens €3; Youth Card holders €3; under-12s free

■ The tower is at its prettiest in the early morning or late afternoon. Tour groups tend to visit early, so go as late as you can for a quieter visit.

■ Nearby restaurants (including Vela Latina – *Doca do Bom Sucesso*) often fill up quickly; if you can't find a table, cross the railway line by the footbridge and walk to the Centro Cultural de Belém. Este Oeste, the restaurant here, has great food and a terrace.

TOP 10 ⭐ Museu Nacional do Azulejo

Ceramic tiles, or *azulejos*, are a distinctive aspect of Portuguese culture, featuring in contexts both mundane and sacred. The art of making them is a Moorish inheritance, much adapted – most noticeably in the addition of human figures, which Islam forbids. This museum dedicated to tiles is enjoyable both for the excellent displays and for its beautiful setting, a 16th-century convent transformed over the centuries to include some of the city's prettiest cloisters and one of its most richly decorated churches.

Lisbon Panel **1**
This vast tiled panorama of Lisbon (right), 23 m (75 ft) in length, is a captivating depiction of the city's waterfront as it looked in about 1710, before the great earthquake. It was transferred here from one of the city's palaces.

2 **Manueline Cloister**
This small but stunning cloister (above) is one of the few surviving features of the original convent of Madre de Deus. This is the Manueline style at its most restrained. The geometrical wall, with its 17th-century tiles, was added in the 19th century.

3 **Nossa Senhora da Vida Altarpiece**
Almost 5 m (16 ft) square and containing over 1,000 tiles, this 16th-century Renaissance altarpiece is the work of João de Góis. It depicts the *Adoration of the Shepherds*, flanked by St Luke and St John.

4 **Tile-Making Exhibit**
Step-by-step exhibits on tile-making, from a lump of clay to final glazing, illuminate how the medium combines the practical and decorative.

5 **Renaissance Cloister**
Part of the first major alteration to the convent in the 16th century, this airy, two-level cloister is the work of Diogo de Torralva. Glassed in to protect visitors and the collection from the weather, it is the light heart of the building.

6 **Temporary Exhibitions**
The ground and first floors have temporary exhibitions on subjects like contemporary tile art, an important art form in Portugal.

7 Moorish Tiles
With their attractive geometric patterns, varied colour palettes and glazing techniques, Moorish tiles **(left)** continue to inspire tile-makers and home decorators alike.

8 Shop
Numerous quality reproductions of classic tile designs are available, as well as modern tiles and other gifts.

A NOD FROM THE 19TH CENTURY

When the southern façade of the church was restored in the late 19th century, the architect used as his model a painting now in the Museu de Arte Antiga *(see pp160–161)*. This shows the convent and church as they looked in the early 16th century. Indoors, the quest for authenticity was less zealous. In one of the cloisters, 19th-century restorers have left a potent symbol of their own era: an image of a steam locomotive has been incorporated into one of the upper-level capitals.

Key to Floorplan
- Second floor
- First floor
- Ground floor

Museum Floorplan

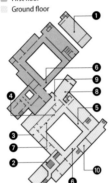

9 Cafeteria and Winter Garden
Suitably tiled with food-related motifs, the museum cafeteria is worth a stop for coffee or a light lunch. The courtyard is partly covered and forms a winter garden.

NEED TO KNOW

MAP F6 ■ Rua da Madre de Deus 4 ■ 218 100 340 ■ www.museudoazu lejo.gov.pt

Open 10am–6pm Tue–Sun. Closed 1 Jan, Easter Sun, 1 May, 13 Jun, 24 & 25 Dec

Adm €5; senior citizens €2.50; Youth Card holders €2.50; under-12s free

■ The rather awkward location of the Tile Museum can be turned into an asset if you combine it with a visit to Parque das Nações *(see pp162–3)*, a shopping trip to Santa Apolónia, or lunch at D'Avis *(Avenida Dom João II)*.

■ The best place for a drink is the museum's cafeteria; otherwise, head for Santa Apolónia.

10 Madre de Deus Church
The magnificent barrel-vaulted convent church **(above)**, packed with paintings, is the result of three centuries of construction and decoration. Its layout dates from the 16th century; the tile panels and gilt woodwork are 17th and 18th century.

TOP 10 ⭐ Palácio Nacional de Queluz

Queluz is like a miniature Versailles – an exquisite Rococo palace with formal gardens and parkland, just 15 minutes from central Lisbon. Prince Pedro, younger son of Dom João V, had it built as a summer palace in 1747–52. Thirteen years later, when he married his niece, the future Dona Maria I, he commissioned extensions from the French architect Jean-Baptiste Robillon, in order to make it the permanent royal residence. Queluz had a brief golden era before the royal family fled to Brazil after Napoleon's invasion in 1807.

1 Robillon Pavilion

This impressive building **(above)**, replete with windows, balustrades and pillars, is a bit too fussy for purists. It was designed by the French architect Robillon.

2 Gardens

A pair of formal gardens – the Hanging Garden **(above)** and Malta Garden – occupy the space between the palace's two asymmetric wings. Laid out by Robillon, they are adorned with fountains, statues and topiary.

3 Sala dos Embaixadores

The magnificent Ambassadors' Room was used for diplomatic audiences, and is opulently decorated with stuccowork and painted and gilded carved woodwork. Concerts were also held in these grand surroundings and the *trompe l'oeil* ceiling depicts the royal family at such an event.

NEED TO KNOW

MAP E5 ■ Largo do Palácio ■ 219 237 300 ■ www.parquesdesintra.pt

Open 9am–7pm daily (6pm in winter). Closed 1 Jan, 25 Dec

Adm €10; senior citizens €8.50; children 6–17 €8.50; under-6s free (check website for winter prices); gardens only €5

■ An early-morning visit to Queluz can be combined with a trip to Sintra (see pp172–3).

■ The terrace at the Pousada is the best place for a drink – unless you are lucky enough to have an invitation to an event in the palace itself.

7 Corredor das Mangas

The hallway linking the old and newer parts of Queluz was named for the glass sleeves *(mangas)* of its candles. Painted wall tiles **(left)** give it its other name, the *Corredor dos Azulejos*.

4 Throne Room

Competing in grandeur with the Sala dos Embaixadores, the dome-ceilinged Throne Room also served as the palace's ballroom, church and theatre.

THE PIOUS QUEEN

Dona Maria I was the first undisputed Queen regnant of Portugal and the first monarch of Brazil. She was a noteworthy ruler but after the death of her son she suffered with mental illness. In 1807, she was exiled to Brazil with her younger son to escape the invasion of Portugal led by the French Emperor Napoleon.

8 Cozinha Velha and Pousada Dona Maria I

The old palace kitchens have long housed the fine Cozinha Velha restaurant. A drink on the terrace of the newer Pousada Dona Maria I, in the former quarters of the Royal Guard, is as close as you'll get to living at Queluz.

Palace Floorplan

9 Lion Staircase

This beautiful staircase links the lower parkland to the palace. It is flanked by an arcaded gallery with a cascade flowing into a tiled canal; the royal family went boating here.

10 Chapel

The first room to be completed in 1752, the chapel also held concerts, some by Dona Maria I's own chamber orchestra. It is thought that she and her sisters painted some of the wall panels.

5 Don Quixote Chamber

The inlaid circular-pattern floor and domed ceiling make this square room seem round. It is named for its painted scenes from *Don Quixote*.

6 Music Room

The Music Room **(right)** was used for concerts and even opera performances, and doubled as a venue for important christenings. It still serves as a concert venue.

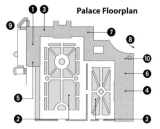

TOP 10 ★ Museu Calouste Gulbenkian

Based on the private collections of Calouste Gulbenkian, this museum features the Founder's Collection, which spans over 4,000 years of art history, and is a part of the Gulbenkian Foundation. Internationally recognized for its quality, the museum is part of a complex that houses the headquarters of the Calouste Gulbenkian Foundation, a concert hall and auditoria, an art library, and a park. The Foundation also features the Modern Collection, established after the death of Gulbenkian, which is housed in another building within the complex.

1 3rd Dynasty Egyptian Bowl

Found in a tomb north of Thebes, this elegant alabaster bowl was modelled on an everyday ointment bowl. The ancient Egyptians adorned tombs with copies of everyday objects made from noble materials. This one is 4,000 years old.

2 Ancient Greek Vase

This 5th-century BC wide-rimmed terracotta vase **(right)** is decorated with mythological motifs: the abduction of Phoebe and Hilaira by Castor and Pollux, and a bacchanalian scene.

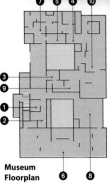

4 Diana Statue

A graceful marble statue by the French sculptor Jean-Antoine Houdon (1741–1828), dating from 1780, is unusual for the era in that it depicts the goddess in movement, and completely naked. It belonged to Catherine the Great of Russia and was exhibited at the Hermitage, where its nudity caused quite a scandal.

3 St Catherine and St Joseph

Two paintings by the 15th-century Flemish master Rogier van der Weyden (1399–1464) are believed to be parts of an altarpiece; a third element is in London's National Gallery. The female **(above)** is thought to be Catherine of Alexandria.

5 Lalique Collection

Gulbenkian was a close friend of the French Art Nouveau jeweller René Lalique and bought a great number of his graceful pieces, many on show in this part of the museum.

Museum Floorplan

6 Oriental Islamic Art

This large gallery displays a wide-ranging collection of manuscripts, carpets, textiles, ceramics **(above)** and other objects from Turkey, Syria, the Caucasus (including Armenia), Persia and India.

7 Boy Blowing Bubbles

Édouard Manet's (1832–83) 1867 painting **(right)** is not just a version of the popular allegory on the transience of life and art, but a portrait of Léon-Édouard Koëlla, stepson of the artist.

9 Portrait of an Old Man

This engaging *chiaroscuro* portrait of a bearded man is an example of Rembrandt's preoccupation with ageing. The gaze is tired, and the large hands intricately lined. Nothing is known about the model.

8 Yuan Dynasty Stem Cup

This blue-glazed piece, dating from an earlier period (beginning of the 14th century) than most of the Far Eastern collection, is decorated with delicate reliefs of Taoist figures under bamboo leaves.

10 Louis XV and XVI Furniture

Considered ostentatious by some, the 18th-century French pieces **(above)** in the decorative art collection fascinate for their materials and craftsmanship. Highlights include a Louis XV chest inlaid with lacquer panels, gold leaf, mother-of-pearl, bronze and ebony; and a table with a shelf that flips over to reveal a mirror.

🔟⭐ Sintra

Recognized in 1995 as a UNESCO World Heritage Site, Sintra was the summer residence for Portuguese kings from the 13th to the late 19th centuries. It still possesses many of the classic qualities of a hill retreat: a cooler climate than the city, ample greenery and an atmosphere conducive to romantic whims. The old town is pretty but crowded, while the surrounding landscapes and sights are an essential part of any visit.

Quinta da Regaleira ③
This lavish palace **(right)** looms on a steep bend in the old road to Sintra. It was built around 1900 for António Augusto Carvalho Monteiro, an eccentric millionaire who also owned Peninha *(N247)*. He was a bibliophile and keen dabbler in alchemy and other esoteric subjects.

① Monserrate
A fantastic Moorish-style palace **(above)** dominates the gardens of Monserrate, which were laid out by English residents.

④ São Pedro Market
Antiques are a feature of the lively market held in the suburb of São Pedro on the second and fourth Sundays of each month.

⑥ Palácio de Seteais
Built in 1787, Seteais (now a hotel) got its Neo-Classical façade later. It's best to visit well dressed, for tea or a meal.

② Palácio Nacional da Pena
Dom Fernando II, Dona Maria II's German-born king consort, had this fabulous toyland palace built in the mid-19th century. The work of a lively imagination, it exhibits his eclectic tastes, and is preserved as it was when the royal family lived there **(above)**.

⑤ Parque da Pena
Filled with exotic trees and shrubs, the park around the Palácio da Pena is another of Dom Fernando II's contributions to Sintra's magic. It contains the chalet he had built for his second wife, Elise Hensler, an American opera singer.

ESTEFÂNIA

ESTRADA MACIEIRA
SOTTO MAIOR
LARGO DE MANUEL I
R. D. FRANCISCO D'ALMEIDA
PR. DA REPÚBLICA
RUA M. EUGÉNIA
RUA B. DA OTA PAÇO DOLIVEIRA
RUA B. C. DA CLÉRIGOS
RIBEIRO
6 km (4 miles)
SANTA EUFÉMIA
CALÇADA DA PENA
SÃO PEDRO DE SINTRA

Map Sintra

9 Palácio Nacional de Sintra

Twin conical chimneys mark the former royal palace **(left)**. Begun in the 14th century and extended in the 16th, it is a captivating mix of styles from Moorish to Renaissance.

THE ARTIST KING

Ferdinand Saxe-Coburg-Gotha was known in Portugal as Dom Fernando II, the "artist" king. Like his cousin Prince Albert, who married the English Queen Victoria, he loved art, nature and the new inventions of the time. He was himself a watercolour painter. Ferdinand enthusiastically adopted his new country and devoted his life to patronizing the arts. His lifelong dream of building the extravagant and beautiful Palace of Pena was achieved in 1854; he died in 1885.

10 Centro Cultural Olga Cadaval

Sintra's main cultural venue, a modern centre hosting dance, theatre, concerts and films, was built in 1987, after a fire destroyed much of the Carlos Manuel cinema.

7 Parque da Liberdade

The town park, with its steep paths running among the trees, occupies the valley below the old town.

Castelo dos Mouros 8

This 10th-century castle **(right)** was captured by Afonso Henriques in 1147. Dom Fernando II partially rebuilt it in the 19th century. A chapel, with an exhibition about the castle's history, and a Moorish cistern are inside.

NEED TO KNOW

30 km (18 miles) NW of Lisbon; trains from Lisbon's Rossio and Entrecampos stations

Tourist information: Praça da República 23, Sintra; 219 231 157; www.cm-sintra.pt, www.parquesdesintra.pt.

■ Sintra's romantic and refreshing qualities may be seriously challenged on summer weekends, when tour groups and locals collide in the square in front of the Palácio Nacional de Sintra. Go during the week, and avoid midday in summer.

■ Bars and cafés in the old town fill up quickly and charge inflated prices. For a different atmosphere, walk past the Tourist Office to Lawrence's Hotel *(Rua Consigliéri Pedroso 38–40)* and enjoy a refreshment in one of its cosy, colonial-style public rooms.

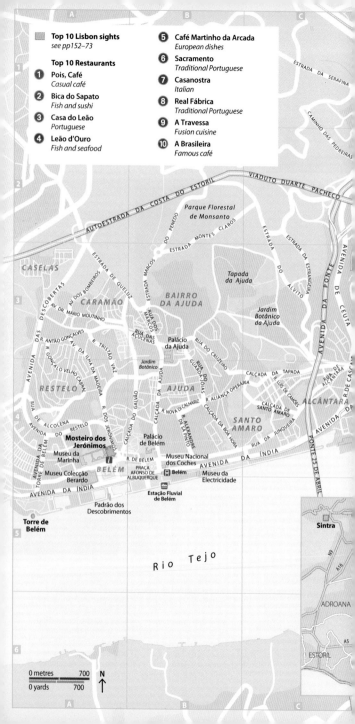

Top 10 Lisbon sights
see pp152–73

Top 10 Restaurants

1. **Pois, Café**
   Casual café

2. **Bica do Sapato**
   Fish and sushi

3. **Casa do Leão**
   Portuguese

4. **Leão d'Ouro**
   Fish and seafood

5. **Café Martinho da Arcada**
   European dishes

6. **Sacramento**
   Traditional Portuguese

7. **Casanostra**
   Italian

8. **Real Fábrica**
   Traditional Portuguese

9. **A Travessa**
   Fusion cuisine

10. **A Brasileira**
    Famous café

ESTRADA DA SERAFINA

CAMINHO DAS PEDREIRAS

VIADUTO DUARTE PACHECO

AUTOESTRADA DA COSTA DO ESTORIL

Parque Florestal de Monsanto

ESTRADA MONTES CLAROS

ESTRADA DO PENEDO

ESTRADA DA ESTRANGEIRA

AVENIDA DE CEUTA

AVENIDA DA PONTE

CASELAS

ESTRADA DE QUELUZ

ESTRADA MARCOS

Tapada da Ajuda

ESTRADA DO ALVITO

BAIRRO DA AJUDA

CARAMÃO

R. DOS BOMBEIROS

AV. DR. MÁRIO MOUTINHO

R. ANTÃO GONÇALVES

AV. DA ILHA DA MADEIRA

R. TRISTÃO VAZ

RUA DAS AÇUCENAS

RUA DOS MARCOS

Jardim Botânico da Ajuda

DESCOBERTAS

RESTELO

AVENIDA

R. GONÇALO VELHO CABRAL

RUA DE ALCOLENA

AVENIDA DO RESTELO

R. DOS JERÓNIMOS

CALÇADA DO GALVÃO

CALÇADA DA AJUDA

Jardim Botânico

Palácio da Ajuda

RUA DO CRUZEIRO

RUA DO GUARDA-JOIAS

R. NOVA DO CALHARIZ

R. ALEXANDRE DE SÁ PINTO

CALÇADA DA BOA HORA

AJUDA

CALÇADA DA TAPADA

R. LUÍS DE CAMÕES

CALÇADA DE SANTO AMARO

R. ALIANÇA OPERÁRIA

ALCÂNTARA

R. DR. ALFAIATA

R. DE CASAL

SANTO AMARO

RUA DA JUNQUEIRA

Mosteiro dos Jerónimos

Museu da Marinha

AVENIDA DA TORRE DE BELÉM

Museu Colecção Berardo

BELÉM

R. DE BELÉM

PRAÇA AFONSO DE ALBUQUERQUE

Palácio de Belém

Museu Nacional dos Coches

Belém

Museu da Electricidade

AVENIDA DA ÍNDIA

PONTE 25 DE ABRIL

AVENIDA DA ÍNDIA

Padrão dos Descobrimentos

Estação Fluvial de Belém

Torre de Belém

Rio Tejo

Sintra

N9

A16

ADROANA

A5

ESTORIL

0 metres   700
0 yards   700

N ↑

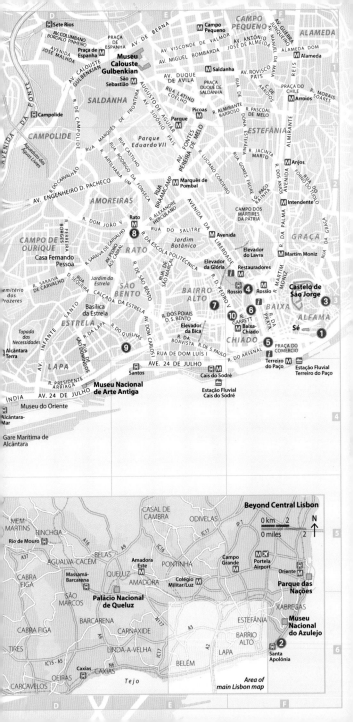

Sete Rios

AV. COLUMBANO
BORDALO PINHEIRO

PRAÇA
DE
ESPANHA

AV. DE BERNA

CAMPO
PEQUENO

ALAMEDA

Campo
Pequeno

AV. DA GUERRA
JUNQUEIRO

ALAMEDA DA

AV. VISCONDE DE VALMOR

AVENIDA
JOSÉ MALHOA

AV. MIGUEL BOMBARDA

AV. ANTÓNIO
JOSÉ DE ALMEIDA

REIS

AV. ROVISCO PAIS

Alameda

Praça de
Espanha

Museu
Calouste
Gulbenkian

São
Sebastião

AV. CALOUSTE GULBENKIAN

R. DE CAMPOLIDE

Campolide

CAMPOLIDE

AVENIDA DA PONTE

Aqueduto das
Águas Livres

SALDANHA

AV. DUQUE
DE ÁVILA

Saldanha

PRAÇA
DUQUE DE
SALDANHA

RUA DE ARROIOS

PRAÇA DO
CHILE

R. MORAIS
SOARES

Arroios

R. PASCOAL
DE MELO

ESTEFÂNIA

RUA DOM JOÃO V

Parque Eduardo VII

AV. FONTES PEREIRA DE MELO

Marquês de
Pombal

CAMPO DOS
MÁRTIRES
DA PÁTRIA

Anjos

Intendente

GRAÇA

AMOREIRAS

AV. ENGENHEIRO D. PACHECO

Rato

Jardim
Botânico

Avenida

Martim Moniz

CAMPO DE
OURIQUE

Casa Fernando
Pessoa

RATO

Jardim da
Estrela

SÃO
BENTO

Elevador
do Lavra

Elevador
da Glória

Restauradores

Rossio

Rossio

Castelo de
São Jorge

emitério
dos
Prazeres

Basílica
da Estrela

ESTRELA

BAIRRO
ALTO

CHIADO

Baixa-
Chiado

Sé

Tapada
das
Necessidades

Alcântara
Terra

LAPA

Elevador
da Bica

PRAÇA DO
COMÉRCIO

ÍNDIA

Santos

AVE. 24 DE JULHO

Museu Nacional
de Arte Antiga

Cais do Sodré

Estação Fluvial
Cais do Sodré

Terreiro
do Paço

Estação Fluvial
Terreiro do Paço

Museu do Oriente

Alcântara-
Mar

Gare Marítima de
Alcântara

Beyond Central Lisbon

MEM-
MARTINS

RINCHOA

Rio de Mouro

CASAL DE
CAMBRA

ODIVELAS

0 km   2

0 miles   2

N

BELAS

AGUALVA-CACÉM

PONTINHA

Campo
Grande

Portela
Airport

Oriente

Parque das
Nações

CABRA
FIGA

Massamá-
Barcarena

Amadora
Este

Colégio
Militar/Luz

SÃO
MARCOS

Palácio Nacional
de Queluz

AMADORA

XABREGAS

Museu
Nacional
do Azulejo

CABRA FIGA

BARCARENA

CARNAXIDE

ESTEFÂNIA

BARRIO
ALTO

LAPA

Santa
Apolónia

TIRES

LINDA-A-VELHA

BELÉM

Caxias

CAXIAS

OEIRAS

Tejo

Area of
main Lisbon map

CARCAVELOS

Top 10 Rome

**Theatrical mosaic masks of Comedy
and Tragedy, Musei Capitolini**

Exploring Rome

Rome is packed with magnificent piazzas, beautiful palazzi, ancient monuments and churches. There is a lot to see and do, and to help you make the most of your visit here are some ideas for a two- and four-day Roman holiday. Bear in mind that you can save time by reserving tickets beforehand, and that advance booking is obligatory at Galleria Borghese.

| 0 metres | 800 |
| 0 yards | 800 |

Key

— Two-day itinerary

— Four-day itinerary

St Peter's Basilica towers magnificently over Rome; it's not only a beautiful church, but is also packed with works of art by great masters.

Two Days in Rome

Day ❶
MORNING
See the **Colosseum** (see pp196–7), then walk past the **Roman Forum** (see pp190–93) and **Imperial Fora** (see pp196–7) to the virtually recreated villa of a patrician family at Palazzo Valentini (Foro Traiano). Visit **Musei Capitolini** (see pp198–201), and don't miss the bird's-eye view of the Forum.

AFTERNOON
Stroll through the centro storico to Piazza Navona and the **Pantheon** (see pp188–9) for atmosphere, ice cream and window shopping. Cross the Tiber by Ponte Sisto to lively Trastevere for a drink.

Day ❷
MORNING
Get up early to see **St Peter's** (see pp182–7) without the crowds when it opens at 7am – an unforgettable experience. Then visit the Vatican Museums (Viale Vaticano), preferably having booked tickets in advance.

AFTERNOON
Spend some time at the lovely Villa Borghese park (Piazzale Napoleone I), followed by a visit to the Bernini sculptures at **Galleria Borghese** (see pp194–5) and the Etruscan finds at Villa Giulia (see pp208–9). Walk back through the park to Piazza del Popolo to visit **Santa Maria del Popolo** (see pp206–7), before ending the day at Piazza di Spagna.

Four Days in Rome

Day ❶
MORNING
Begin with the **Pantheon** (see pp188–9), then wander over to Piazza Navona, stopping to admire Caravaggio's works in San Luigi dei Francesi (Piazza di S. Luigi de' Francesi) and Sant'Agostino (Via di S. Eustachio). Marvel at the Bernini fountains and street performers, then browse the piazza shops.

AFTERNOON
Head to the fantastic **Museo Nazionale Romano's Palazzo**

The Colosseum, built in the 1st century AD, has served as the prototype for all stadiums since.

The Pantheon, constructed in the 1st century BC, is the world's best preserved Roman temple.

Massimo alle Terme (see pp202–5), which has an entire frescoed room from the Villa of Livia. Wind down with an evening in appealing Monti.

Day ❷
MORNING
Explore **Ostia Antica** (see pp210–11) and return for lunch in Testaccio.
AFTERNOON
Visit **Santa Maria del Popolo** (see pp206–7), then explore the Piazza di Spagna area. Climb the Spanish Steps for a great city view. Walk back to the centre via the Trevi Fountain.

Day ❸
MORNING
Explore the **Colosseum** (see pp196–7), then visit Palazzo Valentini (Foro

Traiano) and the **Musei Capitolini** (see pp198–201), stopping for lunch in the museum's roof terrace café.
AFTERNOON
See the evocative ruins of the **Roman Forum and Palatine Hill** (see pp190–93), then wander through the Jewish Ghetto and vibrant Campo de' Fiori.

Day ❹
MORNING
Start early to see **St Peter's** and the **Vatican** (see pp182–7) then take the tram to the stop outside Galleria Nazionale d'Arte Moderna (Viale delle Belle Arti) for lunch.
AFTERNOON
Visit **Villa Giulia** (see pp208–9) before taking a stroll through the park to **Galleria Borghese** (see pp194–5) – make sure to book in advance.

TOP 10 Rome Highlights

The unique appeal of Rome is that it is a 2,800-year-old indoor-outdoor museum, with ancient monuments, art treasures and timeless architecture. With religion at its heart and history in its soul, it dazzles and inspires visitors time and time again.

1 Vatican City
This is home to the pope, the world's largest church, and the most incredible work of art ever created – the Sistine ceiling *(see pp182–7)*.

2 The Pantheon
The most perfectly preserved of all ancient temples, this marvel of engineering has a giant oculus forever open to the sky *(see pp188–9)*.

3 Roman Forum
Formerly at the heart of ancient power, the forum is now evocatively empty, broken by grand arches, solitary columns and carved rubble *(see pp190–93)*.

4 Galleria Borghese
This stunning palace is filled with Graeco-Roman, Renaissance and Baroque works *(see pp194–5)*.

5 Colosseum and Imperial Fora
Imperial Rome built many impressive monuments, including this splendid amphitheatre *(see pp196–7)*.

6 Musei Capitolini

At the ancient centre of religious Rome are some of the world's greatest masterpieces, from 4th-century BC Greek sculptures to Caravaggio's revolutionary, even scandalous, paintings *(see pp198–201)*.

7 Museo Nazionale Romano

These collections, housed at five sites, feature some of the world's finest ancient art, including stunning frescoes and mosaics and Classical sculpture *(see pp202–5)*.

8 Santa Maria del Popolo

Built over emperors' tombs, this church offers a rich display of Renaissance and Baroque art, including masterpieces by Bernini, Raphael and Caravaggio *(see pp206–7)*.

9 Villa Giulia

This elegant 16th-century villa is home to the national collection of Etruscan antiquities *(see pp208–9)*.

10 Ostia Antica

Extending over several square kilometres, the remarkable ruins of ancient Rome's main port city hold many surprises and convey a powerful sense of everyday Imperial life *(see pp210–11)*.

TOP 10 ⭐ Vatican City

The Vatican is the world's smallest nation, covering just 50 ha (120 acres), and is a theocracy of just over 550 citizens, headed by the pope, but its sightseeing complex is beyond compare. Within its wall are the ornate St Peter's Basilica, the astonishing Sistine Chapel, apartments frescoed by Fra Angelico, Raphael and Pinturicchio, and ten museums. The latter include collections of Egyptian, Greek, Etruscan and Roman antiquities; Paleochristian, Renaissance and modern art; and a world-class ethnographic collection.

Sistine Chapel ③
Michelangelo's ceiling (right) is one of the most spectacular works of art in the world (see pp184–5).

④ Etruscan Museum
Finds from the Regolini-Galassi tomb of a noble woman (7th century BC) are the highlights here, including a bronze bed and gold and amber jewellery (left).

① Raphael Rooms
Raphael (1483–1520) decorated Julius II's rooms with frescoes that included the *School of Athens*, a convention of ancient philosophers bearing portraits of Renaissance artists such as Leonardo da Vinci as bearded Plato in the centre.

⑤ Chapel of Nicholas V
The Vatican's hidden gem is this closet-sized chapel frescoed in with early martyrs by Fra Angelico (1400–55).

⑥ Raphael's Transfiguration
Raphael was labouring on this gargantuan masterpiece (1517–20) when he died at 37, leaving students to finish the base. It shows Christ appearing to the Apostles in divine glory.

② Pio Clementino Museum
This museum has several famous Classical sculptures, including the contorted Hellenistic *Laocoön* (right), found in an Esquiline vineyard – Michelangelo saw the unearthing. There are also the *Apollo Belvedere* and *Belvedere Torso*, both huge influences on Renaissance artists.

Plan of Vatican City

9 Egyptian Museum

The collection consists mostly of sculpture brought from Egypt for temples and private villas and gardens. There are also decorated mummy cases (below), mummies and finds from a tomb that include a nit-comb.

8 Caravaggio's Deposition

Caravaggio's (1571–1610) *chiaroscuro* technique accentuates a diagonal composition filled with grisly realism.

10 Borgia Apartments

Borgia pope Alexander VI had these beautiful rooms frescoed by Pinturicchio (1454–1513) – Raphael was once his junior collaborator – between 1492 and 1495. The walls are now hung with lesser pieces from the Modern Art collection.

7 Leonardo da Vinci's St Jerome

Sketchy and unfinished – Leonardo (1452–1519) was often a distracted genius – this 1482 painting is nevertheless an anatomical masterpiece.

NEED TO KNOW

MAP B3 ■ www.vatican.va

Museums and Sistine Chapel: Viale Vaticano 100; 06 6988 3145; open 9am–6pm Mon–Sat (last admission 4pm), 9am–2pm last Sun of the month (free); closed 1 & 6 Jan, 11 Feb, Easter, Easter Mon, 1 May, 29 Jun, 15 & 16 Aug, 1 Nov, 25, 26 & 31 Dec; adm €17 (€8 ISIC under-26s, under-18s)

St Peter's Basilica: Piazza San Pietro; 06 6988 3731;

open 7am–7pm daily (until 6:30pm Oct–Mar); adm free (basilica); €8 (treasury), €8 (dome via steps), €10 (dome via lift)

■ Within the museums complex, take a break at the cafeteria (with a terrace in the Cortile della Pigna) or the pizzeria in the gardens near the Pavilion of Carriages.

■ When in town, the pope gives a mass audience on Wednesday mornings. Book free tickets in

advance (Prefecture of the Papal Household, fax 06 6988 5863).

Museum Guide

The Vatican Museums (a 15-minute walk from St Peter's) consist of ten collections, the Sistine Chapel and the Papal Apartments. To see highlights only, first visit the Pinacoteca, to the right of the entrance turnstile. The Sistine and other collections are to the left.

Sistine Chapel Works of Art

Detail from Michelangelo's fresco *The Creation of Adam*

1 Adam and Eve
God imparts the spark of life to Adam in one of western art's best known scenes, *The Creation of Adam*, then pulls Eve from Adam's rib.

2 Creation
God separates darkness from light, water from land and creates the sun and moon. Michelangelo veers towards blasphemy by depicting God's dirty feet.

3 The Sacrifice, Flood and Drunkenness of Noah
After disassembling his scaffolding and gazing up from floor level, Michelangelo noticed that these three tumultuous scenes were too minutely drawn.

4 Life of Moses Scenes
Left wall highlights include Botticelli's *The Trials of Moses* and Signorelli and della Gatta's *Moses Giving his Rod to Joshua*.

Plan of Sistine Chapel

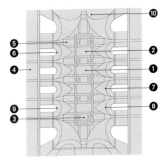

5 Sibyls and Prophets
Hebrew prophets, including Jonah, mingle with the Sibyls who foretold Christ's coming.

6 Old Testament Salvation Scenes and Ancestors of Christ
Portraits from Jesus's family tree are above the windows, and bloody Salvation scenes, including David and Goliath, are on corner spandrels.

7 Life of Christ Scenes
The chapel's right wall stars Botticelli's *Cleansing of the Leper*, Ghirlandaio's *Calling of Peter and Andrew*, and Perugino's *Christ Giving the Keys to St Peter*.

8 Christ Giving the Keys to St Peter
Classical buildings form the backdrop to this pivotal scene of transferring power from Christ to the popes. Each scene is divided into three parts.

9 Botticelli's Punishment of the Rebels
Schismatics question Aaron's priestly prerogative to burn incense. A vengeful Moses opens the earth to swallow them.

10 Last Judgement
This vast work depicts figures nude, equalized and stripped of their earthly rank. This was considered indecorous and the figures were covered by fig leaves. Saints are identified by their medieval icons.

UNDERSTANDING THE SISTINE CHAPEL ART

The Sistine Chapel's frescoes are not merely decorations by some of the greatest artists of the Renaissance – the images tell a story and make a complex theological argument. Pope Sixtus IV commissioned wall frescoes for the Pope's Chapel in 1481–83. They were intended to underscore papal authority, in question at the time, by drawing a line of power from God to the pope. In the Life of Moses cycle, Moses' and Aaron's undisputed roles as God's chosen representatives are affirmed by the fate of those who oppose Aaron – significantly and anachronistically wearing a papal hat – in the *Punishment of the Rebels*. Directly across from this work, Perugino's *Christ Giving the Keys to St Peter* bridges the Old Testament with the New as Christ hands control of the church to St Peter – and therefore to his successors, the popes (who are pictured between the Sistine windows). Michelangelo's breathtaking frescoes on the ceiling (1508–12) later added Genesis, Redemption and Salvation to the story.

TOP 10
PAINTERS OF THE SISTINE CHAPEL

1 **Fra Diamante** *(1430–98)*

2 **Rosselli** *(1439–1507)*

3 **Sandro Botticelli** *(1445–1510)*

4 **Bartolomeo della Gatta** *(1448–1502)*

5 **Domenico Ghirlandaio** *(c.1449–94)*

6 **Luca Signorelli** *(c.1450–1523)*

7 **Perugino** *(1450–1523)*

8 **Pinturicchio** *(1454–1513)*

9 **Piero di Cosimo** *(1462–1521)*

10 **Michelangelo** *(1475–1564)*

The Fall and Expulsion from the Garden of Eden, from Michelangelo's Genesis cycle, shows Adam and Eve being expelled from Eden for eating fruit from the forbidden Tree of Knowledge.

The Trials of Moses by Botticelli depicts scenes from the life of the prophet.

Features of St Peter's Basilica

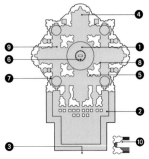

Plan of St Peter's Basilica

1 Dome
When Michelangelo designed a dome to span St Peter's massive transept, he made it 42 m (138 ft) in diameter, in deference to the Pantheon's 43.3 m (142 ft) dome. You can ride a lift much of the way, but must still navigate by foot the final 330 stairs between the dome's inner and outer shell to the 132-m-(435-ft-)high lantern and sweeping vistas across the city.

2 Pietà
Michelangelo carved this statue in 1499 at the age of only 25. It is at once graceful and mournful,

Michelangelo's
Pietà

stately and ethereal. It has been protected by glass since 1972, when a man screaming "I am Jesus Christ!" attacked it with a hammer, damaging the Virgin's nose and arm.

The magnificent Piazza San Pietro

3 Piazza San Pietro
Bernini's (1598–1680) remarkable semi-elliptical colonnades transformed the basilica's approach into a pair of welcoming arms embracing the faithful. Sadly, the full effect of entering the piazza from a warren of narrow medieval streets was spoiled when Mussolini razed the neighbourhood to lay down pompous Via della Conciliazione. The obelisk came from Alexandria in Egypt.

4 Apse
Bernini's exuberantly Baroque stained-glass window (1666) centres on a dove representing the Holy Ghost, surrounded by rays of the sun and a riot of sculptural details. Beneath the window sits the Chair of St Peter (1665), another Bernini concoction; inside is a wood and ivory chair said to be the actual throne of St Peter. Bernini also crafted the multicoloured marble *Monument to Urban VIII* (1644) to the right, based on Michelangelo's Medici tombs in Florence. It is of far

better artistic quality than Guglielmo della Porta's (c.1490–1577) similar one for Pope Paul III (1549) to the left.

5 Statue of St Peter

A holdover from the medieval St Peter's, this 13th-century bronze statue by the sculptor Arnolfo di Cambio (c.1245–1301/10) has achieved holy status. The faithful can be seen lining up to rub (or kiss) Peter's well-worn foot for good luck.

6 Baldacchino

Whether you view it as ostentatious or glorious, Bernini's Baroque sculpted canopy above the high altar is at least impressive. Its spiralling bronze columns are said to have been made from the revetments (portico ceiling decorations) of the Pantheon *(see pp188–9)*, taken by Pope Urban VIII. For his desecration of the Roman temple the Barberini pope and his family were castigated with the quip:

Crux Vaticana or the Cross of Justin II

"What even the barbarians wouldn't do, Barberini did."

7 Treasury

Among the ecclesiastical treasures here is a 6th-century jewel-encrusted bronze cross – the Crux Vaticana – various fragments of the medieval basilica including a 1432 ciborium by Donatello (c.1386–1466), and Antonio Pollaiuolo's (c.1432–98) masterful bronze slab tomb (1493) for Sixtus IV, the pope's effigy surrounded by representations of theological virtues and liberal arts.

8 Grottoes

Many of the medieval basilica's monuments are housed beneath the basilica's floor. During excavations in the 1940s, workers discovered in the Necropolis the legendary Red Wall behind which St Peter was supposedly buried. The wall was covered with early medieval graffiti invoking the saint, and a box of bones was found behind it. The late Pope John Paul II was buried in the crypt after his death in 2005.

9 Alexander VII's Monument

One of Bernini's last works (1678) shows figures of Justice, Truth, Chastity and Prudence gazing up at the pontiff seated in the deep shadows of the niche. A skeleton crawls from under the flowing marble drapery to hold aloft an hourglass as a reminder of mortality.

10 Vision of Constantine

The most dramatic statue in the basilica, this rearing equestrian figure shows Emperor Constantine at the moment in which he had a vision of the Cross at the Battle of the Milvian Bridge in 312 AD. Victorious, Constantine converted to Christianity and made it the official religion of the Empire.

Bernini's ornate *baldacchino*

🔟⭐ The Pantheon

When Emperor Phocas donated this pagan temple to Pope Boniface IV in 608, he unwittingly ensured that one of the marvels of ancient Rome would be preserved unaltered in its new guise as the Christian church of Santa Maria ad Martyres. Designed by Emperor Hadrian in AD 118–25, it has been lightly sacked over the ages, yet the airy interior and perfect proportions remain: a wonder of the world even in its own time.

1 Dome
The widest masonry dome in Europe is precisely as high as it is wide: 43.3 m (142 ft). Its airy, coffered space, cleverly shot through with a shaft of sunlight from the oculus, is what lends the Pantheon an ethereal air.

4 Oculus
The bold 8.3 m (27 ft) wide hole at the centre of the massive dome **(right)** provides light and structural support: the tension around its ring helps hold the weight of the dome.

6 Doors
The massive bronze doors are technically original, but were so extensively renovated under Pope Pius IV (1653) that they have been practically recast.

7 Marble Decorations
Red porphyry, giallo antico, and other ancient marbles grace the interior. More than half the polychrome panels cladding the walls are original, the rest careful reproductions, as is the floor **(below)**.

2 Walls
The 6.2 m (20 ft) thick walls incorporate built-in brick arches to help distribute the weight downwards, relieving the stress of the heavy roof.

5 Portico
The triangular pediment **(above)** is supported by 16 pink and grey granite columns, all original save the three on the left (17th-century copies).

3 Royal Tombs
Two of Italy's kings are honoured by simple tombs. Vittorio Emanuele II (1861–78) unified Italy and became its first king. His son, Umberto I, was assassinated in 1900.

⑧ Fountain

Giacomo della Porta designed this stoop; Leonardo Sormani carved it in 1575. The marble basin was replaced by a stone one and the Egyptian obelisk of Rameses II was added in 1711 **(left)**.

Raphael's ⑨ Tomb

Raphael, darling of the Renaissance art world but dead at 37, rests in a plain, ancient stone sarcophagus **(right)**. Poet Bembo's Latin epitaph says: "Here lies Raphael, whom Nature feared would outdo her while alive, but now that he is gone fears she, too, will die." Other artists buried here include Baldassare Peruzzi.

⑩ Basilica of Neptune Remains

Of the Pantheon's old neighbour, all that remains are an elaborate cornice and fluted columns against the Pantheon's rear wall.

THE FIRST PANTHEON

Emperor Augustus's son-in-law, Marcus Agrippa, built the first Pantheon in 27 BC, replaced in AD 118-125 by Hadrian's rotunda. The pediment's inscription, "M. Agrippa cos tertium fecit" ("M. Agrippa made this") was Hadrian's modest way of honouring Agrippa. The pediment also provided the illusion of a smaller temple, making the massive space inside even more of a surprise (the Pantheon was originally raised and the dome behind it wasn't visible). Bernini's "ass ears", tiny towers he added to the pediment, were removed in 1883.

NEED TO KNOW

MAP D3 ■ Piazza della Rotonda ■ 06 6830 0230

Open 8:30am–7:30pm Mon–Sat, 9am–6pm Sun (9am–1pm during hols); Mass: 10:30am Sun and 5pm Sat; closed 1 Jan, 1 May, 25 Dec

■ There's a good gelateria, Cremeria Monteforte (Via della Rotonda, on the Pantheon's right flank, and an excellent coffee shop, La Tazza d'Oro (Via degli Orfan), just off the square.

■ Rather than bemoan a rainy day in Rome, head to the Pantheon to watch the water fall gracefully though the oculus and spatter on the marble floor and down a drain.

TOP 10 ⭐ Roman Forum

Gazing on the picturesque ruins today, one would hardly guess that the Forum was the symbol of civic pride for 1,000 years. Its beginning, more than 3,000 years ago, was as a cemetery for the village on Palatine Hill. When the marshy land was drained in the 6th century BC, the Forum took on a more central role. It was at its most elegant starting with the reign of Augustus, who is said to have turned the city from brick to marble.

① Temple of Vesta and House of the Vestal Virgins

A graceful round temple and its adjacent palace were the centre for one of the city's most revered cults. Noble priestesses tended the sacred flame and enjoyed the greatest privileges.

② Curia

The 3rd-century-AD Senate retains its original polychrome inlaid floor, its risers, where the 300 senators sat in deliberation, and the speaker's platform. For 2nd-century views of the Forum, examine the large marble reliefs, showing Emperor Trajan's good works.

③ Arch of Septimius Severus

This well-preserved triumphal arch **(below)** celebrates the emperor's Middle Eastern victories. It was erected in AD 203 by his sons, Geta and Caracalla, then co-emperors.

④ Temple of Castor and Pollux

Three Corinthian columns remain of this temple **(left)** to the Dioscuri – twin brothers of Helen of Troy and sons of Jupiter and Leda. It marked the spot where they miraculously appeared in 499 BC to announce a crucial Roman victory.

⑥ Arch of Titus

The oldest extant arch in Rome was built in AD 81 by Emperor Domitian to honour his brother, Titus, and his father, Vespasian, for putting down the Jewish Revolt. Reliefs show the sacking of Jerusalem's Holy of Holies and sacred objects, such as a golden menorah, being taken.

⑤ Basilica of Maxentius and Constantine

Three vast, coffered barrel vaults proclaim the Forum's largest structure, built around AD 315 and used as the legal and financial centre of the Empire.

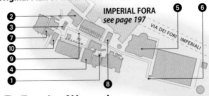

Original Plan of the Roman Forum

IMPERIAL FORA
see page 197

VIA DEI FORI IMPERIALI

7 Temple of Vespasian

Until 18th-century excavations, these graceful columns (AD 79) from a temple to the former emperor stood mostly buried beneath centuries of detritus.

8 Temple of Antoninus and Faustina

Dedicated by Antoninus Pius in AD 41 to his deified wife Faustina, this is one of the best-preserved temples **(above)**. With its Baroque-style top-knot, it is also one of the oddest. Note the carvings of griffins along the side frieze.

9 Via Sacra

Paved with broad, flat, black basalt stones, Rome's oldest road wound from the Arch of Titus through the Forum and up to the Capitoline. Triumphal processions were staged here, but it degenerated into a hangout for gossips, pick-pockets and other idlers.

10 Temple of Saturn

Eight grey-and-red Ionic columns **(left)** constitute what's left of this temple (also the state treasury) to the ruler of agriculture and of a mythic "Golden Age". Saturnalia, celebrated each December, was very similar to modern-day Christmas.

NEED TO KNOW

MAP E4 ▪ Via dei Fori Imperiali ▪ 06 3996 7700

Open 16 Feb–15 Mar: 8:30am–5pm daily; 16–31 Mar: 8:30am– 5:30pm daily; Apr–Aug: 8:30am–7:15pm daily; Sep: 8:30am–7pm daily; Oct: 8:30am–6:30pm daily; 1 Nov–15 Feb: 8:30am–4:30pm daily; closed 1 Jan, 25 Dec

Adm €12 (includes Palatine & Colosseum; valid for 48 hrs); free for under-18s; free for all first Sun of the month

▪ The only option in the immediate area for drinks and snacks is one of the mobile refreshment vendors. For something more substantial, there are plenty of cafés and restaurants on Via Cavour.

▪ In summer, it's best to visit the Forum either early or late in the day, to avoid the intense heat.

Forum Guide
You can access the Forum from Via dei Fori Imperiali. However, for a great view

of the whole site, enter from one of the high points at either end. From the northwest end, begin on the Capitoline (to the right and behind the huge, white Victor Emmanuel Monument) and take the stairs down from Largo Romolo e Remo. From the southeast end, start at the Colosseum *(see pp196–7)* and climb the small hill just to the northwest. Enter by the Arch of Titus, which is also near the main entry gate to the Palatine.

Palatine Hill Features

The ruins of Domus Flavia

Domus Flavia

Marked today mainly by the remains of two fountains, this imposing edifice was the official wing of a vast emperors' palace, built by Domitian in AD 81.

2 Livia's House

This 1st-century BC structure, now below ground level, formed part of the residence of Augustus and his second wife. Here you can examine a number of mosaic pavements and wall frescoes.

3 Palatine Museum and Antiquarium

This former convent houses a wealth of artifacts unearthed here, including pottery, statuary, ancient graffiti and very fine mosaics. You can also study a model of the Iron Age Palatine.

4 Romulus's Iron Age Huts

Traces of the three 9th-century BC huts were uncovered in the 1940s. Legend says that this tiny village was founded by Romulus, who gave Rome its name.

5 Stadium

Possibly a racetrack, or just a large garden, this sunken rectangle formed part of Domitian's palatial 1st-century abode.

6 Domus Augustana

All that remains of the private wing of Emperor Domitian's Imperial extravaganza are the massive substructure vaults.

Temple of Cybele

The orgiastic cult of the Great Mother was the first of the Oriental religions to come to Rome, in 191 BC. Still here is a decapitated statue of the goddess. Priests worshipping Cybele ritually castrated themselves.

8 Farnese Gardens

Plants and elegant pavilions grace part of what was once an extensive pleasure garden, designed by the noted architect Vignola and built in the 16th century over the ruins of Tiberius's palace.

Pavilions at the Farnese Gardens

9 Cryptoporticus

This series of underground corridors, their vaults decorated with delicate stucco reliefs, stretches 130 m (425 ft). It connected the Palatine to Nero's Domus Aurea or Golden House *(Via della Domus Aurea)*.

10 Domus Septimius Severus

Huge arches and broken walls are all that remain of this emperor's 2nd-century AD extension to the Domus Augustana.

A DAY IN THE LIFE OF A ROMAN HOUSEHOLD

Most Romans lived in *insulae*, apartment buildings of perhaps six floors, with the poorest residents occupying the cheaper upper floors. An average Roman male citizen arose before dawn, arranged his toga, and breakfasted on a piece of bread. Then out into the alleys, reverberating with noise. First, a stop at a public latrine, where he chatted with neighbours. Next a visit to his honoured patron, who paid him his daily stipend. Lunch might be a piece of bread dipped in wine or olive oil, perhaps with a bit of cold meat. Bathing waited until late afternoon, when he met his friends at the public baths. There he lingered – conversing, exercising, reading, or admiring the artwork – until dinnertime. The main meal of the day was taken lying on couches, with his slaves in attendance. Then it was bedtime. Roman matrons, apart from their time at the baths (usually earlier than the men), spent the entire day at home, running the household.

Roman toga

TOP 10
ANCIENT ROMAN BELIEF SYSTEMS

1 State Religion of Graeco-Roman Gods (especially the Capitol Triad: Jupiter, Juno, Minerva)

2 Household Gods: Ancestors and Genii

3 Cult of Cybele, the Great Mother

4 Deification of Emperors, Empresses and Favourites

5 Orgiastic Fertility Cults

6 Mithraism

7 Cult of Attis

8 Cult of Isis

9 Cult of Serapis

10 Judeo-Christianity

Feasts held by wealthy Romans were usually extravagant affairs, served by slaves and eaten lying on couches, sometimes under garden pergolas.

TOP 10 ⭐ Galleria Borghese

The Borghese Gallery is one of the world's greatest small museums. Some of Bernini's best sculptures and Caravaggio's paintings sit alongside Classical, Renaissance and Neo-Classical works in a beautiful frescoed 17th-century villa set in the Villa Borghese park, all of which once belonged to the great art-lover of the early Baroque, Cardinal Scipione Borghese. He patronized the young Bernini and Caravaggio, in the process amassing one of Rome's richest private collections.

5 Sleeping Hermaphrodite

A Roman marble copy **(left)** of a notorious Greek bronze sculpture mentioned by Pliny. Walk around what appears to be a sleeping woman, to discover the reason for its notoriety.

1 Bernini's Apollo and Daphne

A climactic moment frozen in marble (1622–5). As Apollo is inches from grabbing Daphne, the pitying gods transform her into a laurel.

3 Bernini's David

Young Bernini's *David* (1623–4) was the Baroque answer to Michelangelo's Renaissance version. The frowning face is a self-portrait.

6 Canova's Pauline Bonaparte

Napoleon's sister caused a scandal with this half-naked portrait (1805–8), lounging like a Classical goddess on a cushion carved of marble.

2 Titian's Sacred and Profane Love

Titian's (1488/90–1576) allegorical scene (1514), painted for a wedding, exhorts the young bride that worldly love is part of the divine, and that sex is an extension of holy matrimony **(above)**.

4 Bernini's Rape of Persephone

Bernini carved this masterpiece **(right)** at the age of 23 (1621–2). Muscular Hades throws his head back with laughter, his strong fingers pressing into the maiden's soft flesh as she struggles to break free of his grasp.

7 Caravaggio's Self-Portrait as a Sick Bacchus

This early self-portrait (1593) as the wine god was painted with painstaking detail, supposedly when the artist was ill. It shows finer brushwork than later works.

8 Raphael's Deposition

The Borghese's most famous painting (1507), although neither the gallery's nor Raphael's best **(below)**. The Perugian matriarch Atalanta Baglioni commissioned it to honour her assassinated son (perhaps the red-shirted pall-bearer).

Museum Floorplan

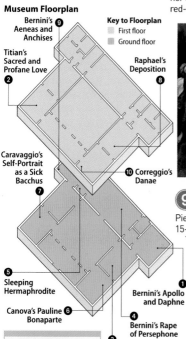

Bernini's Aeneas and Anchises ⑨

Titian's Sacred and Profane Love ②

Caravaggio's Self-Portrait as a Sick Bacchus ⑦

Key to Floorplan
■ First floor
■ Ground floor

Raphael's Deposition ⑧

⑩ Correggio's Danae

⑤ Sleeping Hermaphrodite

Canova's Pauline ⑥ Bonaparte

Bernini's Apollo ① and Daphne

Bernini's Rape ④ of Persephone

③ Bernini's David

9 Bernini's Aeneas and Anchises

Pietro Bernini was still guiding his 15-year-old son in this 1613 work. The carving is more timid and static than in later works, but the genius is already evident.

10 Correggio's Danae

A sensual masterpiece (1531) based on Ovid's *Metamorphoses*. Cupid pulls back the sheets as Jupiter, the golden shower above her head, rains his love over Danae.

THE BORGHESE COLLECTORS

Scipione used this 17th-century villa as a showplace for a stupendous antiquities collection given to him by his uncle, Pope Paul V, to which he added sculptures by the young Bernini. When Camillo Borghese married Pauline Bonaparte, he donated the bulk of the Classical sculpture collection to his brother-in-law Napoleon in 1809. They now form the core of the Louvre's antiquities wing in Paris.

NEED TO KNOW

MAP E1 ■ Villa Borghese, off Via Pinciana ■ 06 328 10 ■ www.galleriaborghese. beniculturali.it, www.tosc. it (for reservations)

Open 9am–7pm Tue–Sun; closed 1 Jan, 25 Dec

Adm €13; €6.50 students (18–25); €2 under-18s and journalists (prices may change during exhibitions); free first Sun of the month; max. viewing time 2 hours (mandatory exit after that)

■ There's a decent café in the museum basement, although the Caffè delle Arti *(06 3265 1236)* at the nearby Galleria Nazionale d'Arte Moderna is better, with a park view.

■ Entrance to the gallery is strictly by reservation. Make sure you book well ahead of time – entries are strictly timed and tickets often sell out days, even weeks, in advance, especially if an exhibition is on.

TOP 10 ★ The Colosseum and Imperial Fora

Trajan's Column

This rich archaeological zone, rudely intruded upon by Mussolini's Via dei Fori Imperiali, contains some of the most grandiose and noteworthy of Rome's ancient remains. Dominating the area is the mighty shell of the Colosseum, constructed in AD 72–80 under the Flavian emperors and originally known as the Flavian Amphitheatre. The Comune di Roma is constantly working on excavating the area and new discoveries are made every year.

1 Trajan's Forum and Column

Trajan's Forum left all who beheld it awed by its splendid nobility. Now cut off by modern roads, all that stands out is the magnificent column, commemorating in fine graphic detail the emperor's victories in what is now Romania. Access to part of it is through Trajan's Markets.

3 Trajan's Markets

The emperor and his visionary architect, Apollodorus of Damascus, built this attractive, very modern-looking shopping and office mall (below) in the early 2nd century AD. There were 150 spaces in all, the top floor utilized by welfare offices, the lower levels by shops of all kinds.

5 Colosseum

Built by Jewish slaves, this magnificent structure was where the Imperial passion for bloody spectacle reached its peak of excess. When Emperor Titus inaugurated the amphitheatre (above) in AD 80, he declared 100 days of celebratory games, some involving the massacre of 5,000 wild beasts, such as lions. This slaughter-as-sport was finally banned in AD 523.

2 Domus Aurea

A result of the mad emperor Nero's self-indulgence, this "golden house" was the largest Rome ever saw, yet it was for amusement only. It covered several acres and had every luxury. Currently closed for restoration.

4 Mamertine Prison

Legend holds that Sts Peter and Paul were imprisoned here. Prisoners were dropped down through a hole in the floor and the only exit was death, often from starvation.

6 House of the Knights of Rhodes

This 12th-century priory was owned by the crusading order of the Knights of Rhodes. Inside are the original portico, three shops and the Chapel of St John.

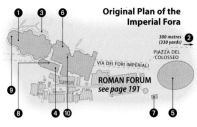

Original Plan of the Imperial Fora

300 metres (330 yards)

PIAZZA DEL COLOSSEO

VIA DEI FORI IMPERIALI

ROMAN FORUM
see page 191

7 Arch of Constantine

This arch marks the victory of the first Christian emperor over his rival, Emperor Maxentius. Yet it is mostly a pastiche of pagan elements taken from several earlier monuments – the beautiful hunt-scene roundels come from a temple dedicated to Emperor Hadrian's male lover, Antinous.

8 Forum of Julius Caesar

The first of Rome's great Imperial Fora. Caesar's line, the Julians, traced their ancestry back to Venus herself, so he erected the Temple of Venus Genetrix in 46 BC and placed there statues of himself and his great love Cleopatra, the queen of Egypt.

9 Palazzo Valentini

In 2005 two Imperial Roman villas, retaining a spa bath, courtyards and traces of frescoed walls and mosaic floors, were found below Palazzo Valentini *(Foro Traiano)*.

10 Forum of Augustus

Julius Caesar's successor made the focus of his forum the Temple of Mars the Avenger **(above)**, identified by the broad staircase and four Corinthian columns.

⭐ Musei Capitolini

Ancient Rome's religious heart, Capitoline Hill now houses a magnificent museum. Take the Cordonata uphill, a theatrical experience planned by Michelangelo in the 16th century. At the top stands a statue of Marcus Aurelius in a star-shaped piazza, which is bordered by twin palaces containing some of Rome's greatest treasures. The collections in the Palazzo Nuovo (this page) and Palazzo dei Conservatori (overleaf) were established in 1471 with a donation of bronzes by Pope Sixtus IV.

Fresco depicting Hannibal crossing the Alps

1 Mosaic of the Masks

This floor mosaic of two Greek theatre masks is probably from the 2nd century AD. The use of perspective, light and shadow is highly skilled, employing small squares of marble to create dramatic effects.

2 Capitoline Venus

This fine 1st-century BC copy of a Praxiteles Aphrodite from the 4th century BC shows the goddess of love risen voluptuously from her bath, attempting to cover herself, as if reacting to someone's arrival.

3 Hall of the Emperors

The hall contains several portraits of the emperors and empresses of the Imperial Age. Among them is a bust of the brutal ruler Emperor Caracalla from the 3rd century AD.

4 Resting Satyr

Used to adorn an ancient grove or fountain, this young mythological creature is a copy of a 4th-century BC original by Greek sculptor Praxiteles. His pointed ears, panther-skin cape and flute are attributes of the nature god Pan. It inspired Nathaniel Hawthorne's novel *The Marble Faun*.

NEED TO KNOW

MAP D4 ▪ Piazza del Campidoglio ▪ 06 0608 ▪ www.museicapitolini.org

Open 9:30am–7:30pm daily; closed 1 Jan, 1 May, 25 Dec

Adm: €15 (free for under-6s); prices may change during major exhibitions

▪ **Capitolini Card** costs €16 (valid for 7 days) and also gives admission to Centrale Montemartini.

▪ The café behind the **Palazzo dei Conservatori (Caffè Capitolino)** has a terrace with a spectacular panorama of the city.

▪ Part of the underground passage between the two museums is the ancient **Tabularium**, imperial Rome's Hall of Records, which offers an unusual view of the Roman Forum.

Museum Guide
The Palazzo Nuovo, on the left as you enter the piazza, contains mostly restored ancient sculpture. The finest pieces are on the upper floor. Take the stairs down to the underpass leading to the Palazzo dei Conservatori (*see pp200–201*) – the courtyard displays ancient marble fragments. The next floor up displays 16th-and 17th-century decorations and Classical statuary. On the top floor are paintings from the Renaissance and Baroque periods.

Marforio 5
This hirsute reclining giant **(right)** was originally a river god, and is believed to have come from the Forum of Augustus *(see p197)*. A Renaissance sculptor added the attributes of the god Ocean and placed him here, as overseer of this courtyard fountain.

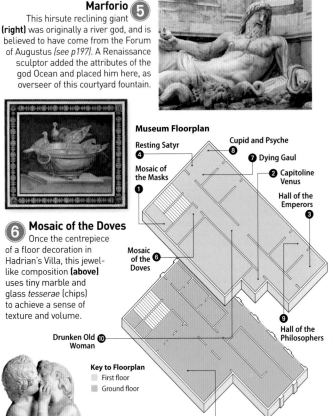

6 Mosaic of the Doves
Once the centrepiece of a floor decoration in Hadrian's Villa, this jewel-like composition **(above)** uses tiny marble and glass *tesserae* (chips) to achieve a sense of texture and volume.

Museum Floorplan

Resting Satyr
4

Cupid and Psyche
8

7 Dying Gaul

Mosaic of the Masks
1

2 Capitoline Venus

Hall of the Emperors
3

Mosaic of the Doves 6

9

Hall of the Philosophers

Drunken Old Woman 10

Key to Floorplan
First floor
Ground floor

5 Marforio

7 Dying Gaul
The collection's most renowned piece conveys great pathos. It is probably a 1st-century AD Roman copy of a Hellenistic bronze from the 3rd century BC.

8 Cupid and Psyche
The Roman god of love embraces the personification of the soul; here, the lovers are eternally united **(left)**. This Roman copy of a Hellenistic original has inspired a great many sentimental variations.

9 Hall of the Philosophers
This room is filled with Roman copies of idealized Greek portrait busts of the greatest Hellenic poets and thinkers, including the blind epic poet Homer.

10 Drunken Old Woman
This copy of a Hellenistic original dating from the 3rd century BC is from a series of sculptures, which represent the wages of vice.

Palazzo dei Conservatori Exhibits

Head, Colossal Statue of Constantine

1 Colossal Statue of Constantine Fragments

Found in the ruins of the Basilica of Maxentius and Constantine, these surreal outsized body parts (c. AD 313–24) formed the unclothed segments of an overwhelming seated effigy of the first Christian emperor, recognizable by his protuberant eyes. The rest of the sculpture was made of carved wood dressed in sheets of bronze.

2 Lo Spinario

One of the precious bronzes that comprised Sixtus IV's donation to the people of Rome, this charming sculpture dates from the 1st century BC. Hellenistic in its everyday subject matter, the head recalls more archaic models. The boy's unusual and graceful pose inspired many works during the Renaissance.

3 Caravaggio's St John the Baptist

Shocking in its sensuality, the boy's erotic pose, his arm around the ram, created an iconographic revolution when it was unveiled around 1600. Masterful *chiaroscuro* brought the holy image even more down to earth.

4 Bronze She-Wolf

The most ancient symbol of Rome, from the 5th century BC, of Etruscan or Greek workmanship. The she-wolf stands guard, at once a protectress and a nurturer, as the twins Romulus and Remus feed on her milk. This was also part of the 1471 donation of Pope Sixtus IV.

Bronze statue of the Roman She-Wolf

5 Guercino's Burial of St Petronilla

The influence of Caravaggio is clearly evident in this huge altarpiece, executed for St Peter's Basilica between 1621 and 1623. Powerful effects of light and dark combined with pronounced musculature and individuality of the figures bring the work directly into the viewer's physical world.

6 Caravaggio's Gypsy Fortune-Teller

An earlier work by Caravaggio, but just as revolutionary as his St John

Palazzo dei Conservatori Floorplan

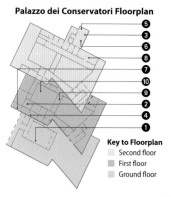

Key to Floorplan
- Second floor
- First floor
- Ground floor

Pietro da Cortona's Baroque artwork *Rape of the Sabines*

the Baptist. This subject is taken from everyday street life in late 16th-century Rome, which the painter knew intimately. Notice that the gypsy is slyly slipping the ring from the unsuspecting young dandy's finger.

7 Bust of Lucius Junius Brutus

Dating from between the 4th and 3rd centuries BC, this bronze bust is possibly the rarest object in the museum. Its identification as the first Roman consul is uncertain, because it also resembles Greek models of poets and philosophers. Its intense, inlaid glass eyes make it one of the most gripping portraits.

8 Pietro da Cortona's Rape of the Sabines

Baroque painting is said to have begun with this work (c.1630), where symmetry is abandoned and all is twisting, dynamic move-ment. It shows an early episode in Roman history: the new city had been founded but the population lacked women, so they stole those of the neighbouring Sabine tribe.

9 Bust of Commodus as Hercules

The 2nd-century emperor, who loved to fight wild animals in the Colosseum, had himself represented as the demigod Hercules, to promote his own divinity. The club held in his right hand, the lion's mantle and the apples of the Hesperides in his left hand are all symbols of the labours of Hercules.

10 Equestrian Statue of Marcus Aurelius

A copy of this 2nd-century AD bronze masterpiece stands in the centre of the Capitoline star; the larger-than-life original is displayed in a glassed-in courtyard within the Palazzo dei Conservatori.

Equestrian statue of Marcus Aurelius

TOP 10 ⭐ Museo Nazionale Romano

The National Museum of Rome (MNR) is split across five sites. Much of the sculpture is at Palazzo Altemps (overleaf), while some of the best individual pieces, mosaics and frescoes are at Palazzo Massimo alle Terme (this page). Aula Ottagona has oversized bathhouse statues and the Baths of Diocletian house the epigraphic and *stele* collection. Crypta Balbi features remnants of ancient Roman city blocks and a 13 BC portico.

1 Statue of Augustus

The statue of Rome's first emperor once stood on Via Labicana. It shows him wearing his toga draped over his head – a sign that, in AD 12, he added the title *Pontifex Maximus* (high priest) to the list of honours he assigned himself.

2 Boats of Nemi

These elaborate bronzes (including lions, wolves and a head of Medusa) once decorated the two luxury boats that Emperor Caligula kept on the Lake of Nemi. The boats, used for parties, even had central heating.

3 House of Livia

These frescoes (20–10 BC) depicting a lush garden came from the villa of Augustus's wife, Livia **(above)**. They were in the *triclinium*, a dining room half-buried to keep it cool in summer.

4 Leucotea Nursing Dionysus

Discovered in 1879, a luxuriously frescoed villa included this bedroom scene of a nymph nursing the wine god **(above)**, with additional scenes in the niches.

5 Wounded Niobid

Sculpted around 440 BC for a Greek temple and later acquired by Julius Caesar, this hauntingly beautiful figure of Niobid (daughter of Queen Niobe) is reaching for the fatal arrow that killed her siblings.

6 Discus Thrower

This 2nd-century AD marble copy **(right)** of the famous 450 BC Greek original by Myron is faithful to the point of imitating the original bronze's imperfect dimensions.

7 Four-Chariotters Mosaic

The imperial Severi family must have been passionate about sports to have decorated a bedroom of their 3rd-century AD villa with these charioteers **(right)**. They are dressed in the traditional colours of the four factions of the Roman circus.

8 Bronze Dionysus

Few large Classical bronzes survive today, making this 2nd-century AD statue special beyond its obvious grace, skill and preserved decoration. You can still see the yellow eyes, red lips and a comb band in the grape-festooned hair.

9 Ivory Mask of Apollo

This exquisite mask was discovered by illegal excavators in 1995 near Lake Bracciano, northwest of Rome, and intercepted by the Carabinieri. It formed part of a larger chryselephantine statue – one whose face, hands and feet were made of ivory, placed on a wooden frame and "dressed" with textiles and gold.

10 Boxer at Rest

No idealised athlete, this is a muscled, tough, middle-aged man, resting between bouts, naked except for the leather strips binding his fists. Red copper highlights make his bruises look fresh **(below)**.

NEED TO KNOW

Palazzo Massimo alle Terme: MAP F3; Largo di Villa Peretti 1; 06 3996 7700; open 9am–7:45pm Tue–Sun, closed 1 Jan & 25 Dec

Palazzo Altemps: MAP C3; Piazza Sant'Apollinare 46; 06 3996 7700; open 9am–7:45pm Tue–Sun, closed 1 Jan & 25 Dec

Adm €12; extra €3 for exhibitions; free first Sun of the month

The ticket (valid for 3 days) gives admission to all Museo Nazionale Romano sites

■ From Palazzo Massimo alle Terme, walk down Via Nazionale for bars and restaurants. After exploring Palazzo Altemps, go to Tre Scalini, 28 on Piazza Navona, for refreshments.

■ Call ahead for Palazzo Massimo alle Terme tickets, as the frescoes and mosaics on the top floor are timed-entry only.

Gallery Guide

Palazzo Massimo alle Terme exhibits its Republican and Early Imperial Rome (up to Augustus) statuary on the ground floor, along with a few older Greek pieces. The first floor art exhibits reflect the political, cultural and economic spheres of Imperial Rome up to the 4th century. The second floor, which requires a timed-entry ticket, displays ancient mosaics and frescoes. In the basement, the numismatic collection illustrates the history of money from its origins. There is also gold jewellery and a mummified eight-year-old girl.

Palazzo Altemps Collection

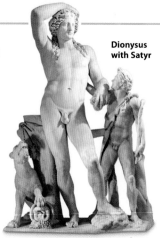

Dionysus with Satyr

1 Athena Parthenos
The 1st-century BC Greek sculptor Antioco carved this statue to match the most famed sculpture in antiquity, the long-lost Athena in Athens' Parthenon.

2 "Grande Ludovisi" Sarcophagus
This mid-3rd century AD sarcophagus, deeply carved and remarkably well-preserved, shows the Romans victorious over the barbarian Ostrogoth hordes.

3 Orestes and Electra
This 1st-century AD statue was carved by Menelaus, an imitator of the great Greek artist Praxiteles. The scraps of 15th-century fresco nearby depict some wedding gifts from the marriage of Girolamo Riario and Caterina Sforza.

4 Garden of Delights Loggia
The loggia frescoes (c.1595) are a catalogue of the exotic fruits, plants and animals then being imported from the New World.

5 Dionysus with Satyr
Imperial Rome was in love with Greek sculpture, producing copies such as this grouping of Dionysus, a satyr and a panther.

6 Ludovisi Throne
This set of 5th-century BC reliefs came to Rome from a Calabrian Greek colony and were discovered in the 19th century.

7 Apollo Playing the Lute
There are two 1st-century AD Apollos in the museum, both restored in the 17th century.

8 Suicidal Gaul
This suicidal figure supporting his dead wife's arm was part of a trio, including the Capitoline's Dying Gaul *(see p199)*, commissioned by Julius Caesar to celebrate a Gaulish victory.

9 Egyptian Statuary
The Egyptian collections are divided into three sections related to that culture's influence on Rome: political theological, popular worship and places of worship. The showpiece is the impressive granite *Bull Api*, or *Brancaccio Bull* (2nd century BC).

10 Colossal Head of Ludovisi Hera
Goethe called this his "first love in Rome". It is believed to be a portrait of Claudius's mother, Antonia.

Garden of Delights Loggia

ANCIENT ROMAN ART

Ancient Rome's art was as conservative as its culture. From the middle Republican to the Imperial era, Romans shunned original sculpture for copies of famous Greek works. The Caesars imported Golden Age statuary from Greece, and Roman workshops churned out toga-wearing headless figures in stock poses to which any bust could be affixed. Romans excelled at bust portraiture, especially up to the early Imperial age when naturalism was still in vogue. Roman painting is divided into styles based on Pompeii examples. The First Style imitated marble; the Second Style imitated architecture, often set within the small painted scenes that became a hallmark of the Third Style. The Fourth Style was *trompe l'oeil* decoration. Mosaic, first developed as a floor-strengthening technique, could be simple black-on-white, or intricate work with shading and contour. *Opus sectile* (inlaid marble) was a style that was imported from the East.

TOP 10
ANCIENT ART COLLECTIONS

1 **Museo Nazionale Romano** (see pp202–3)

2 **Vatican Museums** (see pp182–3)

3 **Musei Capitolini** (see pp198–201)

4 **Centrale Montemartini** (Via Ostiense)

5 **Ara Pacis** (Lungotevere en Augusta)

6 **Villa Giulia** (see pp208–9)

7 **Trajan's Column** (see p197)

8 **Column of Marcus Aurelius** (Piazza Colonna)

9 **Palatine Antiquarium** (see p192)

10 **Museo Barracco** (Corso Vittorio Emanuele II)

The Ludovisi Throne is a sculpted marble block depicting the birth of Aphrodite. The goddess is seen rising from the sea wearing finely carved diaphanous drapery.

A 2nd-century BC Roman mosaic at the Museo Nazionale Romano

⭐ Santa Maria del Popolo

Few churches are such perfect primers on Roman art and architecture. Masters from the Early Renaissance (Bramante, Pinturicchio), High Renaissance (Raphael) and Baroque (Caravaggio, Bernini) exercised their genius in all disciplines here: painting, sculpture, architecture and decoration. It's also one of the few churches with major chapels still intact, preserving the artworks that together tell a complete story.

② Crucifixion of St Peter

Caravaggio has avoided the goriness of his earlier works and filled this *chiaroscuro* work (1601) with drama **(left)**. The naturalistic figures quietly go about their business – the tired workers hauling the cross into place; Peter looking contemplative.

① Pinturicchio's Adoration

Raphael's contemporary retained more of his teacher Perugino's limpid Umbrian style in this 1490 work in the della Rovere chapel. Also in the chapel is Cardinal Cristoforo's tomb by Francesco da Sangallo (1478), while Domenico's tomb (1477) features a *Madonna with Child* by Mino da Fiesole.

③ Conversion of St Paul

Again, Caravaggio leaves all drama to the effects of light, depicting an awe-struck Paul transfixed by blinding light (1601).

④ Sansovino Tombs

Tuscan Andrea Sansovino (c.1467–1529) gave a Renaissance/Etruscan twist to the traditional lying-in-state look (1505–07). These effigies of Cardinal della Rovere and Cardinal Sforza recline on cushions as if asleep.

Santa Maria del Popolo

⑤ Daniel and Habakkuk

Sculpture as theatre by Bernini, as an angel seizes Habakkuk by the hair **(right)** to fly him to the imprisoned, starving Daniel, shown kneeling with a lion licking his foot.

⑥ Raphael's Chigi Chapel

Pagan and Christian imagery are fused in this exquisite chapel designed for Agostino Chigi. The skeleton inlaid in the floor **(left)** plays a role in Dan Brown's *Angels and Demons*.

MORS AD CAELOS

7 Marcillat's Stained-Glass Window

The only Roman work by Guillaume de Marcillat (1470–1529), the undisputed French master of stained glass, this depicts the Infancy of Christ and Life of the Virgin **(left)**.

THE PEOPLE'S CHURCH

The ghost of Emperor Nero, buried in the Domitia family crypt on the Pincio, is said to have terrorized this neighbourhood in the form of demon crows that lived in a cursed tree. Pope Paschal II reassured the locals in 1099 by replacing the tree with a chapel paid for by the people (il popolo). It was enlarged in 1227 and rebuilt in Lombard style in 1472–7. Andrea Bregno may have added the Renaissance façade, and Bernini a Baroque touch to the interior.

Church Floorplan

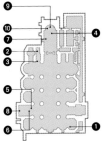

8 Sebastiano del Piombo's Nativity of the Virgin

This altarpiece in the Chigi Chapel (1530–34) is in contrast to the dome's Neo-pagan themes, the Eternal Father blessing Chigi's horoscope of planets symbolized by pagan gods.

NEED TO KNOW

MAP D2 ■ Piazza del Popolo 12 ■ 06 361 0836

Open 7:30am–12:30pm, 4–7pm Mon–Thu; 7:30am–7pm Fri–Sat; 7:30am–12:30pm, 4:30–7pm Sun

■ Canova and Rosati cafés are both on Piazza del Popolo.

■ Some of the church's treasures are behind the high altar in the choir and apse. When Mass is not in session, go behind the curtain to the left of the altar and switch on the lights to see them.

9 Bramante's Apse

The Renaissance architect's first work in Rome, commissioned by Julius II around 1500, was this beautiful light-filled choir and scallop shell-shaped apse.

10 Delphic Sibyl

Pinturicchio, one of the most fashionable artists of the early 16th century, decorated the apse with antique grotesqueries including Sibyls and an intricate tracery of freakish and fantastic beasts.

TOP 10 ⭐ Villa Giulia

Villa Giulia was built in the mid-16th century by Vignola as a pleasure palace for Pope Julius III, who used to float up the Tiber on a flower-decked barge to the building site to keep an eye on progress. It is now a museum devoted to the Etruscans, whose upper classes at least shared Julius's love of luxury. Occupying the area bounded by the Arno and Tiber, they dominated Rome until ousted by an uprising in 509 BC.

1 Frescoed Tomb from Tarquinia

A reconstruction of a tomb at the Etruscan necropolis at Tarquinia, this is frescoed with scenes from a banquet, with dancers, acrobats and athletes providing entertainment **(above)**.

3 Lion Sarcophagus

This marvellous 6th-century BC terra-cotta sarcophagus **(below)**, with four roaring lions on its lid, was so huge that it had to be cut in two in order to fit in the kiln for firing.

5 Euphronios Krater

This exquisite red-figured Greek *krater* – used for mixing wine and water – holds 45 litres and depicts a scene from the Trojan War, in which the Olympian deity Hermes directs Hypnos, the god of sleep, and Thanatos, the god of death, to carry away the body of a slain warrior. It was sold to New York's Metropolitan Museum of Art after being looted from a tomb in the 1920s, and was returned to Italy in 2008 **(right)**.

2 Hydria

This vase, used for carrying water, was imported from Greece by the Etruscans and shows a lion and panther attacking a mule **(below)**.

4 Ficoroni Cista

A cylindrical bronze coffer in which women stored mirrors, cosmetics and beauty accessories, incised with intricately detailed scenes from the myth of Jason and the Argonauts.

6 Ex Votives

As with similar practices in contemporary Catholicism, models of body parts, including faces, feet, uteri and various other internal organs were offered to Etruscan gods by sick people and their families, in the hope that they would be cured.

7 Sarcophagus of the Spouses

When it was discovered in 1881, this splendid 6th-century BC sarcophagus **(right)** was in 400 pieces. Painstakingly reconstructed, the intimate portrait of a married couple reclining on the lid, smiling as if sharing a joke, is perhaps the most evocative and human work of Etruscan art in existence.

8 Etruscan Temple

In the gardens is a 19th-century reconstruction of the Temple of Alatri.

9 Chigi Vase

Imported from Corinth, Greece, this vase **(right)** is painted with hunting and battle scenes, including a fascinating frieze showing hoplites (foot soldiers) in formation with decorated shields.

10 Faliscan Krater of the Dawn

The Faliscans, who lived in southern Lazio, were an indigenous Italic tribe with their own language and culture. This elaborate 4th-century BC vase is decorated with scenes showing a personification of Dawn rising in a chariot.

NEED TO KNOW

MAP D1 ▪ Piazzale di Villa Giulia 9 ▪ 06 320 1706 ▪ www.villagiulia.beniculturali.it

Open 9am–8pm Tue–Sun

Adm €8; free for under-18s and over-65s; free for all first Sun of the month

▪ Villa Giulia's vast collection continues in the Villa Poniatowski (*Piazzale di Villa Giulia*), which also hosts temporary exhibitions. Check the website for more information.

▪ The Villa Giulia Café has tables on a terrace shaded by orange trees, and serves coffee, cold drinks, pastries and sandwiches.

▪ There are excellent audio guides available in English and Italian.

Museum Guide

This is a lovely museum with a lot to see and pleasant gardens to stroll around when you need to take a break. There are two main floors, plus a small basement section – an atmospheric home for the reconstructed tombs from Etruscan necropolises at Tarquinia and Cerveteri. The ground floor is organized geographically, with sections devoted to the main Etruscan archaeological sites, including Cerveteri, Vulci and Veio. The first floor has a room devoted to important objects that have been returned after being illegally excavated and sold, as well as private collections that have been donated to the museum. There is also an interesting and well-explained epigraphic section.

🔟 ⭐ Ostia Antica

Some 2,000 years ago, this lively international port city was at the seashore (*ostium* means "river mouth"), but over the millennia the sea retreated and the river changed course. Ostia was founded in the 4th century BC as a simple fort, but as Rome grew, the town became important as an import hub. Its heyday ended in the 4th century AD, and it died completely as an inhabited area about 1,000 years ago.

3 Museum
Beautifully organized, the displays include precious sculptures, sarcophagi and mosaics found among the ruins. A highlight is a statue **(left)** of the god Mithras about to sacrifice the Cosmic Bull.

4 Forum
The rectangular heart of officialdom was originally encircled by columns. In the centre was a shrine to the Imperial Lares (household gods).

1 Decumanus Maximus
You enter this vast archaeological park by way of the ancient Via Ostiensis. The white marble goddess on the left marks the start of the city's main street, lined with buildings: the Decumanus Maximus.

5 Mithraeum of the Serpents
One of 18 Ostian temples to Mithras. The cult was popular with Roman soldiers, and flourished especially well in port towns. The snake frescoes invoked the earth's fertility; the platforms were for lying on during mystic banquets.

6 Theatre
The original theatre was twice as tall as it now stands **(above)**. Behind the stage was a temple, of either Ceres (goddess of grain) or Dionysus (god of theatre).

7 Piazzale delle Corporazione
This large piazza is surrounded by the ruins of what were once the offices of various maritime businesses, each with a black and white mosaic advertising its trade – chandlers, ropemakers, importers of grain, ivory, wild animals. One has a charming elephant mosaic.

2 Casa di Diana and Thermopolium

You can climb up to the top of this *insula* (apartment block) for a great view across the site. Across the street is the Thermopolium, a tavern with a delightful wall painting of menu items **(above)**.

8 Terme di Nettuno

Built in the 2nd century, this bath complex (left) was enhanced with fine mosaics of sea gods and sea monsters, which you can view from a small terrace. You can also go down to the left to study close-up the ingenious heating system of the baths.

9 Terme dei Sette Sapienti

This elaborate bath complex contains a painting of Venus; floor mosaics of hunters, animals, nude athletes and marine scenes; and humorous texts in Latin.

10 House of Cupid and Psyche

The wealthy had villas like this refined example of a 3rd-century AD *domus* (right). You can still admire the Doric columns, the fountain (*nymphaeum*) and the inlaid marble decorations.

NEED TO KNOW

MAP B6 ■ Viale dei Romagnoli 717 ■ 06 5635 8099

Metro B, trams 3 and 30, or buses 23, 75, 95, 280 to Piramide, then local train from Porta San Paolo Station (next to the metro station) to Ostia Antica

Open Nov–Feb: 8:30am–3:30pm Tue–Sun; Mar–Aug: 8:30am–4:30pm Tue–Sun; Sep–Oct: 8:30am–5:30pm Tue–Sun (last admission one hour before closing); closed 1 Jan, 1 May, 25 Dec

Adm €10 (€5 EU citizens 18–25); under-18s free; free first Sun of the month

The port area (Trajan's Port) can be visited on request, 06 6501 0089

■ There's a snack bar behind the museum.

■ The ruined walls look confusingly similar – rent an audio guide where you buy your entrance ticket.

Park Guide
The trip by local train is easy, short and costs the same as one regular bus ticket. From the Ostia Antica train station, walk straight out to the foot-bridge that goes over the motorway. Continue past the restaurant until you get to the ticket booth. The park is extensive and a decent visit will take at least 3 hours. Wear sturdy shoes, and bring sunscreen and water on hot days.

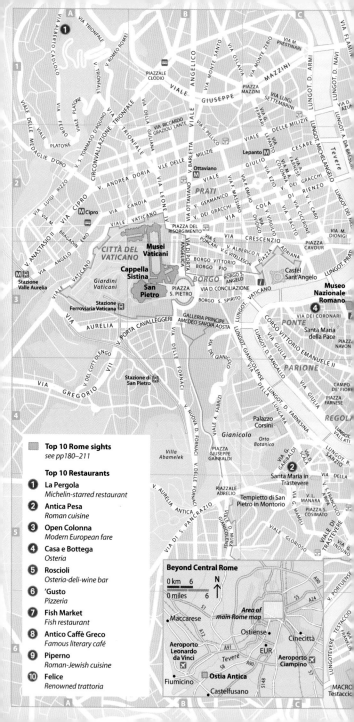

Top 10 Rome sights
see pp180–211

Top 10 Restaurants

1. **La Pergola**
   Michelin-starred restaurant
2. **Antica Pesa**
   Roman cuisine
3. **Open Colonna**
   Modern European fare
4. **Casa e Bottega**
   Osteria
5. **Roscioli**
   Osteria-deli-wine bar
6. **'Gusto**
   Pizzeria
7. **Fish Market**
   Fish restaurant
8. **Antico Caffè Greco**
   Famous literary café
9. **Piperno**
   Roman-Jewish cuisine
10. **Felice**
    Renowned trattoria

Beyond Central Rome

0 km   6
0 miles   6

N

Area of main Rome map

Maccarese
Ostiense
Cinecittà
Aeroporto Leonardo da Vinci
EUR
Aeroporto Ciampino
Fiumicino
Ostia Antica
Castelfusano
MACRO Testaccio

Top 10 Venice Highlights

Basilica di Santa Maria della Salute
viewed from Ponte dell'Accademia

Exploring Venice

Venice is a sightseeing paradise for people of all ages. To make the most of a holiday and see the best the city has to offer, here are some time-efficient ideas for both two- and four-day stays.

The Grand Canal cuts a meandering path through Venice and offers a delightful perspective from the water.

Two Days in Venice

Day ❶
MORNING
Start off at the **Basilica di San Marco** *(see pp220–23)* before wandering around the **Piazza San Marco** *(see pp228–31)*. The Campanile tower gives a superb view over the city.
AFTERNOON
A visit to the **Doge's Palace** *(see pp224–7)* can be followed by a laid-back ride on a *vaporetto* all the way up the glorious **Grand Canal** *(see pp232–5)*, past many elegant *palazzi* and under the Accademia and Rialto bridges.

Day ❷
MORNING
Begin with Venetian art at the **Accademia Galleries** *(see pp236–7)* before strolling through to **Campo Santa Margherita** *(see pp244–5)* for a bite to eat.
AFTERNOON
It's a short walk to the Venetian Gothic masterpiece **Santa Maria Gloriosa dei Frari** *(see pp238–9)* and, from there, on to the lovely Campo San Polo square with its great neighbourhood feel.

Four Days in Venice

Day ❶
MORNING
The natural place to start any visit is the magnificent main square, **Piazza San Marco** *(see pp228–31)*. Visit the panoramic Campanile or the Torre dell'Orologio (booking essential), then have a coffee at the legendary – but expensive – Caffè Florian. Refreshed, head into the **Basilica di San Marco** *(see pp220–23)* to wonder at the ancient mosaics.
AFTERNOON
After lunch, take time to explore the **Doge's Palace** *(see pp224–7)*, once the powerhouse of the Maritime Republic. Don't miss the Bridge of Sighs and the dank prisons.

The impressive Doge's Palace dominates the waterfront leading to Piazza San Marco

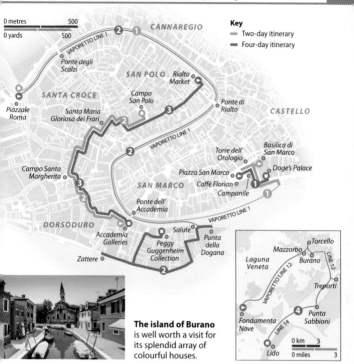

The island of Burano is well worth a visit for its splendid array of colourful houses.

Day ❷
MORNING
Catch a *vaporetto* at Piazzale Roma or the railway station for the spectacular trip along the **Grand Canal** *(see pp232–5)*, passing beneath Rialto Bridge. Alight at Salute to visit the Punta della Dogana *(Campo della Salute)*.
AFTERNOON
After lunch on the sun-blessed Zattere, backtrack to see the impressive **Peggy Guggenheim Collection** *(see pp246–7)*.

Day ❸
MORNING
Make an early start to enjoy the best of **The Rialto**, a fish and produce market, which is open mostly in the morning *(see pp240–41)*. It's then just a short walk to the church of **Santa Maria Gloriosa dei Frari** *(see pp238–9)*, a masterpiece of Venetian Gothic architecture.

AFTERNOON
Campo Santa Margherita *(see pp244–5)* is a bustling square with inviting cafés and restaurants ideal for lunch. After you have eaten, proceed to the **Accademia Galleries** *(see pp236–7)* for an overview of Venetian painting through the centuries.

Day ❹
MORNING
Take a leisurely ferry trip over the Northern Lagoon to the island of **Torcello** *(see pp242–3)*, where you can admire the Byzantine mosaics in the Basilica. Then continue to neighbouring Burano or Mazzorbo for lunch.
AFTERNOON
Pick up a ferry to take you cruising via Treporti and Punta Sabbioni to the Lido for a trip to the beach. Afterwards, head back to Venice proper.

TOP 10 Venice Highlights

The uniquely romantic city of Venice was built entirely on water and has managed to survive into the 21st century without cars. Narrow alleyways and canals pass between sumptuous palaces and magnificent churches, colourful neighbourhood markets and quiet backwaters, unchanged for centuries. Few cities possess such an awe-inspiring line-up of sights for visitors.

Basilica di San Marco ①

Venice's fairy-tale cathedral is distinctly Byzantine, and its façade and interior have been embellished with resplendent mosaics and works of art through the ages *(see pp220–3)*.

Doge's Palace ②

This was the powerhouse of the city's rulers for nearly 900 years. Passing through the maze of gilded rooms gives visitors a fascinating insight into the extravagant lifestyle that so often accompanied state affairs *(see pp224–7)*.

Piazza San Marco ③

Elegance and opulence sit side by side in what Napoleon named "the finest drawing room in Europe". This magnificent square is adorned with monuments that bear testimony to Venice's history *(see pp228–231)*.

Grand Canal ④

The city's majestic water-course swarms with all manner of boats, while its embankments boast a dazzling succession of palaces dating back as early as the 13th century *(see pp232–5)*.

Accademia Galleries
This unsurpassed collection of Venetian paintings includes masterpieces by Titian, Bellini and Giorgione. It is a must, not only for art lovers *(see pp236–7)*.

Santa Maria Gloriosa dei Frari
A Gothic interior with grandiose works of art lies in store behind this church's brick façade *(see pp238–9)*.

The Rialto
A fresh produce market has enlivened this quayside since medieval times and is arguably still the best market in the world *(see pp240–41)*.

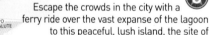

Map showing Venice with campos including CAMPO SAN STAE, CAMPO DEI SANTI APOSTOLI, CAMPO SAN CASSIANO, CAMPO S. GIACOMO DI RIALTO, SAN POLO, CAMPO SAN POLO, Ponte di Rialto, RIVA DEL VIN, Canal Grande, CASTELLO, CALLE DEI FABBRI, CAMPO SAN LUCA, CAMPO MANIN, SAN MARCO, CAMPO S. ANGELO, CAMPO S. FANTIN, FREZZERIA, CAMPO S. MAURIZIO, C. LARGA XXII MARZO, CPO SAN MOISE, CAMPO SAN SAMUELE, CAMPO S. STEFANO, Ponte dell' Accademia, Canal Grande, CAMPO DELLA SALUTE

0 metres 300
0 yards 300

Torcello
Escape the crowds in the city with a ferry ride over the vast expanse of the lagoon to this peaceful, lush island, the site of Venice's original settlement *(see pp242–3)*.

Campo Santa Margherita
Thanks to its market stalls and outdoor cafés, this lovely square is always bustling with life. An added bonus are the many architectural styles *(see pp244–5)*.

Peggy Guggenheim Collection
Italy's leading museum for 20th-century European and American art is housed in a palace on the Grand Canal *(see pp246–7)*.

▣10 ⭐ Basilica di San Marco

The breathtaking Byzantine basilica dominating Piazza San Marco *(see pp228–31)* was constructed in such ornate fashion for two reasons: as an embodiment of the Venetian Republic's power and as a fitting resting place for St Mark. Serving as the doges' chapel, it was the site of coronations, funerals and processions, all gloriously framed by more than 4,000 sq m (43,000 sq ft) of mosaics, eastern treasures and 500 columns, some dating back to the 3rd century.

Western Façade ①

A marvellous succession of domes, columns, arches and spires, **(right)** interspersed with marble statues, screens and glittering mosaics, greets tourists in Piazza San Marco. The northernmost arch houses 13th-century mosaics that depict the basilica itself. Other mosaics are 17th- and 18th-century copies.

② Atrium Mosaics

These glorious mosaics **(left)** of precious gold-leaf over glass tiles were created in the Byzantine tradition by expert craftsmen, and give detailed accounts of the Old Testament. The 13th-century cupola's concentric circles recount 24 episodes from Genesis, including the Creation and Adam and Eve.

③ Flooring

The elaborate paving is a mosaic masterpiece of multicoloured stones on uneven levels, evocative of the sea. Intricate geometrical designs sit alongside animal shapes.

Basilica Floorplan

Pala d'Oro ④

The dazzling jewel-encrusted gold screen **(right)** was commissioned in Constantinople in 976 but frequently added to at later dates. It has 250 panels bearing 1,927 authentic gems and cloisonné plaques.

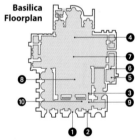

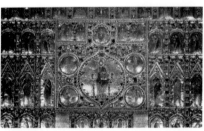

BUILDING THE BASILICA

Construction first began in 829, but it was burned down in 976, in a revolt. The building dates from 1071 and has a Greek cross lay-out capped by five domes. The architect is shown over the central portal, biting his fingers in frustration. The basilica became the city cathedral in 1807.

Ascension Dome (7)

The central dome has a spectacular array of early 13th-century mosaics, depicting the New Testament. *Christ in Glory* is shown above depictions of the Virtues **(right)**.

(8) Pentecost Dome

What is probably the first dome of the basilica to be adorned with mosaics depicts the Descent of the Holy Ghost, seen as a flame over the heads of the 12 Apostles.

(9) Basilica Museum

Here you'll find the famed quartet of horses crafted from bronze and covered in gold. Booty from the Fourth Crusade, these restored Graeco-Roman equine figures originally graced the Hippodrome in Constantinople.

Loggia dei Cavalli (10)

Replicas of the horses **(right)**, now in the museum, stand on this balcony overlooking Piazza San Marco. Visitors can also see clutches of columns, whose dimensions and decorative styles indicate their origins.

The Tetrarchs (5)

The inspiration for these red porphyry rock figures is unknown. They probably represent the four emperors of the eastern and western Roman empires **(right)**. The statue was pillaged from Constantinople during the Fourth Crusade in 1204.

(6) Treasury

The basilica's glittering riches include precious chalices of rock crystal enamelled by medieval silver- and goldsmiths and reliquaries from Venice's eastern conquests, including parts of the True Cross.

NEED TO KNOW

MAP E5 ▪ Piazza San Marco ▪ 041 270 83 11 ▪ www.basilicasanmarco.it

Guided visits: book on www.alata.it

Basilica: Open mid-Apr–Oct: 9:30am–5pm Mon–Sat, 2–5pm Sun & pub hols; Nov–mid-Apr: 9:30am–5pm Mon–Sat, 2–4:30pm Sun & pub hols

Pala d'Oro, treasury and Loggia dei Cavalli: Open mid-Apr–Oct: 9:35am–5pm; Nov–mid-Apr: 9:45am–4:45pm Mon–Sat, 2–4:30pm Sun & pub hols; adm Pala d'Oro €2; treasury €3

Museum: Open mid-Apr–Oct: 9:35am–4:45pm daily; adm €5

▪ Pre-book tickets online to beat the queues.

▪ Visit at dusk, when the setting sun lights up the façade.

▪ Take binoculars to examine the mosaics, but you must leave backpacks in the luggage room.

Basilica Architectural Features

1 Galleries
The airy catwalks over the body of the basilica reflect the eastern tradition of segregation in worship, as they were exclusively for women. They are closed to visitors.

2 Stone Wall-Slabs
Brick-faced until the 1100s, the walls of the basilica were then covered with stone slabs from the East, sliced lengthways to produce a kaleidoscopic effect.

3 Romanesque Stone Carvings
The exquisite semicircular stone carvings over the central doorway were executed between 1235 and 1265 and still bear traces of their original colouring.

4 The "Victory Bringer"
This revered Byzantine icon is given pride of place in the Madonna of Nicopeia Chapel. Rumoured to have been executed by St Luke, it was carried into battle for its miraculous powers.

5 Baptistry
Aglow with 14th-century mosaic scenes of the life of St John, this is also home to the tomb of Italian architect Jacopo Sansovino. Open for prayer only.

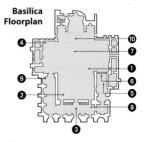

Basilica Floorplan

6 Zen Chapel
The ornate decoration in this chapel was executed for the funeral of its namesake, Cardinal Zen, in 1521, in recognition of his gifts to the state. Open for prayer only.

The ornate Iconostasis

7 Iconostasis
This elaborate screen separates the worship area of the chancel from the nave. Atop its eight columns are Gothic-style statues of the Virgin and the Apostles, sculpted by the Dalle Masegne brothers in 1394.

8 Byzantine Pierced Screens
Influenced by eastern architecture, delicate geometrical designs and lattice-work stone screens are featured on all three façades, in the atrium and loggia.

9 Porta dei Fiori
This doorway on the northern façade bears a 13th-century nativity scene surrounded by Moorish arches.

10 Altar Columns
Four finely carved alabaster and marble columns support a canopy at the altar, beneath which lies the body of St Mark.

Font in the Baptistry

ST MARK, PATRON SAINT OF VENICE

Although the well-loved saint of Byzantium, St Theodore, had been appointed protector of Venice by the Byzantine emperor, the fledgling republic felt in need of a saint of its own. According to legend, in AD 828, two adroit Venetian merchants filched the body of St Mark from a monastery in Alexandria, transporting it under layers of pork fat to conceal it from Muslim guards. The welcome in Venice was triumphant, and the story was recounted in countless paintings and mosaics. The remains, however, were mislaid for years, until an arm miraculously broke through a column in 1094 (marked by a small cross, left of the Altar of the Sacrament) in answer to a prayer. St Mark now rests in peace beneath the basilica's main altar. The ubiquitous winged lion representing St Mark could be found throughout the republic as the trademark of Venetian dominion: it is

often shown with two paws in the sea and two on land, to symbolize the geography of Venice.

TOP 10
VENICE RELICS

1 Milk of the Virgin Mary, Basilica Treasury (*see p221*)

2 Blood of Christ, Basilica Treasury

3 Nail from the True Cross, Chiesa di San Pantalon

4 Thorn from Christ's crown, Basilica Treasury

5 Body of St Mark, Basilica San Marco (*see pp220–221*)

6 Body of St Lucy, Chiesa di San Geremia

7 Three rocks used to stone St Stephen to death, Basilica Treasury

8 Skull of St John the Baptist, Basilica Treasury

9 Leg of St George, Basilica Treasury

10 Foot of St Catherine of Siena, Santi Giovanni e Paolo

The Miracle of the Relic of the True Cross on the Rialto Bridge (1494) by Vittore Carpaccio

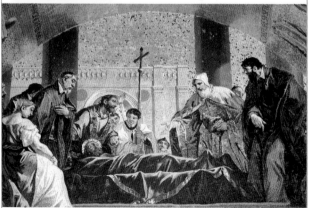

This mosaic in Basilica San Marco depicts the veneration of the body of St Mark by the Doge.

🔟 ⭐ Doge's Palace

A magnificent combination of Byzantine, Gothic and Renaissance architecture, the Palazzo Ducale (Doge's Palace) was the official residence of the 120 doges who ruled Venice from 697 to 1797. A fortress-like structure stood here in the 9th century, to be replaced by the elegant Gothic version seen today, despite a string of fires in the 1500s. Artists such as Titian, Tintoretto and Bellini vied with each other to embellish the palace with painting and sculpture, not to mention architects Antonio Rizzo and Pietro Lombardo, the latter responsible for the western façade.

1 Façade
Elegant twin façades face the piazzetta and the quayside. Pink-and-cream stonework and a loggia stand above an arcade of columns with 36 sculpted Istrian stone capitals **(above)**.

2 Sala del Senato
Senate members met in this lavish hall **(below)** to debate war, foreign affairs and trade with the doge. Time was measured by two clocks – one with a 24-hour face, the other with zodiac signs.

3 Armoury
This is a gripping, if spine-chilling, collection of beautifully crafted firearms, ceremonial weapons and suits of armour **(left)** from Asia and the West. Among the war trophies is a Turkish standard brought back from the Battle of Lepanto (1571).

4 Prisons
A fascinating maze of cells is linked by corridors and staircases on both sides of the canal. One of the most famous inmates, Casanova, made a dramatic escape across the roof in 1756. The "new prisons" were in use until the 1940s and feature poignant graffiti by internees.

PALACE GUIDE

Rooms are labelled with explanatory panels in English and Italian and are spread over three floors and several wings. Follow the red arrows. Highly recommended is the Secret Itineraries Tour through chambers which were once used for administrative purposes and torture.

Scala d'Oro ⑦

The magnificent Golden Staircase (right), so-called for its Classical stucco decorations in 24-carat gold-leaf framing frescoes, led guests of honour to the second floor. Designed by Sansovino, it was later completed by Scarpagnino in 1559.

⑤ Bridge of Sighs

One of the world's most famous bridges (above), the Ponte dei Sospiri is an early 17th-century Baroque structure that crosses to the palace prisons. It reputedly caused the condemned to "sigh" at their last glimpse of sky and sea.

⑥ Sala dello Scudo

Enormous globes (below) and painted wall maps showing the known world in 1762 make this room a must. The map of Eastern Asia traces Marco Polo's travels to China, complete with camels, rhinos and the mythical Uncharted Lands of the People Eaters.

⑧ Porta della Carta

The palace's main entrance (now the visitors' exit) has a beautifully sculpted 1438 portal by the Bon family. The name "paper door" arose because edicts were posted here.

⑨ Sala del Maggior Consiglio

The Great Council Chamber (left) is lined with canvases of Venetian victories and a cornice frieze of 76 doges – a black curtain represents traitor Marin Falier (see p227).

⑩ Doge's Apartments

The communicating rooms of the doge's living quarters include rich brocades, triumphal friezes, gilded ceilings and works of art.

NEED TO KNOW

MAP E5

■ Piazza San Marco
■ 041 240 52 11 ■ www.visitmuve.it

Open Apr–Oct: 8:30am–7pm daily (to 11pm Fri & Sat); Nov–Mar: 8:30am– 5:30pm daily (last admission 60 min before closing time); closed 1 Jan, 25 Dec

Adm €20 (includes entry to the Museo Correr Complex)

Secret Itineraries Tour: 848 08 20 00 (advance booking essential at palace, by phone or online); 9:55am, 10:45am & 11:35am daily in English; tickets: €20 (€14 concessions)

■ A quiet, modern café in the former stables on the ground floor serves snacks and drinks.

■ The Museo dell' Opera, near the ticket office, houses many of the original 14th-century façade capitals – those outside are mostly 19th-century copies.

Doge's Palace Art and Architecture

Veronese's *Rape of Europa*

1 Rape of Europa
Paolo Veronese's (1528–88) allegorical work (1580) in the AntiCollegio shows Europa sitting on a bull, alias Jove, who is nuzzling her foot.

2 Paradise
Possibly the world's largest oil painting (1588–90), *Paradise* by Jacopo (1518–94) and Domenico Tintoretto (1560–1635) is said to contain 800 figures (Sala del Maggior Consiglio).

3 Arcade Capital
Proclaimed the "most beautiful in Europe" by art critic John Ruskin, this eight-sided carved capital on the southwest corner shows the zodiac signs and planets.

4 The Triumph of Venice
Dominating the Sala del Senato is Jacopo Tintoretto's glorious work of propaganda (1580–84), showing allegorical and mythological figures proffering fruits of the sea to Venice.

5 Central Balcony
This magnificent early 15th-century stone terrace, embellished with columns, spires and a host of saints, opens off the Sala del Maggior Consiglio with a breathtaking view of the lagoon.

6 Arco Foscari
This triumphal archway of pink-and-cream stone layers leading to the Giants' Staircase was commissioned by Doge Foscari in 1438.

7 Wellheads
Elaborate 16th-century wellheads were constructed to drain water from the gutters to the palace's central courtyard.

8 Drunkenness of Noah
A powerful sculpture from the early 15th century adorns the façade's southeast corner. Noah, inebriated and half-naked before his sons, is intended to portray the weakness of man.

Drunkenness of Noah

9 Coronation of the Virgin
The faded but inspired remains of Guariento's fresco, discovered beneath Jacopo Tintoretto's *Paradise*, are housed in a side room, with panels explaining the restoration techniques.

10 Giants' Staircase
So named for its two colossal statues of Mars and Neptune, which were sculpted by Sansovino in 1567 as symbols of Venice's power. Visiting dignitaries would ascend the marble-lined stairs to the palace.

Giants' Staircase

THE EXTENT OF THE VENETIAN REPUBLIC

Doge Gradenigo with the Venetian fleet at the siege of Chioggia, 1379

In its earliest days, Venice was little more than a huddle of islands in the middle of a shallow marshy lagoon, settled by a band of refugees from the Veneto region. Yet over the centuries it developed into a mighty republic reaching south to the Mediterranean and north to the Alps, based on the concept of trade. Salt was stored in massive warehouses, there were dealings in exotic spices and wondrous fabrics from the East, crusades were organized and fitted out here, and relics procured. Its main population probably never exceeded 160,000; however, well beyond its walled port towns, which stretched down the Dalmatian coast, were far-flung outposts such as Crete and Cyprus. These dominions protected key passages in commerce with the Arabic countries. Westward across the Po plain, Venice's influence took in Treviso, Vicenza and Verona, extending all the way to Bergamo on the outskirts of Milan and the mighty Visconti dynasty.

The Republic's gaining of maritime power is celebrated in *The Victorious Return of Doge Andrea Contarini after Triumph in Chioggia* by Paolo Veronese (1525–88).

TOP 10 EVENTS IN THE VENETIAN REPUBLIC

1 Venice founded on 25 April (St Mark's Day, AD 421)

2 First doge, Paoluccio Anafesto, elected (697)

3 St Mark's body brought to Venice (828)

4 Ruthless siege of Constantinople during the Fourth Crusade under Doge Enrico Dandolo (1204)

5 Venice loses 60 per cent of its population to the Black Death (1348)

6 Doge Marin Falier decapitated for conspiracy (1355)

7 Genoese defeated at Battle of Chioggia, leaving Venice to reign over the Adriatic and Mediterranean (1381)

8 Victory over Turks at Battle of Lepanto (1571)

9 After 25 years of war, Crete is lost to the Turks (1669)

10 Napoleon invades the Veneto, bringing about the fall of the Venetian Republic (1797)

TOP 10 ★ Piazza San Marco

Long the political and religious heart of Venice, it's hard to believe Piazza San Marco was once just a monastery garden crossed by a stream. The glittering basilica and Doge's Palace command the east side of the square, while other stately buildings along its borders have been the backdrop for magnificent processions. The western end was remodelled by Napoleon, who wished to construct a royal palace here. Today the piazza continues to bustle, with a museum complex *(see p230)*, cafés and costumed Carnival crowds.

1 **Basilica di San Marco**
See pp220–23.

2 **Doge's Palace**
See pp224–7.

3 **Torre dell'Orologio**

A marvel to behold, the imposing and impressive Renaissance-style clock tower is topped by two bronze Moors **(left)** hammering out the hours on the upper terrace. At Epiphany and Ascension there is an hourly procession of clockwork Magi that are led by an angel. According to legend, the craftsmen were subsequently blinded to prevent them repeating the work.

The Piazzetta and the Palace

NEED TO KNOW
MAP E5

Campanile: Open 1–15 Apr: 9am–5:30pm; mid-Apr–Oct: 8:30am–9pm; Nov–Mar: 9:30am–5:30pm; book guided tours on www.venetoinside.com; Adm €8

Torre dell'Orologio: 041 427 308 92 (from abroad); 848 082 000 (from Italy); Guided tours: 10am & 11am Mon–Wed, 2pm & 3pm Thu–Sun. Adm €12

Museo Correr Complex: Open 10am–7pm; Nov–Mar: 10am–5pm (last admission 1 hour before closing). Adm €20 (includes Doge's Palace)

■ The best time to appreciate the beauty of the square is early morning, when only the city sweepers are here.

Campanile **4**
Incomparable views of the city and lagoon can be had by taking the lift to the top of this 98-m (323-ft) bell tower **(right)**. It was masterfully rebuilt to its 16th-century design following its clamorous collapse in 1902.

5 **Piazzetta**
Once an inlet for boats and witness to the arrival of distinguished visitors during the Republic's heyday, this now fully paved mini square fronts the lagoon.

6 Column of San Marco

This is one of two granite columns erected in 1172 by Nicolò Barattieri **(left)**; the other symbolizes San Teodoro. Public executions were held here.

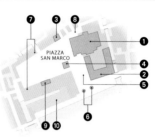

Plan of Piazza San Marco

VENICE'S BELLS

Booming through the city, the five bells in the Campanile have been employed to mark Venice's rhythms for centuries. The Maleficio bell was sounded to announce an execution, the Nona rang at midday, the Trottiera spurred on the nobles' horses for assemblies in the Doge's Palace and the Mezza Terza was used to indicate that the Senate was in session. The Marangona bell is still sounded to mark midnight.

7 Procuratie Vecchie and Nuove

The Procurators, who were responsible for state administration, lived in these elegant 15th-century buildings **(below)**.

8 Piazzetta dei Leoncini

This is the site of a former vegetable market, where a pair of small lions *(leoncini)* carved from red Verona stone **(right)** have been crouching since 1722.

9 Caffè Florian

Reputedly Europe's first coffee house, the premises still retain their original 1720 wood-panelling, marble-topped tables and gilt-framed mirrors.

10 Giardinetti Reali

These shady public gardens, created during the Napoleonic era, took the place of boatyards and grain stores, situated just behind the panoramic waterfront.

Museo Correr Complex

1 Biblioteca Marciana Ceiling

In 1545, the ceiling vault of the reading room *(sale monumentali)*, inside the Libreria Sansoviniana, collapsed and its architect Sansovino was imprisoned – he was released to complete the job at his own expense. Titian selected artists for the decorations; Veronese was awarded a gold chain for the best work.

2 Libreria Sansoviniana Staircase

Bedecked with gilt and stucco decorations by Alessandro Vittoria, the 16th-century staircase leads from a monumental entrance on the piazza to the halls of the old library.

3 Veneziano Paintings

This prolific Byzantine artist is featured in the Pinacoteca's Room 25 (part of Museo Correr), with glowing two-dimensional religious portraits (1290–1302).

Correr Ballroom

4 Correr Ballroom

This showy Neo-Classical creation was built for Napoleon. It is now used for exhibitions.

5 Two Venetian Ladies

Vittore Carpaccio's (c.1460–1525) masterpiece of well-dressed ladies (1500–10) is in Room 38 of the Museo Correr. It was first thought to depict courtesans because of the ladies' décollété dresses, but the women are, in fact, awaiting their menfolk's return from hunting.

6 Canova Statues

In the Museo Correr, works by Antonio Canova (1767–1822), foremost sculptor of his time, include his acclaimed statues of Orpheus and Eurydice.

Canova's statue of Orpheus

7 Map of Venice

Pride of place in Room 32 of the Museo Correr goes to Jacopo de' Barbari's (1440–1516) prospective map-layout of Venice (1497–1500), which was painstakingly engraved on six pear-wood panels.

8 Bellini Room

Works by the talented Bellini family are on display in Room 36 of the Pinacoteca: the poignant *Dead Christ Supported by Two Angels* (1453–5) by the best known, Giovanni; head of the family Jacopo's *Crucifixion* (1450); and son Gentile's portrait of *Doge Giovanni Mocenigo* (1475).

9 Narwhal Tusk

Once prized as the horn of the fabled unicorn, this 1.6-m- (5-ft-) long tusk from the rare whale has been superbly carved with Jesse's and Jesus's family tree (Room 40 in Museo Correr).

10 Crafts and Guilds

Wooden sandals 60-cm (24-inches) high, inlaid with mother-of-pearl, illustrate the stiff demands put upon followers of 15th–17th-century fashion (Room 48).

ACQUA ALTA FLOODING

Acqua Alta ("high water") has long been disruptive to the city between October and March. As warning sirens fill the air, people drag out their waterproof boots, shopkeepers rush to put up protective barriers and street-sweepers lay out duck-boards in low-lying spots. Venice and its lagoon are subject to the tides of the Adriatic Sea, but flood levels are caused by the coincidence of low atmospheric pressure, strong sirocco winds from the south and natural high tides due to moon phases. Piazza San Marco is among the most vulnerable spots. The flood gates designed for the Lido sea entrances are held by many experts to be both useless and harmful to the lagoon. However, there are plans for an elaborate drainage system on the piazza, dredging canals and raising paving levels.

Bullfight in St Mark's Square by Canaletto and Giovanni Battista Cimaroli

Piazza San Marco is located in a vulnerable position on the edge of the lagoon and has been flooded by high tides throughout its history.

TOP 10
HISTORIC EVENTS IN PIAZZA SAN MARCO

1 Foundations of Doge's Palace laid (AD 814)

2 Construction of basilica started (828)

3 First bullfight held (1162)

4 Square paved with brick, herringbone-style (1267)

5 Square paved with volcanic trachyte blocks (1722–35)

6 Napoleon demolishes San Geminiano church to make way for Ala Napoleonica (1810)

7 Campanile crumbles to the ground (1902)

8 Record flood 1.94 m (6.4 ft) above sea level (4 November 1966)

9 Pink Floyd rock concert attracts 100,000 (1989)

10 Campanile stormed by Venetian separatists (1997)

TOP 10 ★ Grand Canal

Venice's majestic "highway", the Canal Grande, is only one of the 177 canals flowing through the city, but at some 4 km (2.5 miles) in length, 30–70 m (98–230 ft) in width and averaging 4.5 m (15 ft) in depth, it certainly earns its name. Snaking its way through the city with a double curve, its banks are lined with exquisite palaces, while on its waters colourful flotillas of gondolas, ferries, taxi launches, high-speed police boats and barges groaning under loads of fresh produce provide endless fascination. In 1818, when the water was cleaner, Lord Byron swam all the way down the Grand Canal from the Lido.

1 Fondaco dei Turchi
With an exotic air and its round arches, this Veneto-Byzantine building (1225) **(above)** was the Turkish trade centre for 200 years. It is now the Natural History Museum *(Santa Croce 1730)*.

2 Ca' Pesaro
This colossal Baroque palace *(Santa Croce, 2076)*, decorated with diamond-point ashlar work, was the final creation of architect Longhena. Home to the city's modern art collections, it is beautifully floodlit at night.

The view towards Santa Maria della Salute

3 Rialto Bridge
One of the city's most familiar sights, the striking 28-m- (92-ft-) wide, 8-m- (26-ft-) high Istrian stone Ponte di Rialto **(below)** dates from 1588.

4 Riva del Vin
A sunny quayside with a string of open-air restaurants, this is one of the few accessible banks of the Grand Canal. Barrels of wine *(vino)* used to be off-loaded here, hence the name.

5 Ca' Rezzonico
The finest feature of this imposing palace is its grandiose staircase **(right)**. Today it is a museum of 18th-century Venice.

6 Accademia Bridge

The lovely wooden Ponte dell'Accademia (above), built in 1932 by the engineer Miozzi, was intended as a temporary measure until a more substantial structure was designed, but it is now a permanent fixture. It affords stunning views of the Grand Canal.

7 Ca' Dario

With an ornamental Renaissance façade studded with multicoloured stone medallions, this lopsided palace is supposedly cursed due to a number of misfortunes that have overtaken its various owners.

8 Santa Maria della Salute

Longhena's 17th-century masterpiece of sculpted whorls beneath a towering dome (right), this church commemorates the end of a devastating plague in the city.

WAVE DAMAGE

Damage to buildings caused by wash has worsened of late with the rise in motor-propelled craft. Waves provoked by all boats eat into foundations of buildings on the water's edge, as well as making life harder for the gondoliers. Speed limits aim to curb this: 7 kmph (4.5 mph) for private craft and 11 kmph (7 mph) for waterbuses on the Grand Canal. Narrower canals mean 5 kmph (3 mph), while 20 kmph (12.5 mph) is the lagoon maximum.

NEED TO KNOW

The Grand Canal runs from Piazzale Roma, the bus terminal and car park area, to Piazza San Marco. It is easily navigable courtesy of ferries Nos. 1 (all stops) and 2 (main stops only).

■ Take the *vaporetto* line No. 1 to enjoy the best views of the sights along the canal.

■ To beat the crowds, start out from Piazzale Roma heading towards San Marco in the late afternoon or evening, or take the reverse direction in the morning.

9 Punta della Dogana

The figure of Fortune (right) stands atop the erstwhile customs house, now an arts centre (Campo della Salute), and doubles as a weather vane. The Grand Canal joins St Mark's Basin here.

10 Harry's Bar

The legendary watering hole (Calle Vallaresso 1323) of Ernest Hemingway is where the Bellini *aperitivo* was invented. Opened in 1931, it was named after the American who funded it.

Watercraft of Venice

Typical Venetian gondola

1 Gondola

These are most often seen transporting tourists around the canals. A larger version *(traghetto)* is also used for the cross-canal ferry, while the smaller *gondolino* is a slender racing craft.

2 Vaporetto

Strictly speaking, this is the capacious rounded waterbus, now also seen in an "ecological" electric model. A slimmer *motoscafo* serves the outer runs and narrow canals with relatively low bridges.

3 Sandolo

A slim, lightweight boat perfectly suited to hunting and fishing in the shallow waters of the lagoon, not to mention racing. Painted black, these "imitation gondolas" can deceive tourists on the back canals.

4 Topo

The most common barge for transporting goods around the canals, the *topo* can be seen loaded with everything from washing machines to demijohns, often with a live dog "figurehead" on the prow.

5 Sanpierota

This flat-bottomed rowing boat is named after the inhabitants of San Pietro in Volta in the southern lagoon. Once used for transporting fish to Venice, nowadays it is fitted with an outboard motor and photogenic oblique sail.

6 Bragozzo

With its gently rounded prow and stern, this brightly coloured sailing boat was traditionally used for fishing by the inhabitants of Chioggia.

7 Fire Boat

From their station near Ca' Foscari, the red launches are called both to deal with fires and to rescue submerged obstacles and crumbling façades.

8 Garbage Vessel

The city's hefty waste-collecting AMAV barges trundle over the lagoon with the day's rubbish, in addition to carrying out environmental monitoring.

Ambulance launch

9 Ambulance and Police Launches

These modern craft attract plenty of attention as they roar down the canals – only the emergency categories are allowed to disregard the city's speed limits.

10 Car Ferry

These giants convey all manner of motor vehicles from the Tronchetto to the Lido.

VENICE'S GONDOLAS

The quintessential sleek Venetian gondola has been plying the city's canals since as early as the 11th century, although it did not take on its present graceful form until the late 1400s. Compared to a mere 405 gondolas on the waterways today, as many as 10,000 were in use in the late 19th century: bridges were once few and far between and gondolas acted as ferries between one island and another, a custom that continues to this day across the Grand Canal by the *traghetti*. A handful of gondola yards still construct the boats as well as carry out repairs, such as San Trovaso in Dorsoduro. It's a costly and complex craft – eight different types of wood are needed for a total of 280 pieces to make the asymmetrical craft, 11 m (36 ft) in length and 1.42 m (4.5 ft) in width, at a cost approaching €25,000.

**TOP 10
GONDOLA FEATURES**

1 *Forcola* (rowlock)
2 *Ferro* (prow bracket)
3 *Hippocampus* (side ornament)
4 Night lamp
5 Bronze stern decoration
6 Ribbed oar
7 *Felze* (cabin)
8 Gondolier's foot rest
9 Gondolier's striped shirt
10 Gondolier's straw hat

The iron bracket (ferro) on the prow weighs 30 kg (66 lb) to offset the weight of the rower, and adds to the more than 350-kg (770-lb) weight of the gondola. Originally painted in bright colours, the black gondolas that you see today were decreed by the Senate to prevent excessive shows of wealth.

Gondola repair yard

TOP10 ⭐ Accademia Galleries

A dazzling collection of masterpieces spanning the full development of Venetian art from Byzantine to Renaissance, Baroque and Rococo, the Gallerie dell'Accademia is Venice's equivalent of the Uffizi in Florence. Giovanni Battista Piazzetta started the collection in 1750 to serve as models for the art school; in 1807 it was boosted by Napoleon with the addition of works from suppressed churches. The same year the collection moved to its present premises, occupying three former religious establishments: the 12th–15th-century Scuola Grande di Santa Maria della Carità and its adjoining church, and a 12th-century monastery remodelled by Palladio in the 1500s. In the 1940s, architect Carlo Scarpa modernized the interior spaces.

San Giobbe Altarpiece ①

Giovanni Bellini's (c.1435–1516) inspirational altarpiece **(right)** (Room 2) was painted in 1487 for the Church of San Giobbe. It is regarded as one of the finest examples of Sacra Conversazione, which was central to 15th-century Venetian art. The presence of St Sebastian and St Giobbe beside the Virgin suggests the aftermath of plague, while angel musicians pay homage to San Giobbe, patron saint of music.

② The Tempest

This enigmatic 1506 portrayal of a woman suckling her child **(left)** is

by Giorgione (c.1477–1510) (Room 23). The overall impression is of the figures and the dream-like, stormy landscape blended into one whole.

③ Supper in the House of Levi

The forceful canvas by Veronese (1573) occupies an entire wall of Room 10 and caused controversy in its time. The church authorities, who commissioned it as "The Last Supper", were angered by the inclusion of "dogs, buffoons, drunken Germans, dwarfs and other such absurdities" – so Veronese changed the title.

④ Pietà

Titian's last work (1576) is unfinished but it is also considered his best (Room 10), imbued as it is with golden light and a piercing sense of anguish.

5 **Meeting and Departure of the Betrothed Ursula and Ereo**

Part of Carpaccio's magnificent narrative cycle (1495) about a Breton princess and an English prince can be seen in Room 21.

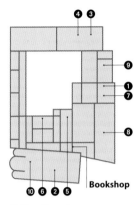

Gallery Floorplan

6 **Procession in St Mark's Square**

Part of Gentile Bellini's (c.1429–1507) spectacular cycle (1496) of the St Mark's Day procession in 1444 **(above)** can be seen in Room 20.

7 **Madonna dell'Arancio**

This work (1496–8) by Cima da Conegliano (c.1459–1517), painted for a Murano Franciscan church, is enlivened with partridges and plants (Room 2).

NEED TO KNOW

MAP C6 ▪ Campo della Carità, Dorsoduro 1050 ▪ 041 522 22 47 ▪ www.gallerieaccademia.it

Open 8:15am–7:15pm daily (to 2pm Mon; last admission 45 minutes before closing); closed 1 Jan, 1 May, 25 Dec

Adm €12

▪ The galleries are currently undergoing extensive expansion, so the floorplan may differ from that shown here until the work is completed in 2019.

Gallery Guide

The vast gallery is organized in chronological order for the most part and the rooms, labelled with roman numerals, are equipped with explanatory cards in English. The Quadreria corridor is filled with masterpieces.

8 **Coronation of the Virgin**

This resplendent polyptych (1350) by Venice's leading 14th-century artist, Paolo Veneziano (1300–65), is the first work in Room 1. Flanking the stunning Byzantine-inspired central piece are depictions of events from the Life of Christ.

9 **Portrait of a Gentleman**

Lorenzo Lotto's (1480–1557) image of a melancholic man in his study (1528) **(above)** may be a self-portrait (Room 7). Lotto was known for works of psychological insight.

10 **Lion of St Mark with Saints John the Baptist, John the Evangelist, Mary Magdalene and Jerome**

This marvellous canvas (in Room 23) by Cima di Conegliano depicts a winged lion flanked by four saints.

🔟 ⭐ Santa Maria Gloriosa dei Frari

A masterpiece of Venetian Gothic ecclesiastical architecture, this cavernous 15th-century church for Franciscan friars took more than 100 years to complete, along with its "brother" SS Giovanni e Paolo, and a further 26 years for the consecration of the main altar. A wonderful series of art treasures is held within the deceptively gloomy interior, which is almost 100-m (330-ft) long and 50-m (165-ft) across, from priceless canvases by Titian and Bellini to tombs of doges and artists such as Canova.

1 Assumption of the Virgin

Titian's glowing 1518 depiction of the triumphant ascent of Mary **(left)** shows her robed in crimson, accompanied by a semicircle of saints, while the 12 Apostles are left gesticulating in wonderment below. This brilliant canvas on the high altar is the inevitable focus of the church.

Santa Maria Gloriosa dei Frari

2 Rood Screen

This beautiful screen, which divides the worship area and nave is carved in a blend of Renaissance and Gothic styles by Pietro Lombardo (1435–1515) and Bartolomeo Bon. It is also decorated with marble figures **(right)**.

5 Campanile

The robust 14th-century bell tower set into the church's left transept is the second tallest in Venice.

3 Choir Stalls

Unique for Venice, the original three tiers of 124 friars' seats deserve close examination for their inlaid woodwork. Crafted by Marco Cozzi in 1468, they demonstrate the influence of northern European styles.

4 Madonna Enthroned with Saints

Tucked away in the sacristy, and still in its original engraved frame, is another delight for Bellini fans (1488). "It seems painted with molten gems," wrote Henry James of the triptych.

STATE ARCHIVES

The labyrinthine monastery and courtyards adjoining the church have been home to Venice's State Archives since the fall of the Republic. Its 300 rooms and approximately 70 km (43 miles) of shelves are loaded with precious records documenting the history of Venice right back to the 9th century, including the Golden Book register of the Venetian aristocracy. Scholars enter the building via the Oratorio di San Nicolò della Lattuga (1332), named after the miraculous recovery of a Procurator of San Marco thanks to the healing qualities of a lettuce (lattuga).

Canova's Mausoleum ⑥

This colossal monument **(right)**, based on Canova's Neo-Classical design for Titian's tomb, which was never built, was a tribute by the sculptor's followers in 1822.

⑧ Monument to Doge Francesco Foscari

This is a fine Renaissance tribute to the man responsible for Venice's mainland expansion. Foscari was the subject of Lord Byron's *The Two Foscari*, which was turned into an opera by Verdi.

Statue of John the Baptist ⑨

The inspirational wood statue of John the Baptist from 1450 **(right)**, which was created especially for the church by artist Donatello (1386–1466), stands in the Florentine chapel. The striking emaciated carved figure is renowned for being particularly lifelike.

⑩ Monument to Titian

Titian was afforded special authorization for burial here after his death during the 1576 plague, although this sturdy mausoleum was not built for another 300 years.

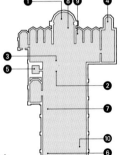

Church Floorplan

⑦ Mausoleum of Doge Giovanni Pesaro

The monsters and black marble figures supporting the sarcophagus of this macabre Baroque monument prompted art critic John Ruskin to write, "it seems impossible for false taste and base feeling to sink lower".

★ The Rialto

The commercial hub of Venice, centred on the Rialto Bridge, is as bustling today as it has always been – records tell of markets here since 1097. The area is also the city's historical heart and took its name from Rivoaltus, the high consolidated terrain that guaranteed early settlers flood-free premises. Most buildings, however, date from the 16th century, because a fire swept through Rialto in 1514. During Carnival the stall-holders don medieval costume to vie with each other for custom and only the new awnings and electronic cash registers hint at the modern world.

① Fresh Produce Market

The market here is a treat for the senses, with artistic piles of luscious peaches and cherries, thorny artichokes and red chicory from Treviso. Fruit, vegetables and fish are strictly seasonal **(above)**.

Rialto market alongside the Grand Canal

③ San Giacomo di Rialto

The oldest church in Venice claims to have a foundation set by a pious carpenter in the 5th century, although the present building is medieval. The Gothic portico and 24-hour clock are well worth a look.

④ Public Rostrum

New laws and names of criminals were announced atop this porphyry column **(right)**, supported by a stone figure known as *il gobbo* (hunchback).

② Pescheria

Writhing eels, huge swordfish, soft-shelled crabs and crimson-fleshed fresh tuna are among the stars of the 1907 Neo-Gothic fish market hall **(above)**, barely out of reach of the scavenging seagulls.

⑤ Palazzo dei Camerlenghi

This lopsided 1525 palace once imprisoned debtors on the ground floor, while the top floors served as offices for the city *camerlenghi* (treasurers).

6 Gondola Ferry
A must for every visitor is a trip on the *traghetto* ferry across the Grand Canal **(left)** – one of only eight still in operation. Custom dictates that passengers should remain standing.

7 Banco Giro Arcade
Merchants from the East and the West gathered to exchange a variety of goods, including silks and spices, outside the city's first bank – set up in 1157 – which is now a wine bar.

PLACE NAMES

Rialto market's narrow alleyways carry names such as Orefici (goldsmiths), Pescaria (fishmongers) and Erberia (vegetables), because the same type of shops once stood together. Local eateries for market traders also had evocative names such as Scimia (Monkey) and Do Mori (Two Moors).

8 Ruga degli Orefici
This lovely covered passageway decorated with frescoes has been home to silversmiths, goldsmiths and silk traders since the 1300s.

9 Fabbriche Nuove
Uniformed *carabinieri* (police) patrol the elongated law courts along the Grand Canal. Designed in 1552–5 by Sansovino they are recognizable by their 25 plain arcades.

NEED TO KNOW

MAP D3 ▪ San Polo ▪ Fresh produce market: 7:30am–1pm Mon–Sat; Pescheria: 7:30am–1pm Tue–Sat

▪ In addition to fresh fruit from the market, picnic supplies can be bought at the delicatessens and bakeries in the neighbourhood.

10 Grand Canal Views
The Erberia, right on the Grand Canal, makes a wonderful spot for boat-watching. Alternatively, wander on to the Rialto Bridge for a different vantage point **(below)**.

TOP 10 ⭐ Torcello

Some of the most breathtaking Byzantine mosaics in the world, found in the lagoon's oldest building, the Torcello basilica, reward those who visit this laid-back island, a beautiful 60-minute ferry ride from northern Venice. From the 5th century, mainlanders fleeing invading Lombards and Huns ventured across tidal flats to found a settlement that grew to 20,000 and lasted 1,000 years. However, few clues to the past remain, as the canals silted up, malaria decimated the population and the power base shifted to Venice once and for all. Today, Torcello is home to a handful of gardeners and fishermen.

Basilica Exterior ①
A miraculous survivor, this striking cathedral was founded in 639, but underwent radical restructuring in 1008. It retains its Romanesque form, light-brick walls and an arcaded 9th-century portico **(right)**.

② Doomsday Mosaics, Basilica
In these 12th–13th-century marvels **(above)**, the Last Judgment is dramatically depicted in superbly restored scenes of devils, angels, wild beasts and fires.

③ Apse Mosaics, Basilica
This moving 13th-century mosaic shows the Virgin in a blue robe with gold fringing, cradling her radiant child. Below are the 12 Apostles standing in a meadow of flowers.

④ Iconostasis, Basilica
Marble panels show peacocks drinking at the fountain of eternal life

(left), small lions posing under a tree full of birds, while six columns support 15th-century paintings of the Apostles with the Virgin.

⑤ Paving, Basilica
In vivid swirls of colours, rivalling the flooring in Basilica San Marco, are brilliant 11th-century tesserae of stone and glass. Cubes, semicircles and triangles are laid into square designs. The floor level was raised 30 cm (12 inches) during the basilica's reconstruction.

7 Campanile

The views from this simple 55-m (180-ft) bell tower **(left)** reach over the vast expanse of the lagoon, with its meandering canals and tidal flats, to the Adriatic Sea, Venice itself and even north to the Alps on a clear winter's day.

8 Throne of Attila

By popular belief this marble armchair **(below)** was the throne of the king of the Huns, though historical sources claim it was for the island's magistrates.

ATTILA THE HUN

The "Scourge of God", or the King of the Huns, ruled from AD 434 to 453 over an empire that stretched from the Alps and the Baltic towards the Caspian Sea. As part of his campaign against the Roman Empire, Attila attacked Milan, Verona and Padua, and refugees fled to Torcello. Burning the cathedral town of Aquileia gave him great satisfaction – his men raised a hill in Udine so he could enjoy the sight.

9 Museo dell'Estuario

An intriguing, if modest, collection of archaeological finds from the island and priceless treasures from the church are housed in the adjoining Gothic buildings.

NEED TO KNOW

MAP B1 ▪ Boat line 12 from the Fondamente Nuove to Burano, then change to boat line 9

Basilica di Santa Maria dell'Assunta: 041 730 119; Open Mar–Oct: 10:30am–5:30pm daily; Nov–Feb: 10am–4:30pm daily; closed 1 Jan, 25 Dec. Adm €5

Campanile: Open Mar–Oct: 10:30am–5:30pm daily; Nov–Feb: 10am–5pm. Adm €5. Audio guide

Santa Fosca: Closed to visitors during services

Museo dell'Estuario: 041 730 761; Open Mar–Oct: 10:30am–5pm Tue–Sun; Nov–Feb: 10am–4:30pm Tue–Sun; closed public hols. Adm €3

6 Santa Fosca

Alongside the basilica is this elegant church based on a Greek cross design, encircled by a five-sided colonnaded portico. The inside of the church is closed to visitors during services.

10 Locanda Cipriani

A favourite of Ernest Hemingway, who stayed here in 1948, this guesthouse **(left)** has a quiet charm that has attracted VIPs since it opened in 1938 *(Piazza Santa Fosca)*.

🌟 Campo Santa Margherita

This cheery, picturesque square in the district of Dorsoduro is a hive of activity day in, day out. It owes its name to the Christian martyr St Margaret of Antioch, possibly a fictitious figure, but highly popular in medieval times. Patron saint of expectant mothers, she is depicted in a niche on the square's northern wall with her emblem, the dragon. The square's capacious form, exploited by local children on bicycles and in-line skaters, is due to an ambitious enlargement project in the 1800s which opened up the south end by filling in canals.

1 Ex Chiesa di Santa Margherita

A writhing 14th-century dragon symbolizing the martyrdom of the saint enlivens the foot of the bell tower of the former church. It has been restored by the university as the Auditorium Santa Margherita.

2 Palazzo Foscolo-Corner

This beautiful palace is virtually unchanged since the 1300s and instantly distinguishable by its deep overhanging eaves. A striking Byzantine-style lunette, bearing an inset with the family crest, tops the entrance portal.

3 Scuola Grande dei Carmini

Glorious rooms **(below)**, decorated with Tiepolo's masterpieces, are highlights of this confraternity. The upstairs ceiling shows *St Simon Stock Receiving the Scapular from the Virgin.*

Campo Santa Margherita

4 Calle del Forno

An unusual series of medieval-style projections from a first-floor dwelling, partly held up by brick columns, is one of the most interesting features of this busy thoroughfare leading to Piazzale Roma and the bus terminal. The street is named after a long-gone *forno* (bakery).

5 Scuola dei Varoteri

A splendid bas-relief of the Virgin sheltering a group of trades-men in adoration adorns the former tanners' guild dating from 1725. Because of its isolated position, it was once mistakenly thought to be the house of the city's executioner.

8 Chiesa di Santa Maria dei Carmini

This richly adorned church **(left)** survived Napoleon's suppression of the Carmelite order of monks in the adjoining monastery. Many of its 13th-century features are intact, such as the sculpted entrance porch.

RIO TERRÀ

Rio is a common name for canal, while *terrà* means filled-in. Dating back to the 1300s, the practice of filling in waterways was widespread in the 1800s to provide extra pedestrian space. Some were covered with low-slung arches to keep water flowing, exemplified by Via Garibaldi in Castello. Later campaigns encouraged the reverse procedure.

9 Corte del Fondaco

A charming covered passageway leads through to this minor courtyard where curious, low, bricked-in arches indicate the former site of a 1700s flour store. The name *fondaco* – or store – is derived from the Arabic word *fonduq*.

10 Rio Nuovo

Excavated in 1932–3 to form a shortcut from Piazzale Roma to the Grand Canal, the canal has been closed to *vaporetti* since the 1990s, due to building damage.

6 The "House of the Moor"

Shakespeare's *Othello* was based on Cristoforo Moro, who was sent to govern Cyprus from 1508. This house at No. 2615 is his former home.

7 Altana Terraces

These timber roof platforms **(right)** were common in Venetian palaces, used by women for bleaching their hair in the sun. They are now used for laundry and partying on summer evenings, and can be seen around Campo Santa Margherita.

NEED TO KNOW

MAP B5

Scuola Grande dei Carmini, Dorsoduro:
041 528 94 20 ■ www.scuolagrandecarmini.it

Open 11am–5pm daily

Adm €5

....

■ Numerous pizza-slice outlets and bars serving *tramezzini* (sandwiches) and *panini* (rolls) make for a cheap lunch option.

TOP10 ⭐ Peggy Guggenheim Collection

The delightfully spacious, light-filled Collezione Peggy Guggenheim is home to works by more than 200 contemporary artists representing powerful avant-garde movements such as Cubism, Futurism and Surrealism. The landmark collection, put together by its far-sighted namesake, is housed in the 18th-century Palazzo Venier dei Leoni, known as the "unfinished palace" because of its one-storey construction. As well as the wonderful works of art on display inside the gallery, there is also a striking sculpture garden and the former home of Peggy Guggenheim to visit.

1 The Poet
A wonderful starting point is this portrait (1911) by legendary Spanish artist Pablo Picasso (1881–1973), from his early Cubist period. The figure is executed from a limited palette of ochre and dark browns.

2 Bird in Space
This polished brass sculpture (1932–40) was once classified by US customs as a "stair-rail" and was therefore subject to duty. Its creator was Romanian artist Constantin Brancusi (1876–1957).

3 Attirement of the Bride
This portrayal (1940) of an orange-robed bride assisted by mutant animals and humans (**below**) is by Max Ernst (1891–1976). The German Surrealist was married to Peggy Guggenheim from 1942 to 1946.

Peggy Guggenheim Collection

Key to Floorplan
- Gallery
- Nasher Sculpture Garden

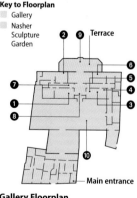

Gallery Floorplan

4 Empire of Light

Magical light effects see darkened trees and a house silhouetted by a street lamp against a contrasting daytime sky with fluffy clouds in this work (1953–4) by René Magritte (1898–1967). The Belgian Surrealist was renowned for his eccentric subjects.

6 Woman Walking

This serene elongated form of a truncated female figure (1932), apparently inspired by Etruscan design, is the recognized trademark of the Swiss artist Alberto Giacometti (1901–66), a short-term participant in the Surrealist movement **(right)**.

7 The Moon Woman

This vibrant canvas (1942) starring a skeletal stick figure with an odd, padded curve is an early work by Jackson Pollock (1912–56), pre-dating his famous "drip" technique.

PEGGY GUGGENHEIM

This heir to a mining fortune (1898–1979) first came to Europe in 1921, quickly fitting into Bohemian Paris. Resolving to "buy a picture a day", she amassed a contemporary art collection before she made Venice her home in 1947. She is fondly remembered by locals here for her faithful dogs and for owning the city's last private gondola.

8 Mobile

This simple masterpiece of movement (1941) by Alexander Calder (1898–1976), which gave its name to all mobiles, hangs in the atrium of Guggenheim's house.

9 Angel of the City

Set on steps leading to the terrace, this bronze horse and rider (1948) by Italian sculptor Marino Marini (1901–80) greet passing boats.

NEED TO KNOW

MAP C6 ■ Fondamenta Venier dei Leoni, Dorsoduro 704 (2nd entrance Calle S Cristoforo, Dorsoduro 701) ■ 041 240 54 11 ■ www.guggenheim-venice.it ■ No flash photography

Open 10am–6pm Wed–Mon; Closed 25 Dec

Adm €15; audio guides

■ Take a break in the coffee shop or on the café's shady verandah for a light snack or a meal.

■ Enjoy the view from the terrace, which looks onto the Grand Canal.

5 Magic Garden

This deliberately child-like piece (1926) by Paul Klee (1879–1940) features blurry shapes and sketched-in faces and buildings.

10 Three Standing Figures

Beautifully placed in the Nasher Sculpture Garden, these sculptures (1953) by Henry Moore (1898–1986) were inspired by Italian bell towers.

Venice Lagoon

Torcello

Laguna
Veneto

Mazzorbo   Burano

Murano

Area of
main Venice map

0 km   2

0 miles   2

N

A   **B**   **C**

1

Parco
Groggia

CAMPO DI
SANT'ALVISE

CAMPIE
P

Rio dei Riformati

Rio di Sant'Alvise

FMTA DELLA SENSA

FMTA MADONN
DELL'ORTO

Rio   della   Sensa

FONDAMENTA DELLE
CAPPUCCINE

FMTA D. ORMESINI

RIO   della   Sensa

CAM
DEI M

CAMPO
DEL GHETTO
NUOVO

Museo
Ebraico

FOND. DE
Rio

2

Crea

San
Giobbe

Canale di   Cannaregio

FONDAMENTA SAVORGNAN

CANNAREGIO

Guglie

R. TERRA S. LEONARDO

RIO TERRA
FARSETTI

RIO TERRA D.
MADDALENA

CAM

CAMPO
SAN
GIOBBE

CALLE RIELLO

Parco
Savorgnan

CAMPO S.
GEREMIA

CAMPO
SAN LEONARDO

Palazzo
Labia

CAMPO SAN
MARCUOLA

Palazzo
Vendramin-
Calergi

Rio della Crea

CALLE DE LA MISERICORDIA

R. TERRA LISTA DI SPAGNA

Riva di
Biasio

San Marcuola

San Stae

**Canal
Grande**

Fondaco
dei Turchi

CAMPO SAN
ZAN DEGOLA

CAMPO
SAN STAE

3

Scalzi

Ponte
degli Scalzi

CMPO
S. SIMEON
PROFETA

LISTA DEI BARI

Chiesa di San
Giacomo dell'Orio

Palazzo
Mocenigo

Ca' Pesaro

Stazione Ferrovie
dello Stato
Santa Lucia

Ferrovia

FMTA SAN SIMEON PICCOLO

S Simeòn
Piccolo

8

CAMPO
NAZARIO
SAURO

CAMPO S.
GIACOMO
DELL'ORIO

C. DELLA CHIESA

CAMPO
S.
CASSIAN

SANTA CROCE

PONTE DELLA LIBERTA

Piazzale
Roma

Ponte della
Costituzione

Giardino
Papadopoli

RIOTERRA
SECONDO

2 **SAN POLO**

6

4

**Piazzale
Roma**

PIAZZALE
ROMA

Tre Ponti

C. DELLE CHIOVERE

Scuola Grande
di San Giovanni
Evangelista

CAMPO
SAN STIN

Sant'Apon

San Nicolò
da Tolentino

**Santa Maria
Gloriosa dei
Frari**

CAMPO
SAN POLO

San Polo

Rio delle Burchielle

FMTA MINOTTO

Scuola
Grande di
San Rocco

Rio D. FRARI

Rio di San Polo

Cana
Gran

Rio Nuovo

RIO TERRA DEI PENSIERI

Rio della Cazziola

CALLE DEI PRETI CROSERA

CAMPO
SAN TOMA

Sant'Angelo

Museo
Fortuny

FONDAMENTA DELLE
PROCURATIE

Ex-Chiesa di
Santa Margherita

Rio di Ca'foscari

CAMPO
SAN PANTALON

San Tomà

Palazzo
Grassi

CAMP
SANT'ANGE

5

Rio del Tintor

C. BAGOSI

**Campo Santa
Margherita**

Scuola
Grande dei
Carmini

R.T. SANT'APONAL

Ca'
Rezzonico

SAL. SAN SAMUELE

7 **SAN MARC**

FONDAMENTA
DELL'ARZERE

Santa Maria
dei Carmini

Ca' Rezzonico

San Samuele

CAMPO
SANTO
STEFANO

CAMPO
SAN BARNABA

5

10

CAMPO SA
MAURIZIO

CAMPO
ANGELO
RAFFAELE

DORSODURO

Rio del Carmini

Rio Malpaga

Rio d. Eremite

CAMPO
SAN VIDAL

Accademia

Ponte
dell'Accademia

San
Sebastiano

**Gallerie
dell'Accademia**

CAMPO
SAN VIO

**Collezio
Peggy
Guggenhe**

6

San Basilio

FMTA ZATTERE PONTE LUNGO

Squero di
San Trovaso

Rio di San Trovaso

Gesuati

RIO TERRA ANTONIO FOSCARINI

Rio di San Vio

Zattere

FMTA ZATTERE AI GESUATI

FMTA ZATTERE ALLO SPIRITO SAN

Spirito Santo

0 metres   300

0 yards   300

N

Canale   della   Giudecca

A   **B**   **C**

Top 10 Venice sights
see pp218–47

Top 10 Restaurants

① Ostaria Boccadoro
Venetian cuisine

② Da Fiore
Fine dining

③ Osteria di Santa Marina
Innovative local cuisine

④ Vini da Gigio
Classic Venetian fare

⑤ La Bitta
Rustic bistro

⑥ Antica Birraria La Corte
Pizzeria

⑦ Al Bacareto
Traditional Venetian dishes

⑧ Gelateria Alaska
Ice cream parlour

⑨ Caffè Brasilia
Snacks and coffee

⑩ Ristorante A Beccafico
Southern Italian eatery

Top 10 Copenhagen

**Fishing boats on the water in the
historic district of Nyhavn**

Exploring Copenhagen

Copenhagen may not be the biggest of capital cities, but it punches well above its weight in terms of culture, history and charm. Despite its compact size, there is a lot to see and do. To help you make the most of your visit, here are some ideas for a two- or four-day trip.

Christiansborg Slot has magnificent interiors.

Key
— Two-day itinerary
— Four-day itinerary

Nyhavn is a waterfront entertainment area.

Two Days in Copenhagen

Day ❶

MORNING

Set sail from **Nyhavn** (see pp264–5) on a canal tour, then stroll along the promenade past the Royal Danish Playhouse. Follow the harbourside path until you reach **Amalienborg** (see pp266–7), where you can watch the changing of the guard. Have lunch at Kompasset (Nyhavn 65 stuen).

AFTERNOON

Head west on Gothersgade until you reach **Kongens Have** (see pp260–61). Continue through the gardens to **Rosenborg Slot** (see pp260–61) to see the crown jewels. Walk north on Øster Voldgade and visit **SMK – National Gallery of Denmark** (see pp268–9), ending with a drink at Torvehallerne KBH (Frederiksborggade 21).

Day ❷

MORNING

Begin the day at **Nationalmuseet** (see pp274–5), making sure to visit the Viking exhibition. Next, go to **Slotsholmen** (see pp272–3) and visit the Royal Stables before taking a tour of the Royal Reception Rooms at Christiansborg Slot. Climb the palace tower for amazing views. Stop at the Tower Restaurant for an innovative spin on a smørrebrød (open sandwich).

AFTERNOON

Head southwest on Stormgade to Ny Carlsberg Glyptotek (Dantes Plads 7), before crossing Tietgensgade and exploring **Tivoli** (see pp258–9). After spending a couple of hours here, exit onto Vesterbrogade and walk east towards the **Latin Quarter** (see pp262–3) for sightseeing and shops.

Four Days in Copenhagen

Day ❶

MORNING

Make **SMK – National Gallery of Denmark** (see pp268–9) your first stop of the day, then cross Georg Brandes Plads and head to **Rosenborg Slot** (see pp260–61).

and arrive at Vor Frelsers Kirke (*Skt. Annæ Gade 29*). Spend the afternoon in Christiania.

Day ❸
MORNING
Start the day with a trip to Zoologisk Have (*Roskildevej 32*), and visit the elephant house here. Stroll through Frederiksberg Have before exiting onto Pile Alle, then make your way into Visit Carlsberg (*Gamle Carlsberg Vej 11*).

AFTERNOON
Stroll northeast and stop at Bakkehuset (*Rahbeks Alle 23*). Turn right to get onto Vesterbrogade then right again onto Gasværksvej, following the road until you reach Kødbyen, where you will find a plethora of trendy bars.

Take a guided tour of the 17th-century palace before exiting into **Kongens Have** (*see pp260–61*). Head east to Marmorkirken, and then on to **Amalienborg** (*see pp266–7*). Stop at Ida Davidsen (*Store Kongensgade 70*) for lunch.

AFTERNOON
Walk west, stopping to admire the Gefionspringvandet and St Alban's Church before crossing the footbridge into Kastellet (*Gl. Hovedgvagt*). See the Little Mermaid from the fortress ramparts, then catch a 1A bus into **Kongens Nytorv** (*see pp264–5*). Stroll along Strøget, then have a drink at one of Amagertorv's cafés.

Day ❷
MORNING
Start the day at **Nationalmuseet** (*see pp274–5*) and museum-hop on **Slotsholmen** (*see pp272–3*) before popping into the Royal Stables. Take a torchlit tour of the ruins under Christiansborg Slot.

AFTERNOON
Cross the **harbour** (*see pp256–7*) and enter Christianshavn. Turn right to visit the Christians Kirke on Strandgade, then head east until you reach the canal, crossing the bridge on Sankt Annæ Gade

Day ❹
MORNING
Begin the day with a coffee at one of the many cafés along Studiestræde before exploring the bustling **Latin Quarter** (*see pp262–3*). Head up Store Kannikestræde to Rundtårn, and then hike to the top. Continue into **Nyhavn** (*see pp264–5*) for lunch.

AFTERNOON
Take a boat tour of the canals and jump off at Holmens Kirke (*Holmens Kanal 21*). Walk west along Gammel Strand, passing Rådhus before turning onto Vesterbrogade. Turn left into **Tivoli** (*see pp258–9*), and spend the afternoon in the pleasure gardens.

Tivoli Gardens has manicured lawns, flowers and fountains.

TOP 10 Copenhagen Highlights

Copenhagen is a vibrant city offering an array of experiences. Walk through the cobbled streets of the medieval city, explore world-class museums, experience the finest restaurants and hippest nightlife, or simply unwind beside the gorgeous waters of one of the nearby peaceful seaside towns. This charming destination has something for everyone.

1 Harbour Sights

The best way to soak up Copenhagen's harbour sights is to take a boat trip along the canals of Slotsholmen and Christianshavn. It is also a good way to understand the city's development (see pp256–7).

Tivoli **2**

This pleasure garden and funfair attracts kids and adults. The rides are great for an adrenaline rush, and if you feel peckish there are many restaurants (see pp258–9).

3 Rosenborg Slot and Kongens Have

Set in one of the city's prettiest parks, the lovely 17th-century Rosenborg Castle houses the royal regalia, including the dazzling Crown Jewels (see p260–61).

4 Latin Quarter

One of the oldest areas in Copenhagen, the Latin Quarter is just off the main pedestrianized street, Strøget (see pp262–3).

5 Kongens Nytorv and Nyhavn

Kongens Nytorv (King's New Square) is a splendid Baroque square at the top of Nyhavn. Previously a seedy haunt for sailors, Nyhavn has been radically transformed. It is now a waterside attraction with bars and restaurants (see pp264–5).

6 Amalienborg and Frederiksstaden

Home to the royal family since 1794, this complex of palaces represents some of the best Rococo architecture in Denmark, plus fascinating displays *(see pp266–7)*.

7 SMK – National Gallery of Denmark

You will find a wonderful collection of Danish and European sculpture as well as paintings at the SMK. It is housed in a beautiful 19th-century building, connected by a glass bridge to a modern wing *(see pp268–9)*.

8 Christiania

This is a wonderland of cafés, bars, music venues, art galleries and fiercely independent shops – and a must-see for anyone interested in the city's thriving counter-culture *(see pp270–71)*.

10 Nationalmuseet

Here is a perfect example of how brilliantly the Danes design their museums. You will find some fabulous ethnographic artifacts from around the world, as well as an excellent children's museum *(see pp274–5)*.

9 Slotsholmen

This is where it all began in the 12th century. The present Neo-Baroque castle was built in 1907–28, but was never inhabited by the monarch. It is shared between the royals and Parliament *(see pp272–3)*.

★ Harbour Sights

A harbour tour is a delightful way to take in the city's brilliant views and varied topography. You will be taken along the wide waters of the Inner Harbour and winding waterways of Christianshavn, then round to Slotsholmen (the island on which the original town of Havn flourished in the 12th century). Vor Frelsers Kirke, in particular, makes a spectacular sight as you look up through the rigging of sailing boats dotting the Christianshavn canal.

1 The Canals

The canals that you glide along on the tour **(above)** were built in a Dutch style in 1618 at the command of Christian IV. It is because of this that Christianshavn is referred to as "Little Amsterdam".

2 Operaen

The Opera House **(below)** was built in just four years. Its massive auditorium seats 1,700 people *(Ekvipagemestervej 10)*. The foyer's sculptures change colour with the weather.

3 Vor Frelsers Kirke

With a soaring twisted spire, this opulent church dominates the Christianshavn skyline. An ascent offers an unparalleled vantage point over the city.

4 Nyhavn

Even today, the utterly charming old harbour of Nyhavn is filled with boats. The old brothels and pubs have now been turned into respectable bars and restaurants serving good, traditional Danish dishes.

5 Den Sorte Diamant

The Black Diamond, a vast, eye-catching structure, holds all the books ever published in Denmark *(Søren Kierkegaards Plads 1)*. It is the largest library in the Nordic countries, and a great place to find original Danish texts.

Map of Harbour Sights

⑦ Havnebadet
Take a refreshing dip in the clean harbour waters **(left)** of this popular open-air pool *(Islands Brygge 14)*, while enjoying superb views of the city. There are three pools to choose from – for adults, for children and a smaller pool for divers.

⑧ Langelinie
One of the city's most scenic areas, this is a wonderful place to walk along the harbour banks. Stroll along, past Kastellet and the Little Mermaid, right up to the final stretch where there is a cruise ship terminal.

⑨ The Little Mermaid
Den Lille Havfrue is a surprisingly small landmark, ordered by brewery magnate Carl Jacobsen in 1909 as a gift to the city of Copenhagen. It was created in 1913 by Edvard Eriksen, whose wife, Eline, was the model.

⑩ Pavilions and the Royal Yacht
On the quayside, just beyond the Little Mermaid, are two green-domed pavilions. It is here that the Danish royal family gathers before boarding their stunning 79-m (259-ft) royal yacht, called the *Dannebrog* **(right)**, which shares its name with the Danish flag (said to have fallen from the sky in the year 1219).

MUTANT MERMAID

Set close to the Little Mermaid, and almost inviting controversy, is a sculpture group called *Paradise Genetically Altered* by Danish artist Bjørn Nørgaard. There is a triumphal arch, with a 9-m (29-ft) genetically altered Madonna atop it, surrounded by figures of Adam, Eve, Christ, Mary Magdalene, the Tripartite Capital – a critical representation of capitalism – and a pregnant man. On its own small island not far away sits the *Genetically Modified Little Mermaid*.

⑥ Houseboats
The houseboats along the canals range from boat-like structures to some with barge-like designs, and other homes built on floating platforms, complete with outdoor spaces.

NEED TO KNOW

MAP F3 ■ www.visit copenhagen.com

■ Both Stromma and Netto Boats offer guided canal and harbour tours.

■ The tours run round the year, with several departures per day.

■ Public buses whose routes run along the harbour include the 901 and 902 from Den Sorte Diamant, Nyhavn, Knippelsbro, Operaen, Nyholm or Larsen Plads.

■ Buses 991, 992 and 993 run between Refshaleøen (Holmen) and Langelinie. Copenhagen Cards are also accepted.

TOP10 ⭐ Tivoli

Famous for its magical fairy-tale ambience, exotic buildings, gorgeous landscaped gardens and upmarket entertainment and restaurants, Tivoli Gardens is more than an amusement park. The atmosphere is magical enough to merit a visit even if you are not interested in the excellent rides on offer. Founded in 1843, Tivoli has long been a favourite with royalty. It also proved to be a great source of inspiration for Walt Disney, who visited in the 1950s and is said to have been fascinated by Tivoli's atmosphere.

2 Thrill Rides
Day or night, Tivoli rings with the shrieks of people whizzing along on thrill rides such as *Aquila*, *The Demon* **(left)**, *Vertigo* and *The Starflyer*, which reaches a height of 80 m (262 ft).

3 Tivoli Concert Hall and Open-Air Stage
The hall hosts varied performances. There is music daily in the Harmony Pavilion, and free rock concerts on Friday nights (May–Sep).

1 Gentle Rides
For children and the faint-hearted, there are plenty of fun, gentle rides. The Ferris wheel is an observation wheel that offers great views over Tivoli. You could also enjoy a trolley-bus ride, a carousel ride with exotic animals and music, a waltzer in the shape of a pirate ship and several charming kids' rides, such as flying dragons and miniature classic cars.

4 Pantomime Theatre
Built in 1874, this theatre **(below)** has an exotic Chinese design and a spectacular stage curtain styled like a peacock's tail. It is known for its very enjoyable mime shows.

5 Dragon Boats
These boats **(above)** are very popular rides at Tivoli. Kids love floating on the lake during the day. In the evenings, the setting turns romantic.

6 Tivoli at Night
At night Tivoli is utterly magical, sparkling resplendently with thousands of fairy lights and Chinese lanterns. You can catch the dazzling Tivoli Illuminations over the lake, an exuberant, late-night show with fireworks, lasers, music and waterjets.

7 Traditional Rides

Tivoli's current Ferris wheel dates from 1943. The Roller Coaster **(left)** was built in 1914 and is one of the oldest of its kind. It reaches speeds of 58 kmph (36 mph). The classic carousel is also very popular, perfect for adults looking for a dose of nostalgia.

CHRISTMAS AT TIVOLI

For six weeks between mid-November and the end of December Tivoli transforms into a winter wonderland: an exciting, no-holds-barred, Father Christmas-strewn, elf-driven, illuminated extravaganza that you and the kids aren't likely to forget in a hurry!

8 Tivoli Akvarium

Don't miss the amazing aquarium in the foyer of the Concert Hall. Based on a tropical coral reef, this extensive salt-water aquarium is home to more than 1,600 fish of over 500 varieties. Among the popular attractions are the eels.

9 Tivoli Youth Guard

A tradition since 1844, the Youth Guard parades through Tivoli – complete with instruments, coach and horses – forming a delightful picture.

NEED TO KNOW

MAP C5

■ Vesterbrogade 3 ■ 33 15 10 01 ■ www.tivoli.dk

Open summer: 11am–11pm Sun–Thu (until midnight Fri & Sat); winter: 11am–9pm Sun–Thu (until 10pm Fri & Sat; hours can vary, check website before visiting)

Adm varies (check website for details)

■ Go on the thrill rides during the day, as long queues can build up in the evenings.

10 Nimb Hotel

This splendid hotel **(below)**, housed in the Nimb building, offers a variety of culinary experiences, such as a *vinoteque*, the Cakenhagen (bakery), a Bar'n'Grill with primed steaks and a brasserie.

TOP10 ⭐ Rosenborg Slot and Kongens Have

Rosenborg Castle was originally built as a summer house in 1606–34 by Christian IV. At that time, it stood surrounded by sprawling gardens (now the Kongens Have park) out in the tranquil countryside. This was Christian IV's favourite castle, and many rooms retain the original Renaissance decor from his residency. When he was on his deathbed at Frederiksborg Castle in 1648, he insisted on being brought to Rosenborg Castle, and eventually died here.

1 Knight's Hall
Known as the Long Hall before 1750, this room **(above)** was completed in 1624 as a celebration hall. Only two Dutch fireplaces still remain from its original elaborate decorations.

2 Royal Residence
Complete with fairy-tale turrets and bronze lions guarding the entrance **(below)**, the castle is wholly regal. In 1838, it became the first royal residence to open to the public.

3 Marble Hall
Originally serving as the bedroom of Kirsten Munk, Christian IV's morganatic wife, this room was turned into a Baroque show of splendour to celebrate the Absolute Monarchy.

4 Crown Jewels
The castle has been used as the treasury of the realm since 1658. In the castle's heavily guarded basement are Denmark's Crown Jewels **(above)**.

5 Dark Room
This room is filled with fascinating objects, such as wax portraits of Frederik III and a 17th-century trick chair.

ROSENBORG'S KINGS

Christian IV: Built many Renaissance buildings.
Frederik III: Introduced Absolute Monarchy to control the aristocracy.
Christian V: Introduced fair taxation.
Frederik IV: Constructed Frederiksberg Castle.
Christian VI: Known as the religious king.
Frederik V: Responsible for the building of the Frederiksstaden district.

8 Frederik IV's Chamber Room

In the 1700s, this room **(above)** was used by Frederik IV's sister as an antechamber and the tapestries that hang here date back to this period. Note the intricate equestrian silver statue of Frederik. The coffered ceiling is the original.

9 Christian IV's Bedroom

Another private royal apartment, this room contains Christian IV's bloodied clothing, from the naval battle of Kolberger Heide (1644) where he lost an eye. The king wanted these clothes preserved as national mementos.

10 Winter Room

This panelled room **(below)** is said to have been one of Christian IV's most important private chambers. Look out for the speaking tubes that connect with the wine cellar and room above.

6 Glass Cabinet

This room was designed as a glass cabinet in 1713–14 by Frederik IV. The cabinet was built to house the extensive collection of glassware presented to Frederik in 1709 by the city of Venice, and its contents are amazing.

7 Kongens Have

Visited by over 2 million people every year, these are Denmark's oldest royal gardens and date back to the 17th century. There is a rose garden, which contains many statues. Various art events and a puppet theatre for children are held during summer.

NEED TO KNOW

MAP D2 ■ Øster Voldgade 4A ■ 33 15 32 86 ■ www.rosenborgslot.dk

Open Jan–mid-Apr & Nov–Dec: 10am–3pm Tue–Sun; mid-Apr–May & Sep–Oct: 10am–4pm daily; Jun–Aug: 9am–5pm daily

Adm 110 Dkr, students 75 Dkr, under-18s free; Kongens Have free; Copenhagen Card accepted

Guided tours (each 60–90 minutes long) are available in English, German and French (advance booking is required)

■ Avoid lurking near the guards at the entrance to the Crown Jewels – you might be considered a security risk.

■ Grab a bite at the restaurant or the small café in Kongens Have.

TOP 10 ⭐ Latin Quarter

The Latin Quarter is home to Copenhagen's university, where Latin used to be the spoken language. One of the oldest areas in the city, it is full of 17th-century buildings that were built by the architect king, Christian IV. Although there have been dwellings here since medieval times, most of them were destroyed in the disastrous fire that spread across Copenhagen in 1728. Today, the Latin Quarter is a lively and bustling student area brimming with shops and cafés.

Højbro Plads ①
The 1902 bronze equestrian statue **(right)** on this popular square depicts the 12th-century Bishop Absalon, founder of Copenhagen, facing the site of his original castle on Slotsholmen.

② Sankt Petri Kirke
Older than Vor Frue Kirke, Copenhagen's German church also suffered from city fires and the British bombardment of 1807 (*Larslejsstræde 11*). Its sepulchral chapel has monuments and tombs dating back to 1681.

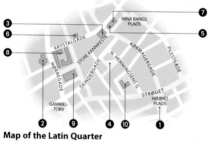

Map of the Latin Quarter

⑤ Rundetårn
The Round Tower (*Købmagergade 52A*) was built in 1642 by Christian IV as an observatory, its official role until 1861. It is 34.8 m (114 ft) high, with an internal ramp that spirals almost to the top. It holds art exhibitions and concerts in the library.

③ Regensen
This 17th-century student residence lies opposite the Rundetårn. A part of it burned down in the great fire of 1728, but was soon rebuilt. Its students retain the old tradition of "storming" Rundetårn every May.

④ Gråbrødretorv
Named after the Grey Brothers who built Copenhagen's first monastery here, this lovely 13th-century square **(right)** is now a popular place for locals and visitors to enjoy alfresco meals or drinks.

7 Trinitatis Kirke

This magnificent church **(left)** was built in 1637–56 for the staff and students of the university *(Pilestræde 67)*. If it happens to be closed when you visit, you can enter Rundetårn and get a view of the church nave through the glass panel at the start of the ramp.

8 Universitetet

Founded in 1479 by Christian I, the University of Copenhagen was the country's first university. The Neo-Classical building that can be seen here today dates to the 19th century. In the courtyard, there are the remains of an old Bishop's Palace (1420). Most of the university is now on the island of Amager.

THE BELLS AND CARILLON OF HELLIGÅNDSKIRKEN

In 1647, 50 years after the clock tower was built, King Christian IV gifted the church a set of bells and a carillon. The carillon consisted of 19 bells. It was also used at funerals; the importance of the deceased decided for how long the bells would chime – sometimes hours.

9 Vor Frue Kirke

In the 12th century, Bishop Absalon founded a Gothic church *(Nørregade 8)*. After burning down twice, the present Neo-Classical cathedral **(below)** was completed in 1829, but the tower is from medieval times.

6 Synagogen

Built from 1830–33, Copenhagen's oldest synagogue survived Nazi occupation. The synagogue for the city's Jewish community, it is not open to visitors except with prior booking.

10 Helligåndskirken

The Church of the Holy Ghost *(Niels Hemmingsens Gade 5)* was built in 1295 as a hospital, and was expanded to include a monastery in 1474.

NEED TO KNOW

MAP D3

Synagogen: Krystalgade 12; 33 12 88 68

Rundetårn: Købmagergade 52A; 33 73 03 73; open May–Sep: 10am–8pm daily, Oct–Apr: 10am–6pm Mon, Thu–Sun, 10am–9pm Tue–Wed; adm 25 Dkr (free

with Copenhagen Card); www.rundetaarn.dk

Trinitatis Kirke: Købmagergade 52A; open 9:30am–4:30pm Mon–Sat; www.trinitatis kirke.dk

Universitetet: Nørregade 10; 35 32 26 26; open 9am–5pm Mon–Fri; www.ku.dk

Vor Frue Kirke: Nørregade 8; open 8am–5pm Mon–Sat

Sankt Petri Kirke: Skt Peders Str 2; 33 13 38 33; open Apr–Sep: 11am–3pm Wed–Sat; adm to the sepulchral chapel

Helligåndskirken: Niels Hemmingsens Gade 5; 33 15 41 44; open noon–4pm Mon–Fri (11am–1pm Sat)

🔟⭐ Kongens Nytorv and Nyhavn

Kongens Nytorv (King's New Square) and Nyhavn (New Harbour) are two of the most picturesque areas in Copenhagen, although ongoing construction work around Kongens Nytorv has at times marred the view. The square was once outside the city gates and the site of the town gallows in medieval times. The Nyhavn canal was planned by Frederik III to connect the Inner Harbour with the square, enabling merchants to unload their goods.

1 Nyhavn Nos 18, 20 and 67

These brightly painted merchants' houses were built together with the harbour. Fairy-tale writer Hans Christian Andersen lived in them – he wrote his first tale, *The Tinder Box* (1835), while living at No 20.

3 Nyhavn Canal

Running down to the Inner Harbour, this canal (right) is flanked by houses that belonged to merchants. A large anchor, installed in honour of the sailors who lost their lives in World War II, marks the starting point of Nyhavn.

Map of Kongens Nytorv and Nyhavn

2 Charlottenborg Slot

An early example of the Danish Baroque style, this palace was built by Frederik III's son Ulrik. It houses the Royal Danish Academy of Fine Arts as well as the Kunsthal Charlottenborg.

4 Hotel d'Angleterre

This is Copenhagen's oldest hotel (below), and one of the oldest in the world (Kongens Nytorv 34). It has hosted royalty and celebrities, including Karen Blixen, Churchill, Grace Kelly and Madonna.

5 Magasin du Nord

Originally the famous Hotel du Nord, this is Copenhagen's oldest department store and is considered to be the city's answer to London's Selfridges or New York's Bloomingdale's.

6 Amber Museum

Set in a house dating back to 1606, this small museum displays an exquisite collection dedicated to Denmark's national gem, amber (also called Nordic Gold).

8 Equestrian Statue

The bronze statue in the middle of Kongens Nytorv commemorates Christian V (1646–99), who rebuilt the square in 1670 in Baroque style. Created by the French-born court sculptor Abraham-César Lamoureux, it shows the king dressed as a Roman emperor **(left)**.

"THE IMPERIAL ETHIOPIAN PALACE"

In the 1950s, Ethiopia's emperor Haile Selassie, with his wife, family and entire entourage, visited Denmark and stayed at the Hotel d'Angleterre. During their stay, all telephone calls to the hotel were answered with "The Imperial Ethiopian Palace".

9 Store Strandstræde and Lille Strandstræde

Once full of pubs and brothels, "Big Beach Street" and "Little Beach Street" are now home to art galleries and stylish designer shops.

10 Det Kongelige Teater

This Baroque-style theatre is home to the Royal Danish Ballet **(below)** and is the third one to stand on this site.

7 Vingårdsstræde 6

At the age of 22, Hans Christian Andersen lived for a year in the attic of this building, one of the city's oldest, built on the site of a vineyard (hence *Vingårdsstræde*). Its 13th-century cellars now host the Michelin-starred Kong Hans Kælder.

NEED TO KNOW

MAP E3

Amber Museum: Kongens Nytorv 2; 33 11 67 00; open May–Sep: 9am–7:30pm daily, Oct–Apr: 10am–5:30pm daily; adm 25 Dkr, child 10 Dkr; www.houseofamber.com

Charlottenborg Slot: Nyhavn 2; 33 74 46 39; open 11am–8pm Tue–Fri, 11am–5pm Sat–Sun; adm 90 Dkr, concessions 40 Dkr, free after 5pm Wed; www.kunsthalcharlottenborg.dk

Magasin du Nord: Kongens Nytorv 13; open 10am–8pm daily; www.magasin.dk

Det Kongelige Teater: Kongens Nytorv; 33 69 69 33; guided tours available, book at the box office or in advance; www.kglteater.dk

■ The restaurants on the south side of Nyhavn are good and usually not as busy as those on the north.

■ Find a quick bite away from the crowds in Nyhavn Pizzeria at 8 Lille Strandstræde.

🔟⭐ Amalienborg and Frederiksstaden

Built in the 1750s, this stately complex was designed by the royal architect, Nicolai Eigtved. Four Rococo palaces, originally home to four noble families, enclose an octagonal square in Frederiksstaden, an aristocratic area built by Frederik V. Christian VII bought the palaces after the Christiansborg Slot burned down in 1794, and the royal family has lived here ever since. It was named after a palace built on this site by Queen Sophie Amalie in the 17th century.

Christian VII's Palace ①

This palace (right) was one of the first to be completed by the time of Eigtved's death in 1754. Also known as Moltke Palace – named after its original owner, Count Adam Gottlob Moltke – it is the most expensive palace in the complex and also boasts one of the best Rococo interiors in the entire country.

③ Frederik VIII's Palace

This palace, which has a clock on its façade, was renamed after Frederik VIII moved in. It is now the residence of Crown Prince Frederik and Crown Princess Mary.

⑤ The Golden Axis

Marmorkirken and Frederiksstaden lie on a short axis called the Golden Axis, which was considered very important when the Opera House was built.

④ Amaliehaven

The Amalie Garden was created in 1983 on the banks of the Harbour, financed by the shipping giant A P Møller and the Christine McKinney Møller Foundation. It has a splendid fountain.

② Palace Guards

When the queen is in residence, the Danish Royal Life Guards (above) stand outside the palace, guarding their monarch in two-hour shifts. At noon, guards from Rosenborg Slot take over, marching through the city streets just before noon.

NEED TO KNOW

MAP E3

Marmorkirken: Frederiksgade 4; 33 15 01 44; open 10am–7pm Mon–Thu, noon–5pm Fri–Sun (tower open mid-Jun: 1–3pm daily, Sep–mid-Jun: 1–3pm Sat & Sun); adm; www.marmorkirken.dk

Amalienborg Museum: 33 12 21 86; open May–mid-Jun: 10am–4pm daily; mid-

Jun–mid-Sep: 10am–5pm daily; mid-Sep–Oct: 10am–4pm daily; closed Nov–Apr: Mon; adm 95 Dkr, students 65 Dkr, free with Copenhagen Card; www.dkks.dk

■ Two palaces are closed to the public: Frederik VIII's and Christian IX's.

■ The guards will not respond well to people sitting on palace steps.

THE RUSSIAN CONNECTION

The onion domes of Alexander Nevsky Kirke, the Russian Orthodox Church, are easy to identify. Consecrated in 1883, it was a gift from Tsar Alexander III to mark his marriage to the Danish Princess Marie Dagmar in 1866.

7 Colonnade

Christian VII's royal architect, Caspar Harsdorff, built this Classical-style colonnade in 1794–5. Supported by eight ionic columns, it connects two palaces.

8 Christian IX's Palace

The first royal family to live here was Crown Prince Frederik VI and his wife (1794). Since 1967, it has been home to Queen Margrethe and Prince Consort Henrik.

6 Marmorkirken

Properly called Frederikskirken, the Marble Church (above) got its name on account of plans to build it with Norwegian marble. Its dome, one of the largest in Europe, has a diameter of 31 m (102 ft).

Map of Amalienborg and Frederiksstaden

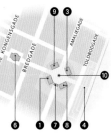

9 Christian VIII's Palace

This is where Crown Prince Frederik lived until his marriage to Australian Mary Donaldson. Part of the palace is open all year round as the Amalienborg Museum (above).

10 Equestrian Statue of Frederik V

Designed and cast (1753–71) by French sculptor Jacques Saly, this statue of Frederik V (right) is said to have cost four times as much as Amalienborg itself.

TOP 10 ⭐ SMK – National Gallery of Denmark

The National Gallery is housed in two buildings, one from the 19th century and the other a stylish, modern extension, linked by a bridge over Sculpture Street. The museum holds international and national paintings, sculptures, prints, drawings and installations from the 14th century to the present, with the national collection specializing in Golden Age and 19th-century paintings.

⑥ Christ as the Suffering Redeemer

This striking painting on the traditional pietà theme by prominent Renaissance artist Andrea Mantegna (1431–1506) shows the Resurrection of Christ on the third day after his crucifixion. Mantegna is known for his profound interest in ancient Roman civilization; in this painting it comes through in the porphyry sarcophagus.

① The Meeting of Joachim and Anne outside the Golden Gate of Jerusalem

Filippino Lippi (1457–1504) was a true Renaissance artist. This is evident in the architectural detail of the Corinthian columns and his paintings **(above)**.

② The Wheel of Life

Belonging to the *Suite of Seasons* series, this painting (1953) by Asger Jorn (1914–73) represents the month of January. Jorn, who was suffering from tuberculosis, was inspired to paint this in the hope of better health.

③ The X-Room

This space has changing installations by young international artists. The black box interior is transformed into multimedia worlds.

④ Please, Keep Quiet!

Visitors have to enter this installation by Elmgreen and Dragset (2003) through swing doors, which open to a hospital ward scene. This represents the neutrality of an exhibition space.

⑤ Sculpture Street

An impressive, varied collection of sculptures by international contemporary artists runs the length of the building under a glass roof.

⑦ Alice

One of over 300 portraits by Amedeo Modigliani (1884–1920) painted between 1915 and 1920, this beautiful painting, with simple, stylized features, reflects the artist's interest in African sculpture **(below)**.

8 Romantic Paintings

Per Kirkeby (1938–2018) was one of Denmark's most important artists. This early collage from 1965 uses clippings from popular magazines and comics as a homage to Pop Art.

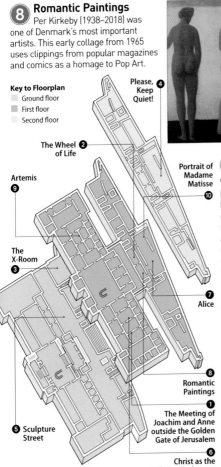

Key to Floorplan
- Ground floor
- First floor
- Second floor

Please, Keep Quiet! ❹

The Wheel ❷ of Life

Portrait of Madame Matisse ❿

Artemis ❾

The X-Room ❸

Alice ❼

Romantic Paintings ❽

❶

The Meeting of Joachim and Anne outside the Golden Gate of Jerusalem

❺ Sculpture Street

Christ as the Suffering Redeemer ❻

Museum Floorplan

9 Artemis

Created in 1893–4, Vilhelm Hammershøi's (1864–1916) painting **(above)** shows Artemis crowned with a crescent moon. The painting's Arcadian nudity, lack of depth, muted palate and enigmatic coolness are typical of Hammershøi's later work.

10 Portrait of Madame Matisse

Also known as *The Green Stripe*, this painting by Henri Matisse (1869–1954) of his wife was to have far-reaching reper-cussions in the art world. It was one of several paintings shown in the 1905 *Salon d'Automne* and helped give rise to the Fauvist movement, known for its bright colours and spontaneous style.

NEED TO KNOW

MAP D2 ■ Sølvgade 48–50 ■ www.smk.dk

Open 11am–5pm Tue–Sun (until 8pm Wed)

Adm 110 Dkr; under-30s 85 Dkr; under-18s free

Free guided tours available

■ The prints and drawings collection dates back to the 15th century.

■ The children's museum provides activities every weekend throughout the summer holidays.

■ The bright, stylish museum café looks out onto Østre Anlæg Lake. In good weather, the park is ideal for a picnic.

Museum Guide
Enter the museum from the corner of Sølvgade and Øster Voldgade. The lobby has temporary exhibitions and a bookshop. The entire ground floor is taken up by Sculpture Street, with 20th-century Danish and international art in the extension of the first and second floor. The old main building houses European art 1300–1800, Danish and Nordic art 1750–1900 and French art 1900–1930.

TOP 10 ⭐ Christiania

A world apart from the opulent splendour of Royal Copenhagen, this self-proclaimed "freetown" sits on the edge of one of the city's most expensive neighbourhoods. It has provided a safe haven for hippies, dreamers and nonconformists since the 1970s, when a band of ideological squatters moved into the abandoned army barracks with the aim of creating a self-sustaining community, free from the shackles of the state. Today, it's a bucolic, tumbledown wonderland of cosy cafés, bars, music venues, art galleries and shops.

Entrance to Christiania and Pusher Street

1 Den Grå Hal
With its graffitied entrance, this is the biggest music and cultural venue in the freetown of Christiania. The former stables doubles up as a unique bazaar during the Christmas period, selling everything – even locally carved instruments.

2 Badehuset
Dare to go bare at this back-to-basics nudist bathhouse; the cheapest and friendliest unisex sauna in the city. For under 50 Dkr, you can try a wonderful Moroccan *rasul* (a mineral cleanser).

3 Christiania Walking Tour
To really get a feel for the area, join one of the regular walking tours of Christiania and learn more about the fascinating history of the self-styled freetown from one of its residents. Tours depart regularly.

4 Nemoland
This former fruit and vegetable market is now one of Copenhagen's most vibrant bars, offering cheap booze and eats to be enjoyed on its terrace **(below)**. The outdoor stage hosts regular free music concerts in the summer.

5 ALIS Wonderland

What started life as a humble skate ramp has become one of the city's best skateparks. The vibrant graffiti murals **(above)** adorning the walls are now an attraction in themselves.

8 Café Månefiskeren

This cosy café with a laid-back vibe is the perfect spot to unwind or enjoy a game of bar billiards. There's regular free jazz and reggae concerts in the quaint cobblestone courtyard.

10 Loppen

This intimate live music venue **(below)** is a cornerstone of the city's alternative music scene. With gigs almost every night of the week, and a great programme that includes everything from Scandinavian punk to Danish dub-reggae, it's the ideal place to end your night out.

Map of Christiania

6 Morgenstedet

Tuck into hearty vegetarian fare at this cosy cottage-style restaurant set just off Christiania's main drag. It was originally established as a volunteer-run collective.

9 Christiania Smedie

Christiania's oldest business, this blacksmith started out producing furnaces in the early 1970s before switching its attention to building cargo bikes.

7 Galloperiet

Christiania's tongue-in-cheek tribute to the SMK – National Gallery of Denmark, this quirky gallery has a collection of wonderful arts and crafts.

TOP 10 ⭐ Slotsholmen

The small fishing village of Copenhagen was founded on the island of Slotsholmen in the 12th century. Bishop Absalon, the king's friend, built a castle here in 1167. Two centuries later, the castle was destroyed by the Hanseatic League, the European trade alliance, which resented Copenhagen's increasing control over trade. Christiansborg Slot, which stands here today, is home to the Danish Parliament, the Jewish Museum and the Palace Church.

① Christiansborg Tårnet

At 106 m (348 ft), the tower of Christiansborg Slot is the highest in Copenhagen and offers a magnificent panoramic view of the city. It is free to enter (closed Monday), but be sure to reserve in advance if you want to eat in the tower's upscale Nordic restaurant.

② Christiansborg Slotskirke

On the site of the original 18th-century church destroyed in the palace fire of 1794, this Neo-Classical church was built in 1813–26 (Slotsplads 9). However, a fire broke out in 1992 and destroyed its roof, dome and parts of the interior. The royal family still uses the chapel for baptisms and when royal family members lie in state.

③ Thorvaldsens Museum

 This museum is home to almost all of the works and some of the personal belongings of Danish sculptor Bertel Thorvaldsen. In the entrance hall (below) are the original plaster casts of his most famous pieces.

④ Danish War Museum

Built as an arsenal in 1604–8, the Royal Danish Arsenal Museum is filled with artillery guns. The Armoury Hall has 7,000 hand weapons, some from the 1300s.

⑤ Christiansborg Slot

Designed in Neo-Baroque style in 1907–28, this palace is where you will find the Folketinget (the Parliament), the Prime Minister's apartment, the High Court and the State Rooms (above) used for royal family functions – note the marble- and silk-adorned Throne Room and Great Hall.

⑥ Teatermuseet

This court theatre, above the Royal Stables, was established in 1767. Now a museum (Christiansborg 18), it depicts Danish theatre in the 18th and 19th centuries. Visitors can also walk onto the stage.

8 Dansk Jødisk Museum

This museum has a striking, modern interior **(left)**, designed by Polish-American architect Daniel Libeskind. The building depicts the lives and culture of the Jewish population staying in Denmark *(Proviantpassagen 6)*.

9 Ruins Under the Palace

These fascinating ruins were discovered during the construction of the present palace. Notable are parts of Bishop Absalon's castle, the second castle that stood here until the 18th century, and details of the routine of daily life.

7 Royal Stables

The stables of Christian VI's Palace survived the fire of 1794. The Queen's horses are still kept here amid splendid marble walls, columns and mangers. There is also a collection of royal coaches and riding gear.

CASTLE ISLAND

Several castles have stood on this island through the centuries. The first one was built in 1167 by Bishop Absalon. A second castle, used by King Erik of Pomerania, was built in 1416. When the building started to fall apart, it was pulled down and demolished in 1731 by Christian VI who, in its place, built a palace suitable for an Absolute Monarch. It was completed in 1740, but was destroyed in the fire of 1794. Another castle, built in 1803–28, burned down in 1884. The present castle was built in 1907–28.

10 Royal Library Gardens

With blossoming beds of flowers and large shadowy trees **(below)**, this garden is centred around a fountain, and there are plenty of benches to sit on and relax, as you look at the statue of philosopher Søren Kierkegaard.

NEED TO KNOW

MAP D4

Christiansborg Slot: 33 92 64 92; open May–Sep: 10am–5pm daily, Oct–Apr: 10am–5pm Tue–Sun; tours of State Rooms May–Sep: 3pm daily, Oct–Apr: 3pm Tue–Sun; adm 90 Dkr, under-18s free; www.christiansborg.dk

Ruins Under the Palace: open May–Sep: 10am–5pm daily, Oct–Apr: 10am–5pm Tue–Sun; adm 50 Dkr, under-18s free

Royal Stables: open May–Sep: 1:30–4pm daily, Oct–Apr: 1:30–4pm Tue–Sun; adm 50 Dkr, under-18s free

Royal Library Gardens: 6am–10pm daily

Christiansborg Slotskirke: open 10am–5pm daily

Danish War Museum: 33 11 60 37; open noon–4pm Tue–Sun

Thorvaldsens Museum: Bertel Thorvaldsens Plads 2; 33 32 15 32; open 10am–5pm Tue–Sun; adm 70 Dkr (free Wed), under-18s free; www.thorvaldsensmuseum.dk

⭐ Nationalmuseet

Denmark's largest museum, the National Museum presents the history and culture of the Danes from prehistoric times through to the present. It also houses a wonderful collection of Greek and Egyptian antiquities, an ethnographic collection and the Children's Museum. Many of the displays derive from King Frederik III's Royal Cabinet of Curiosities, put together around 1650.

NEED TO KNOW

MAP D4 ■ Ny Vestergade 10 ■ 33 13 44 11 ■ www.natmus.dk

Open Jul–Aug: 10am–5pm daily; Sep–Jun: 10am–5pm Tue–Sun

Free guided tours: Jul: 10:30am, noon, 1:30pm daily; Aug–Sep: 10:30am, noon, 1:30pm Sat & Sun; Oct–Dec: 10:30am, 1:30pm Sat & Sun

Victorian Home: Frederiksholms Kanal 18; open 11am–1pm (every hour) Sat & Sun (only via a guided tour, buy tickets at the museum); adm 50 Dkr, under-18s free

■ The Victorian Home, a plush apartment with beautiful, authentic 19th-century interiors, owned by the museum, is located nearby.

■ Have brunch or open sandwiches at the café.

Museum Guide
Fronted by a courtyard, the entrance hall has toilets, lockers and the museum shop, selling books and educational toys with a Viking twist. The Children's Museum is to your left. The ground floor has the prehistoric collection, while the first floor has a range of displays. There's a Danish history collection on the second floor, and the antiquities are on the third floor. Temporary exhibitions rotate regularly.

1 Room 117
This 18th-century bourgeois interior can be traced to the town of Aalborg in Jutland. A room in a sea of glass-display galleries, it features a heavy wooden four-poster bed **(above)**, chest, coffered wooden ceiling and mullioned windows.

2 Denmark's Oldest Coin
The name of Denmark and an image of a Danish king are depicted on this silver coin, displayed in Room 144, that was struck in AD 995.

5 Gundestrup Cauldron
Found near Gundestrup, this lovely silver cauldron from the Iron Age is decorated with animals and mystical figures.

3 Prehistoric Denmark and the Viking Age
The museum's most popular exhibit is this display of the country's 14,000-year history. These intricate golden horns **(right)** were reconstructed in the 20th century.

4 Cylinder Perspective Table
Part of Frederik III's Royal Cabinet of Curiosities, the table shows him and his wife painted ingeniously in a distorted perspective, rectified when viewed in the reflective cylinder.

Sun Chariot 6

The unique Sun Chariot or Solvognen **(right)** was dug up in 1902 by a farmer who was ploughing his field. This 3,400-year-old artifact from the Bronze Age shows a wheeled horse pulling a large sun disk gilded on one side.

Museum Floorplan

Key to Floorplan
- Ground floor
- First floor
- Second floor
- Third floor

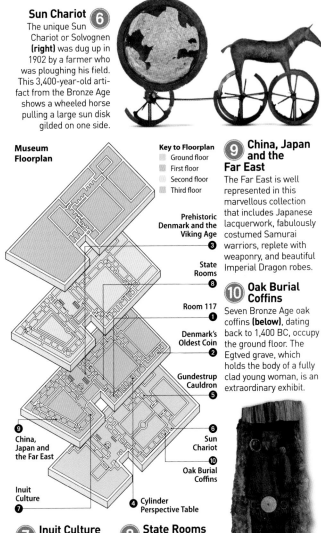

Prehistoric Denmark and the Viking Age
3

State Rooms
8

Room 117
1

Denmark's Oldest Coin
2

Gundestrup Cauldron
5

6
Sun Chariot

10
Oak Burial Coffins

9
China, Japan and the Far East

Inuit Culture
7

4 Cylinder Perspective Table

China, Japan and the Far East 9

The Far East is well represented in this marvellous collection that includes Japanese lacquerwork, fabulously costumed Samurai warriors, replete with weaponry, and beautiful Imperial Dragon robes.

Oak Burial Coffins 10

Seven Bronze Age oak coffins **(below)**, dating back to 1,400 BC, occupy the ground floor. The Egtved grave, which holds the body of a fully clad young woman, is an extraordinary exhibit.

Inuit Culture 7

This collection from Greenland showcases the skill and creative ingenuity of the people of the frozen North. The displays include clothing, such as embroidered anoraks and boots, plus toys and watercolours of daily life.

State Rooms 8

The State Rooms date back to the time when this building was a royal palace. They have been well preserved and are virtually intact from the period 1743–4. Next door, the Great Hall is adorned with original Flemish tapestries.

Top 10 Berlin

The grand auditorium of the Berlin
Staatsoper Unter den Linden

Exploring Berlin

For a sprawling, historic metropolis whose charms are widely scattered, Berlin is a surprisingly easy place to navigate. There's something for every interest and budget, and excellent public transport whisks you from sight to sight with clockwork efficiency. Here are a few ideas to maximize your fun and minimize your planning.

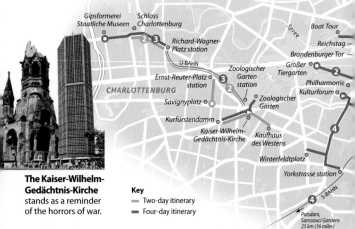

The Kaiser-Wilhelm-Gedächtnis-Kirche stands as a reminder of the horrors of war.

Key
- Two-day itinerary
- Four-day itinerary

Two Days in Berlin

Day ❶
MORNING
Begin at Alexanderplatz and ascend the Fernsehturm *(Panoramastraße 1A)* for an unequalled panorama of Berlin. View Babylonian treasures at the Pergamonmuseum *(Bodestraße 1-3)*.

AFTERNOON
Stroll along historic **Unter den Linden** *(see pp288–91)*. Admire the iconic **Brandenburger Tor** *(see pp284–5)* and take a guided tour of the **Reichstag** *(see pp286–7)* before enjoying a classical concert at the Philharmonie *(Herbert-von-Karajan-Str 1)*.

Day ❷
MORNING
Start with the ruins of the **Kaiser-Wilhelm-Gedächtnis-Kirche** *(see pp302–3)* before exploring stores along **Kurfürstendamm** *(see pp300–301)* and in Kaufhaus des Westens.

AFTERNOON
After lunch, wander through **Schloss Charlottenburg** *(see pp304–7)* and linger in its Baroque-style gardens. Seek out Savignyplatz for cocktails and an evening bite.

Four Days in Berlin

Day ❶
MORNING
Explore the **Reichstag** *(see pp286–7)*, then take a boat tour through Berlin's waterways. There are piers in the Großer Tiergarten next to the Haus der Kulturen der Welt *(John-Foster-Dulles-Allee 10)*.

AFTERNOON
Visit pretty Gendarmenmarkt and have lunch nearby. Promenade on **Unter den Linden** *(see pp288–91)* before admiring the **Brandenburger Tor** *(see pp284–5)*. Catch an evening show at the Friedrichstadt-Palast *(Friedrichstraße 107)*.

The Reichstag, one of Berlin's most symbolic buildings, is a popular sight.

The Neues Museum contains spectacular treasures, including the bust of Nefertiti.

Potsdamer Platz, untouched for nearly 50 years in rubble, has now been regenerated into a vibrant city hub.

Day ❷

MORNING

Take the lift up to the Fernsehturm (Panoramastraße 1A). Peruse the collections of **Museumsinsel** (see pp296–9), particularly the Neues Museum, home to the Nefertiti bust, and the Pergamonmuseum.

AFTERNOON

Head to **Potsdamer Platz** (see pp292–5) for architecture and the Marlene Dietrich exhibit at the Deutsche Kinamathek (Potsdamer Straße 2). Stroll in the Tiergarten.

Day ❸

MORNING

Start at the **Kaiser-Wilhelm-Gedächtnis-Kirche** (see pp302–3), then choose between the **Zoologischer Garten** (see pp312–3) or shopping on **Kurfürstendamm** (see pp300–301).

AFTERNOON

Marvel at Prussian riches at **Schloss Charlottenburg** (see pp304–7) and

wander its beautifully landscaped park. Stop by the Gipsformerei Staatliche Museen (Sophie-Charlotten-Straße 17–18) for gift sculptures.

Day ❹

MORNING

Start the day at the **Kulturforum** (see pp308–11). There are several cultural institutions to be explored in this complex, but a wise use of time is to view the Renaissance masters at the Gemäldegalerie. To enjoy some local specialities for lunch, stop by the last market hall in Berlin, the Marheineke-Markthalle (Marheinekeplatz 15), which is full of vibrant stores.

AFTERNOON

The splendid town of Potsdam and the stunning gardens in the palace complex of Sanssouci (Maulbeerallee) are a short trip away from the city by commuter train.

TOP 10 Berlin Highlights

Berlin is Germany's liveliest city and one of the most fascinating capitals in the world. You'll find no other place where art and culture, museums and theatres, entertainment and nightlife are more diverse and exciting than around the banks of the Spree River. Once reunited, Berlin quickly developed into a cosmopolitan city, and today there is an air of great energy and vibrancy about it.

1 Brandenburger Tor and Pariser Platz

The Brandenburger Tor is in Pariser Platz, where the embassies and the Hotel Adlon Kempinski exude stylish elegance *(see pp284–5)*.

2 Reichstag

No other building is a more potent symbol of Germany's history than the Reichstag. Its vast egg-shaped dome affords fantastic views across the city *(see pp286–7)*.

3 Unter den Linden

This leafy boulevard has always been a central axis along Berlin's most important historic buildings *(see pp288–91)*.

4 Potsdamer Platz

The new heart of the old city is Potsdamer Platz, where exciting modern structures have been erected *(see pp292–5)*.

Museumsinsel
⑤ Among the museums in this complex are the Pergamonmuseum, which houses the Pergamon Altar, the Altes and the Neues museums (see pp296–9).

Kurfürsten-damm ⑥

Berlin's much visited strolling and shopping avenue is the main thoroughfare in the western part of the city (see pp300–301).

Kaiser-Wilhelm-Gedächtnis-Kirche ⑦

The tower ruins of the memorial church, built to commemorate Kaiser Wilhelm I, still stand as a silent reminder of the horrors of war (see pp302–3).

Schloss Charlottenburg ⑧

The former Hohenzollern summer residence and its beautiful Baroque gardens offer visitors a slice of Prussian history (see pp304–7).

Kulturforum ⑨

This complex of museums, which includes the Gemäldegalerie, the Kunstgewerbemuseum and the Neue Nationalgalerie, yields a unique cultural experience (see pp308–11).

Zoologischer Garten ⑩

Germany's oldest and most famous zoo and aquarium, in the centre of the city, boasts over 19,000 animals and nearly 1,500 different species (see pp312–3).

TOP 10 ⭐ Brandenburger Tor and Pariser Platz

The best known of Berlin's symbols, the Brandenburg Gate stands proudly in the middle of Pariser Platz, asserting itself against the modern embassy buildings that now surround it. Crowned by its triumphant Quadriga sculpture, the famous gate has long been a focal point in Berlin's history: rulers and statesmen, military parades and demonstrations – all have felt compelled to march through the Brandenburger Tor.

Brandenburger Tor ①
Built by Carl G Langhans in 1789–91 and modelled on the temple porticoes of ancient Athens, the Brandenburg Gate **(right)** is the undisputed symbol of Berlin. Since the 19th century, this iconic landmark has been the backdrop for many events in the city's turbulent history.

② **Quadriga**
The 6-m (20-ft) high sculpture **(below)** was created in 1794 as a symbol of peace by Johann Gottfried Schadow. As the model for the goddess of peace, he used his niece, who subsequently became famous throughout Berlin.

③ **Hotel Adlon Kempinski Berlin**
Destroyed in World War II, the city's most elegant hotel **(below)** is a reconstruction of the original, which hosted celebrities such as Greta Garbo, Thomas Mann and Charlie Chaplin.

④ **DZ Bank**
This modern building, designed by the American architect Frank Owen Gehry, combines the clean lines of Prussian architecture with some daring elements inside.

⑤ **Akademie der Künste**
Built in 2000–2005 and designed by Günter Behnisch and Manfred Sabatke, the Academy of Arts incorporates, behind a vast expanse of windows, the ruins of the old art academy, which was destroyed in World War II.

⑥ **French Embassy**
Christian de Portzamparc built this elegant building in 2001 on the site of the old embassy, which was ruined in World War II. Its colonnades and windows are a homage to the original.

⑧ Palais am Pariser Platz

This complex by Bernhard Winking is a successful modern interpretation of Neo-Classical architecture. Inside you will find a café, a restaurant and a souvenir shop around a pleasantly shaded courtyard **(left)**.

NEED TO KNOW

MAP E3 ■ Pariser Platz

Visitor information:
Brandenburger Tor southern gatehouse; (030) 25 00 25; open Apr–Oct: 9:30am–7pm daily; Nov–Mar: 9:30am–6pm daily; www.visitberlin.de

DZ Bank: Pariser Platz 3; open 10am–6pm Mon–Fri

■ For a quick pit stop between sights, visit the Starbucks on Pariser Platz 4A.

■ You can trace the Wall along the former border patrol road, following the green-and-white Berliner Mauerweg signs. Sites of historic interest and natural beauty alternate along the trail.

⑩ Haus Liebermann

Josef P Kleihues built this in 1996–8, faithfully re-creating the original that stood on the same site. The house is named after the artist Max Liebermann, who lived here. In 1933, watching Nazi SA troops march through the gate, he famously said: "I cannot possibly eat as much, as I would like to puke."

⑦ American Embassy

The last gap around Pariser Platz was finally closed in 2008 **(above)**. A dispute had delayed building for years: the US wanted a whole street moved for reasons of security, but had to concede the point in the end.

⑨ Eugen-Gutmann-Haus

With its clean lines, the Dresdner Bank **(right)**, built in 1997 by gmp, recalls the style of the New Sobriety movement of the 1920s. In front of it is Pariser Platz's famous original street sign.

🔟 ⭐ Reichstag

Of all the buildings in Berlin, the Reichstag, seat of the Bundestag (parliament), is probably one of the most symbolic. The mighty structure, erected in 1884–94 by Paul Wallot as the proud manifestation of the power of the German Reich, was destroyed by arson in 1933 and bombed during World War II. In 1995, the artist Christo wrapped up the Reichstag and, in 1999, the British architect Lord Norman Foster transformed it into one of the most modern parliamentary buildings in the world.

The Dome
The Reichstag dome by Lord Norman Foster affords breathtaking views of Berlin. It is open at the top to air the building and – a symbolic touch – to allow for the free and open dissemination of debates throughout the country. A ramp winds its way up to the top **(right)**.

② Plenary Hall
The plenary hall **(above)** is the seat of the Deutscher Bundestag – the German parliament – which has convened here again since 20 April 1999. Technologically, the hall is one of the most advanced parliament buildings in the world. The federal eagle caused a row: considered too "fat", it had to be slimmed down.

THE REICHSTAG FIRE

When the Reichstag went up in flames on 27 February 1933, the Dutch communist van der Lubbe was arrested for arson. It is, however, likely that the Nazis started the fire themselves. Hitler used it as an excuse to get the "Enabling Act" passed, which let him dispose of his opponents and marked the start of a 12-year reign of terror.

③ Portico "Dem deutschen Volke"
The dedication "To the German People" was designed in 1916, against the will of Wilhelm II.

④ Restored Façade
Despite extensive renovations, small World War II bullet holes are still visible in the building's façade.

⑤ Restaurant Käfer
This popular luxury restaurant **(right)** on the Reichstag's roof offers an excellent view of the historical centre of Unter den Linden.

8 **The German Flag**
The giant German flag **(left)** was first raised on the occasion of the official national celebrations of German reunification on 3 October 1990.

9 **Weiße Kreuze Memorial**
Opposite the southern side of the Reichstag, a memorial recalls the Berlin Wall, which stood only a few steps away. The white crosses commemorate the people who died there while trying to escape to West Berlin.

10 **Memorial by Dieter Appelt**
Unveiled in 1992, the memorial **(below)** in front of the Reichstag commemorates 97 Social Democratic and Communist delegates who were murdered under the Third Reich.

6 **Platz der Republik**
Celebrations often take place on the lawn in front of the Reichstag, as in 2006, when Germany hosted the Football World Cup **(below)**.

7 **Installation "Der Bevölkerung"**
Hans Haacke's work of art "To the People" is a counterpoint to the portico inscription opposite and uses the same style of lettering.

NEED TO KNOW

MAP E3 ■ Platz der Republik 1
■ Dome: (030) 22 73 21 52; Käfer: (030) 22 62 99 33 ■ www.bundestag.de

Open Dome: 8am–midnight (last entry 10pm); Käfer: 9am–4:30pm & 6:30pm–midnight daily

To visit the Reichstag dome you must register at www.bundestag.de 2–3 days in advance. You can try for same-day admission at the Visitors' Service Centre (open Nov–Mar: 8am–6pm daily; Apr–Oct: 8am–8pm daily) next to the Berlin Pavilion on Scheidemannstraße. You will need your passport/identity card.

■ **If a meal at Käfer exceeds your budget, many stalls near the Reichstag sell tempting *Bratwurst* (sausages).**

🔟⭐ Unter den Linden

"As long as the lime trees still blossom in Unter den Linden, Berlin will always be Berlin," sang Marlene Dietrich about this magnificent avenue. The lime trees blossom more beautifully than ever and the street's old buildings have been extensively restored. The Linden, once a royal bridle path linking the king's town residence (the Stadtschloss) and Tiergarten, became Berlin's most fashionable street in the 18th century, and was synonymous with the city that was then the capital of Prussia.

Deutsches Historisches Museum ①
Germany's largest history museum **(right)** offers an overview of more than 1,000 years of German history. Housed in the Zeughaus, it is the oldest and architecturally the most interesting building [see p290] on Unter den Linden.

② Staatsoper Unter den Linden
The richly ornamented State Opera House **(above)** is one of Germany's most attractive. Neo-Classical in style, it was built by architect Georg Wenzeslaus von Knobelsdorff between 1741–3 as Europe's first free-standing opera house, to plans devised by Frederick the Great himself.

③ St Hedwigskathedrale
Designed by von Knobelsdorff in 1740–2 and modelled on the Pantheon in Rome, this **(below)** is the seat of Berlin's Catholic archdiocese. It was commissioned by Frederick the Great to appease Berlin Catholics after the conquest of Silesia.

④ Humboldt-Universität
Berlin's oldest and most highly regarded university **(above)** was founded in 1890, on the initiative of Wilhelm von Humboldt. Twenty-nine Nobel Prize winners were educated here, including Albert Einstein.

5 Neue Wache

The central German memorial **(above)** for all victims of war was created in 1816–8 by Karl Friedrich Schinkel. A reproduction of Käthe Kollwitz's moving *Pietà* stands here.

9 Kronprinzenpalais

Originally created in 1669 as a private residence by Johann Arnold Nering, the building was remodelled in 1732–3 into a Neo-Classical palace by Philip Gerlach and was a residence for several Hohenzollern heirs. After World War I it became an art museum, before the East German government housed state visitors there. The German reunification agreement was signed here in August 1990. It now holds cultural events and exhibitions.

10 Bebelplatz

Originally named Opernplatz, this wide open space was designed by Georg W von Knobelsdorff as the focal point of his Forum Fridericianum. The elegant square was meant to introduce some of the splendour and glory of ancient Rome to the Prussian capital. In May 1933, it became the scene of the infamous Nazi book burning.

6 Opernpalais

The charming building next to the Staatsoper, built in 1733–7, was also known as the Kronprinzessinnenpalais and once served as a palace for the daughters of Friedrich Wilhelm III.

7 Russische Botschaft

The gigantic Russian Embassy, built in Stalinist "wedding-cake style", was the first building to be erected on Unter den Linden after World War II.

8 Frederick the Great's Statue

One of Christian Daniel Rauch's grandest, this equestrian statue **(above)** shows "Old Fritz" (13.5 m/44 ft high) in his tricorn and coronation mantle.

NEED TO KNOW

Deutsches Historisches Museum: **MAP F3**; Zeughaus, Unter den Linden 2; (030) 20 30 40; open 10am–6pm daily; adm €8; free for under-18s; www.dhm.de

Staatsoper: **MAP E4**; Unter den Linden 7; (030) 20 35 45 55; www.staatsoper-berlin.de

St Hedwigskathedrale & Bebelplatz: **MAP E4**; Bebelplatz; open 10am–5pm Mon–Sat, 1–5pm Sun; www.hedwigs-kathedrale.de

■ Take a break at the Café im Deutschen Historischen Museum (in the Zeughaus), which can be accessed directly from the street.

Deutsches Historisches Museum

1 The Dying Warriors
The 22 reliefs by Andreas Schlüter (1664–1714), displayed on the walls of the courtyard rather than in one of the museum's exhibitions, portray the horrors of war in an unusually immediate way.

2 Europe and Asia
This group of 18th-century Meissen porcelain figures reflects the fascinating relationship between the two continents.

3 Steam Engine
A full-sized steam engine from the year 1847 marks the entrance to the exhibition on the Industrial Revolution.

4 Martin Luther
Luther's portrait, by Lucas Cranach the Elder (1472–1553), is the focal point of exhibition rooms devoted to the Reformation and Martin Luther himself.

Martin Luther **by Lucas Cranach**

5 Clothes from the Camps
Among the many exhibits here that illustrate the years under Nazi rule is the jacket of a concentration camp inmate – a chilling reminder of the Third Reich.

6 V2 Rocket
Exhibited in the section on Nazi Germany is a V2 rocket engine, displayed next to an 88-mm flak gun. The V2 missile was one of the *Wunderwaffen* ("wonder weapons") used by German troops at the end of World War II.

A Nazi Germany V2 rocket engine

7 Soldiers Plundering a House
This painting by Sebastian Vrancx (1573–1647), dating from around 1600, depicts a scene from the wars of religion that tore the Netherlands apart during the 16th century.

8 Saddle
A valuable saddle, dating from the middle of the 15th century, is decorated with elaborately carved plaques made of ivory.

9 The Berlin Wall
An original section of the Berlin Wall, together with the banners of a peaceful pro-unification demonstration in 1989, commemorates the fall of the Wall.

10 Gloria Victis
The moving allegorical figure of Gloria Victis, created by the French sculptor Antonin Mercié (1845–1916), bears witness to the death of his friend during the final days of the Franco-Prussian War of 1870–71.

ZEUGHAUS UNTER DEN LINDEN

Originally the royal arsenal, the Zeughaus was built in 1706 in the Baroque style according to plans by Johann Arnold Nering. It is an impressive structure, with the building surrounding a historical central courtyard that is protected by a modern glass cupola roof. Especially memorable are Baroque sculptor Andreas Schlüter's figures of 22 dying warriors, lined up along the arcades in the courtyard. They portray vividly the horrors of war. Behind the main building stands a cone-shaped glass annexe designed by the Chinese-born architect Ieoh Ming Pei in 2001 for special exhibitions and temporary shows. The permanent exhibition in the main historical building includes a collection entitled "Images and Testimonials of German History". Highlighting the most significant periods and events in the history of the country, the displays include a surprising variety of exhibits dating from the days of the early medieval German Empire up to 1994. Featured are the period of the Reformation, the Thirty Years' War, the wars of Liberation and the failed Revolution of 1848, and, of course, the two World Wars.

TOP 10
UNTER DEN LINDEN EVENTS

1 1573 Elector Johann Georg has a bridle path built, linking the royal Stadtschloss and the Tiergarten

2 1647 During the reign of the Great Elector, the road is planted with *Linden* (lime trees)

3 From 1740 Frederick the Great has grand buildings erected

4 1806 Napoleon and his troops march along Unter den Linden

5 1820 The road turns into a grand boulevard

6 1928 Unter den Linden and Friedrichstraße epitomize the world city

7 1933 Troops celebrate Hitler's victory

8 1945 The avenue is razed to the ground

9 1948–53 Revival of the boulevard

10 October 1989 Demonstrations lead to the fall of the East German regime

Entry of Napoleon into Berlin, 27 October 1806 (1810) by Charles Meynier shows the victorious French at the Brandenburg Gate, Unter den Linden.

TOP 10 ⭐ Potsdamer Platz

The heart of the new metropolis of Berlin beats on Potsdamer Platz. This square, where Berliners and tourists alike now flock to cinemas, restaurants and shops, was a hub of urban life in the 1920s. After World War II, it became a desolate wasteland, but since the fall of the Wall, Potsdamer Platz – for a while Europe's largest building site – has become a city within the city, surrounded by imposing edifices that began to appear in the 1990s, and are still being added to today.

Sony Center ①
The Sony Center **(right)** is the most ambitious, successful and architecturally interesting building in the new Berlin. The cupola structure, designed by Helmut Jahn, is the German headquarters of the Sony company, and with its cinemas and restaurants it is also a social magnet.

② Deutsche Kinemathek
This museum **(below)** takes visitors backstage at Babelsberg and Hollywood with Marlene Dietrich's costumes *(see p294)* and other exhibits.

Weinhaus Huth ④
The only building on Potsdamer Platz to have survived World War II, the restored Weinhaus **(right)** today accommodates restaurants and the excellent Daimler Contemporary, which showcases modern art.

③ Café Josty
Café Josty harkens back to its legendary predecessor, a regular haunt of artists and intellectuals in the 19th century. Today's Josty is partially housed in the historic Kaisersaal (Emperor's Hall) of the former Grand Hotel Esplanade.

⑤ Boulevard der Stars
Berlin's walk of fame features stars such as Marlene Dietrich, Werner Herzog, Fritz Lang, Hans Zimmer, Christoph Waltz, Diane Kruger and Romy Schneider **(left)**. The coloured asphalt evokes the red carpet.

Map of Potsdamer Platz

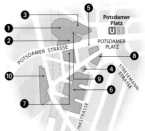

6 Potsdamer Platz Arkaden
The arcades **(above)** draw visitors with three floors hosting 130 shops, exclusive boutiques and restaurants. The lower ground floor is a food court serving a range of meals and snacks.

10 Spielbank Berlin
Berlin's casino invites visitors to *faites vos jeux*. Apart from roulette, Black Jack is also played, and an entire floor is given over to gambling machines.

NEED TO KNOW

MAP E4

Deutsche Kinemathek: Potsdamer Str. 2; (030) 300 90 30; open 10am–6pm Tue–Sun (to 8pm Thu); adm €8, family €16; www.deutsche-kinemathek.de

LEGOLAND® Discovery Centre: Potsdamer Str. 4; (030) 301 04 00; open 10am–7pm daily (last entry 5pm); adm €13; www.legoland discoverycentre.de

CinemaxX: Potsdamer Str. 5; (01805) 24 63 62 99

Sony Center: Potsdamer Platz; www.sonycenter.de/en/

Spielbank Berlin: **MAP F4**; Marlene-Dietrich-Platz 1; open 11–3am daily; adm €2.50; ID must; www.spielbank-berlin.de

■ Apart from visiting Café Josty, try the ice cream at Caffè e Gelato inside the Potsdamer Platz Arkaden.

7 CinemaxX
The CinemaxX **(below)**, with its 17 screens, is one of Berlin's largest cinemas. The bigger screens show current Hollywood blockbusters, while the three smallest are for low-budget art-house and German films.

8 Quartier Potsdamer Platz
Leading architects such as Hans Kollhoff and Renzo Piano designed these skyscrapers. One landmark is the terracotta and glass Atrium Tower.

9 LEGOLAND® Discovery Centre
This LEGO® wonderland *(Potsdamer Straße 4)* features brick models, a miniature Berlin, a train ride to a land of dragons and a DUPLO® Village with blocks for the tots.

Deutsche Kinemathek Exhibitions

Costumes of Marlene Dietrich

industry's victims: some film stars allowed themselves to be used for the Nazis' benefit, others refused to cooperate. The life and work of the actor Kurt Gerron, who was persecuted and murdered, is documented as an exemplary case.

1 Marlene Dietrich
This exhibition of the film star's estate includes her film costumes, her touring luggage, film clips, posters, photographs, letters and notes.

2 Metropolis
This iconic film, directed by Fritz Lang in 1927, has an alarming vision of a futuristic urban dystopian world as its subject. Models and props from the film are on display.

3 Caligari
The best known German film of the 1920s, *The Cabinet of Dr Caligari* (1920), was an influential masterpiece of Expressionist filmmaking by Robert Wiene.

4 Weimar Republic
The exhibits here are dedicated to the works of the legendary directors of German cinema's golden age from 1918 to 1933.

5 Olympia
This exhibition reveals the technical tricks used in the Nazi propaganda film *Olympia*, a staged documentary by Leni Riefenstahl made in 1936–8 after the Olympics.

6 National Socialism
This exhibition has documents relating to the use of film as propaganda, everyday cinema and the

7 Post-War Cinema
The story of films and filmmaking in East and West Germany is shown here with props and costumes of popular stars of post-war German cinema such as Hanna Schygulla, Romy Schneider, Heinz Rühmann and Mario Adorf.

8 Transatlantic
This exhibition of letters, documents, keepsakes and souvenirs retraces the careers of German film stars in Hollywood, both of the silent era and the "talkies" that followed after 1928.

Exhibits in the Transatlantic section

9 Pioneers and Divas
The infant days of cinema are featured here, as well as stars of the silent era such as Henny Porten and the Danish Asta Nielsen.

10 Exile
Documents in this exhibition relate to the difficulties encountered by German filmmakers when making a new start in the USA in 1933–45.

THE NEW CENTRE OF BERLIN

In the 1920s, Potsdamer Platz was Europe's busiest square, boasting the first automatic traffic lights in Berlin. During World War II this social hub was razed to the ground. Ignored for almost 50 years, the empty square shifted back into the centre of Berlin when the Wall came down. During the 1990s, it was Europe's largest building site. New skyscrapers were built, old structures were restored – some preserved rooms of the ruined historic Grand Hotel Esplanade were even physically moved into the Sony Center. Millions of people came to follow progress from the famous Red Info Box, which was removed in 2001. Altogether, around €17 billion was invested to create the present square.

Grand Hotel Esplanade remnants, Sony Center

Skyscrapers at dusk on Potsdamer Platz

TOP 10
POTSDAMER PLATZ ARCHITECTS

1 Helmut Jahn
Sony Center

2 Renzo Piano and Christian Kohlbecker
Atrium Tower, Spielbank Berlin, Musical-Theater, Spielbank, Weinhaus Huth

3 José Rafael Moneo
Hotel Grand Hyatt, Mercedes-Benz Headquarters

4 Hans Kollhoff
Daimler

5 Giorgio Grassi
Park Colonnades

6 Ulrike Lauber and Wolfram Wöhr
Grimm-Haus, CinemaxX

7 Sir Richard Rogers
Office Block Linkstraße

8 Steffen Lehmann and Arata Isozaki
Office and Retail House Linkstraße

9 Heidenreich & Michel
Weinhaus Huth

10 Bruno Doedens and Maike van Stiphout
Tilla-Durieux-Park

Museumsinsel

Formed by the two arms of the Spree River, the Museumsinsel is home to the world's most diverse museum complex. Built between 1830 and 1930, the museums, which hold the Prussian royal collections of art and archaeology, were turned into a public foundation in 1918. Heavily damaged in World War II, the complex was restored and declared a UNESCO World Heritage Site in 1999. Renovation work will go on until 2025 during which a path linking four museums will be created.

Bode-Museum

Located at the northern tip of Museumsinsel, the Bode-Museum is a stately structure dominated by a cupola **(right)**. The building holds the Sculpture Collection, the Museum of Byzantine Art and the Numismatic Collection, made up of a diverse collection of over 500,000 objects.

2 Pergamonmuseum

Built in 1909–30, this is one of the world's most important museums *(see p298)* of ancient art and architecture, with a vast collection of antiquities. The huge Ishtar gate **(above)** dates from the 6th century BC.

3 Neues Museum

Spectacularly revamped by British architect David Chipperfield, the building itself is as fascinating as its exhibits. As well as the Museum of Pre- and Early History, the Ägyptisches Museum is also housed here.

MISSING TREASURES

During World War II, many of the island's exhibits were hidden in underground bunkers. Some pieces of "Priam's Gold", excavated from the site of ancient Troy, were taken by the Red Army as war booty and remain in Moscow. The Neues Museum points out where there are gaps in the collection.

4 Ägyptisches Museum

Housed within the Neues Museum, this museum *(Bodestraße 1)* features portraits of Egyptian royals and monumental architecture.

5 Alte Nationalgalerie

First opened in 1876, the Old National Gallery was beautifully restored in the 1990s **(right)** and now holds 19th-century sculptures and paintings *(Bodestraße 1–3)*, with works by Schadow and Max Liebermann.

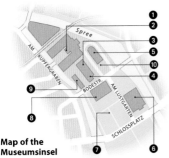

Map of the Museumsinsel

7 Altes Museum

The first building to be completed on Museumsinsel in 1830, the Altes Museum *(Am Lustgarten)* resembles a Greek temple. Originally meant to hold paintings, it now houses the collection of Classical antiquities **(right)**.

8 James Simon Gallery

Named in honour of James Simon (1851–1932), a patron of the Berlin State Museums, this will open in 2019 as the central entrance and visitor centre.

9 Colonnade Courtyard

This columned courtyard between the Neues Museum and the Alte Nationalgalerie frames and connects the museums and provides an atmospheric venue for open-air concerts.

10 Lustgarten

This "pleasure park", with a fountain in its centre, is located in front of the Altes Museum *(Am Lustgarten)*. The lawns are popular with tired visitors.

6 Berliner Dom

The island's most overwhelming structure *(Am Lustgarten 1)*, this Baroque-style cathedral **(above)** is unusually ornate for a Protestant church. Organ concerts and services can be enjoyed in this exquisitely restored church.

NEED TO KNOW

MAP F3 ▪ (030) 266 424 242 ▪ www.smb.museum

Open 10am–6pm daily, until 8pm Thu (most museums); sections of the Pergamonmuseum may be closed due to a phased remodelling until 2025

Adm €10–12 per museum; Museumsinsel day pass €18; 3-day Berlin Museum Pass €29; extra fee for some exhibitions; free for under-18s

▪ Some of the museums have cafés, but the café at the Altes Museum is convenient as it is a little closer than the others to Karl-Liebknecht-Straße, the island's main road.

▪ It's best to set aside a whole day for the extraordinary collections of the Museumsinsel. There are several parks nearby in which you can take breaks. Sundays can be very busy with long queues and large groups.

Pergamonmuseum

Detail, frieze from Darius's palace

5 Pergamon Altar

The Pergamon Altar from the eponymous Greek city (in modern Turkey) dates from 160 BC and is the largest and most significant treasure in the collections of the Berlin museums. Closed until 2023, it can be viewed in 3D in a building nearby.

6 Giant Sculpture of a Bird of Prey

The nearly 2-m- (7-ft-) high Riesensonnenvogel (huge sun bird) was discovered during excavations in Tell Halaf, Syria, the centre of the ancient Aramaic city-state of Guzana.

1 Frieze from the Palace of Darius

A frieze dating to around 510 BC from the palace of Darius in Susa (Iran) is made of exquisitely coloured glazed brick and depicts a row of Persian warriors holding lances and carrying bows and quivers.

2 Ishtar Gate

The Ishtar Gate, built under the reign of Nebuchadnezar II in the 6th century BC in Babylon, and the Processional Way are fully preserved. Original faïence tiles depict the sacred lions.

3 Market Gate of Miletus

This vast gate (AD 100) is over 16 m (52 ft) high. To the right of the entrance, a hairdresser has carved an advertisement for his shop into the stone.

4 Assyrian Palace Room

The reconstructed room of the Assyrian kings' palace (9th century BC) boasts impressive door figures and 13th-century BC wall paintings.

7 Aleppo Room

Taken from a Christian merchant's house in Syria and dating from the early 17th century, this small room features magnificent wooden cladding and is a beautiful example of Ottoman architecture.

8 Mosaic of Orpheus

This delightful mosaic floor, depicting Orpheus playing his lyre amid animals enchanted by his skill, comes from the dining room of a private home in Asia Minor (AD 200).

9 The Mshatta Façade

A gift from Ottoman Sultan Abdul Hamid II to Kaiser Wilhelm II, this stone façade elaborately carved with arabesque and animal forms was the south face of a desert fort built in AD 744 in Mshatta, Jordan.

Market Gate of Miletus

10 Victory Stele of Esarhaddon

This monumental stele, excavated in 1888 in Zincirli, commemorates Esarhaddon's victory over Pharaoh Taharqa (671 BC).

SAVING THE MUSEUMSINSEL

Visitors at the spectacular Neues Museum

The island of museums is a treasury of antique architecture, but until recently it had been slowly decaying. Since 1992, however, €1.8 billion has been spent on the renovation and modernization of Museumsinsel. A master plan created by renowned architects that include David Chipperfield and O M Ungers will transform the complex into a unique museum landscape – just as it was first conceived in the 19th century by Friedrich Wilhelm IV, when he established the "free institution for art and the sciences". Once completed, an "architectural promenade" will serve as a conceptual and structural link between various individual museums, except the old National Gallery. This promenade will consist of a variety of rooms, courtyards and vaults, as well as exhibition halls. The core of the complex will be a new central entrance building. The museums are gradually reopening after extensive individual renovations – the Pergamonmuseum is scheduled to be completed by 2025.

TOP 10 MUSEUMSINSEL EVENTS

1 1810 Plan for a public art collection created

2 1830 The Altes Museum, Prussia's first public museum, opens

3 1859 Completion of the Neues Museum

4 1876 Opening of the Alte Nationalgalerie

5 1904 Completion of the Kaiser-Friedrich-Museum (Bode-Museum)

6 1930 Opening of the Pergamonmuseum

7 1943 Bombs destroy most of the museums

8 1958 Most museums reopen after renovation

9 1999 Museumsinsel declared a UNESCO World Heritage Site

10 2009 The Neues Museum reopens

The Altes Museum with the green Lustgarten in front

🔟 ⭐ Kurfürstendamm

After years of decline, the Kurfürstendamm, or Ku'damm for short, has once again become a fashionable hot spot. Breathtaking architecture, elegant boutiques and a lively street artist scene around Breitscheidplatz have made this shopping boulevard one of Berlin's most attractive and – at 3.8 km (2.5 miles) – also its longest avenue for strolling.

① Breitscheidplatz
Here, in the heart of the western city, artists, Berliners and visitors swarm around J Schmettan's globe fountain, known by locals as "Wasserklops" (water meatball).

② Kaiser-Wilhelm-Gedächtnis-Kirche
While the church itself was destroyed during World War II, the church tower *(see pp302–3)* stands in the centre of the square **(left)**, serving as both memorial and stark reminder of the terrors of war.

③ Europa-Center
The oldest shopping centre **(below)** in West Berlin, opened in 1962, is still worth a visit. Here you will find fashion boutiques, a comedy theatre and an official Berlin Tourist Info centre.

⑤ Bikini Berlin
The Bikini-Haus building **(above)**, built in 1956, was renovated to house the splendid Bikini Berlin, an ultra-hip boutique mall that also offers great views of the nearby zoo.

④ Neues Kranzler Eck
This glass and steel skyscraper was built in 2000 by architect Helmut Jahn. The legendary Café Kranzler was retained as a bar in front of the office block. There is an official Berlin Tourist Info centre here.

> **WHEN KU'DAMM WAS NO MORE THAN A LOG ROAD**
>
> In 1542, today's magnificent boulevard was just a humble "Knüppeldamm", or log road. It served the Electors as a bridle path, linking their town residence (Stadtschloss) and their hunting lodge (Jagdschloss). It was not until 1871 that the area around the Ku'damm developed into a fashionable "new west end". Chancellor Otto von Bismarck had the boulevard modelled on the Champs Elysées in Paris, lined with houses, shops, hotels and restaurants.

7 Lehniner Platz

The square is home to the Schaubühne theatre **(left)**, built as Universum cinema in 1928 by Erich Mendelsohn and converted in 1978.

8 Fasanenstraße

A small street off Ku'damm, Fasanenstraße **(below)**, with its galleries, expensive shops and restaurants, is one of Charlottenburg's most elegant areas.

9 Traffic Turret

On the corner of Joachimstaler Straße stands an old-fashioned traffic turret or *Verkehrskanzel*, the last one in the city and now a heritage monument. A policeman sat in the raised glass cabin to control traffic lights manually from 1955 until 1962, when the signals went automatic.

6 Iduna-Haus

The turreted building at No. 59 at the Leibnitzstraße corner is one of the few surviving bourgeois houses from the late 19th century. The ornamented Jugendstil (Art Nouveau) façade **(below)** has been lavishly restored. The building is home to a number of banks.

10 RT&W Galerie

The Neo-Classical building housing this art gallery gives visitors a glimpse of Ku'damm's erstwhile splendour.

NEED TO KNOW

Europa-Center:
MAP C4; Tauentzienstr. 9; (030) 348 00 80; open 24 hours (shops and Berlin Tourist Info: 10am–8pm Mon–Sat); www.24EC.de

Bikini Berlin: **MAP C4**; Budapester Str. 38–50; open 10am–8pm Mon–Sat, noon–6pm Sun; www.bikiniberlin.de

■ Few original cafés in the Kurfürstendamm area have survived. The most charming of these is the Café Wintergarten, located in the Literaturhaus on Fasanenstraße .

■ Avoid Ku'damm on Saturday mornings when it is teeming with locals and tourists out on shopping trips.

TOP10 ⭐ Kaiser-Wilhelm-Gedächtnis-Kirche

This ruined Neo-Romanesque church is one of Berlin's most haunting symbols. It was consecrated in 1895 and named Kaiser Wilhelm Memorial Church in honour of Wilhelm I. Following severe damage by the 1943 bombing raids, the ruins of the tower were left standing as a memorial. Egon Eiermann built a new church next to it in 1957–63.

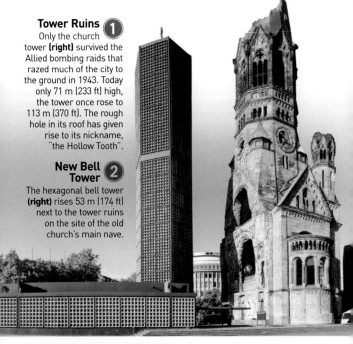

Tower Ruins ①
Only the church tower (**right**) survived the Allied bombing raids that razed much of the city to the ground in 1943. Today only 71 m (233 ft) high, the tower once rose to 113 m (370 ft). The rough hole in its roof has given rise to its nickname, "the Hollow Tooth".

New Bell Tower ②
The hexagonal bell tower (**right**) rises 53 m (174 ft) next to the tower ruins on the site of the old church's main nave.

A CHURCH WITH TWO LIVES
The Kaiser-Wilhelm-Gedächtnis-Kirche has the Berliners to thank for its preservation: in 1947, the Senate had planned to demolish the tower ruins for safety reasons. In a referendum only about 10 years later, however, one in two Berliners voted for its preservation. And so the idea came about to build a new church next to the ruin and to preserve the vestibule of the old church as a striking memorial hall to the horrors of war.

③ Kaiser's Mosaic
One of the preserved mosaics shows Heinrich I on his throne, with imperial orb and sceptre (**right**). Originally decorated with scenes from German imperial history, the interior was meant to place the Hohenzollerns within that tradition.

8 Coventry Crucifix

This small crucifix was forged from old nails that were found in the ruins of Coventry Cathedral in England. It commemorates the bombing of Coventry by the German Luftwaffe in 1940.

Tower Clock 9

The tower clock is based on a Classical design, with Roman numerals. At night, it is lit blue by modern light-emitting diodes to match the lighting inside the new church.

4 Main Altar

The golden figure of Christ (above) created by Karl Hemmeter is suspended above the main altar in the modern church. In the evening light, the windows behind the altar glow an overwhelming dark blue.

10 Russian Orthodox Cross

This gift from the bishops of Volokolomsk and Yuruyev was given in memory of the victims of Nazism.

NEED TO KNOW

MAP C4 ■ Breitscheidplatz ■ (030) 218 50 23 ■ www.gedaechtniskirche-berlin.de

Open Church: 9am–7pm daily; memorial hall: 10am–6pm Mon–Sat, noon–6pm Sun; services 10am and 6pm Sun

Free guided tours at 12:15pm, 1:15pm, 2:15pm & 3:15pm daily and 10:15am & 11:15am Mon, Fri & Sat (donations welcome); group tours in English available for a small fee

■ Visit the new church on a sunny day around lunchtime, when the blue glass window is at its most impressive.

■ There are fantastic views of the church from the Mövenpick Café in the Europa-Center opposite.

5 Mosaic of the Hohenzollerns

The vividly coloured mosaic (above) of the Hohenzollerns adorns the vestibule of the church ruins. It depicts Emperor Wilhelm I together with Queen Luise of Prussia and her entourage.

Original Mosaics 6

Glittering mosaics (right) in Jugendstil style showing Prussian dukes and princes are preserved on the walls and ceilings along the stairways.

7 Figure of Christ

Miraculously, the vast, plain sculpture of Christ, which is suspended from the ceiling, survived the bombing of the church.

TOP10 ⭐ Schloss Charlottenburg

The construction of Schloss Charlottenburg, designed as a summer residence for Sophie Charlotte, wife of the Elector Friedrich III, began in 1695. The Orangerie was extended and a cupola was added by Johann Friedrich Eosander between 1701 and 1713. Subsequent extensions were undertaken by Frederick the Great, who added the Neuer Flügel between 1740 and 1746.

1 Altes Schloss
The Baroque tower of the oldest part of the palace (dating to 1695) by Johann Arnold Nering is crowned by Richard Scheibe's golden statue of Fortuna **(above)**.

2 Porzellankabinett
This small, exquisite mirrored gallery **(below)** has been faithfully restored to its original glory. Among the exhibits on display are valuable porcelain items from China and Japan.

3 Schlosskapelle
The luxurious splendour of the palace chapel recalls the once magnificent interior design of the palace, before it was destroyed in World War II. However, apart from the original altar, the entire chapel – including the king's box – is a costly reconstruction.

4 Monument to the Great Elector

The equestrian statue of the Great Elector Friedrich Wilhelm **(right)** is thought to be one of his most dignified portraits. Made by Schlüter in 1696–1703, it stood on the Rathausbrücke originally, near the destroyed Stadtschloss.

⑤ Neuer Flügel
Built between 1740 and 1747 by Georg W von Knobelsdorff, the new wing contains Frederick the Great's private quarters, as well as a large collection of 18th-century French paintings.

⑦ Schlosspark
The palace has a lovely Baroque garden, beyond which lies a vast park, redesigned by Peter Joseph Lenné in 1818–1828 in the English style with rivers, artificial lakes and small follies.

⑧ Belvedere
Friedrich Wilhelm II liked to escape to the romantic Belvedere **(below)**, a summer residence built in 1788 by Carl Gotthard Langhans, which served as a tea pavilion. Today it houses a collection of precious Berlin porcelain objects.

Map of Schloss Charlottenburg

⑨ Neuer Pavillon
This Italianate villa, designed by Schinkel for Friedrich Wilhelm III in 1825, was inspired by the Villa Reale del Chiatamone in Naples and clearly shows the Hohenzollerns' love of the Italian style.

⑩ Mausoleum
Slightly hidden, this Neo-Classical building **(below)** by Schinkel is the final resting place of many of the Hohenzollerns.

⑥ Museum Berggruen
Situated in the Western Stüler Building opposite the Charlottenburg palace, this modern art gallery houses the permanent exhibition "Picasso and his Time", featuring more than 100 works that span the artist's career. Other highlights of the collection include works by Matisse, Klee and Giacometti.

NEED TO KNOW

MAP A3 ■ Spandauer Damm ■ (030) 32 09 10 ■ Adm ■ www.spsg.de

Altes Schloss: open Apr–Oct: 10am–6pm Tue–Sun (Nov–Mar: until 5pm)

Neuer Flügel: open Apr–Oct: 10am–6pm Wed–Mon (Nov–Mar: until 5pm)

Belvedere: open Apr–Oct: 10am–6pm Tue–Sun

Neuer Pavillon: open Jan–Mar: 10am–5pm Tue–Sun (Apr–Oct: until 6pm; Nov–Dec: noon–4pm Tue–Sun)

Mausoleum: open Apr–Oct: 10am–6pm Tue–Sun

Museum Berggruen: Schlossstr. 1; open 10am–6pm Tue–Sun; www.smb.museum

■ The Orangery Café has an attractive garden.

■ Try a romantic midweek evening stroll to avoid the crowds *(park: 6am–dusk)*.

Schloss Charlottenburg Rooms

Goldene Galerie in the Neuer Flügel

 Goldene Galerie
The festival salon in the Neuer Flügel, 42 m (138 ft) long, was designed in Rococo style by Frederick the Great's favourite architect von Knobelsdorff. The richly ornamented room has a cheerful appearance.

2 Eichengalerie
The wooden panelling of the Oak Gallery is carved with expensively gilded portraits of Hohenzollern ancestors.

3 Gris-de-Lin-Kammer
This small chamber in Friedrich's second palace apartment is decorated with paintings, including some by his favourite artist, Antoine Watteau. The room was named after its wall coverings in violet-coloured damask (*gris-de-lin* in French).

4 Schlafzimmer der Königin Luise
Queen Luise's bedchamber, designed in 1810 by Karl Friedrich Schinkel, features the clear lines typical of the Neo-Classical style. The walls are clad in silk fabrics and wallpaper.

5 Winterkammern
Friedrich Wilhelm II's early Neo-Classical rooms contain fine paintings, tapestries and furniture.

6 Bibliothek
Frederick the Great's small library has outstanding elegant bookcases and a vibrant, light green colour scheme.

7 Konzertkammer
Furniture and gilded panelling in the concert hall have been faithfully re-created as during Frederick the Great's time. Antoine Watteau's (1684–1721) *Gersaint's Shop Sign*, considered to be one of his most significant works, hangs here; the king bought the work directly from the artist.

8 Grünes Zimmer
The green room in Queen Elisabeth's quarters is an excellent example of royal chambers furnished in 19th-century Biedermeier style.

Queen Elisabeth's Grünes Zimmer

9 Rote Kammer
The elegant chamber, decorated entirely in red and gold, is adorned by portraits of King Friedrich I and Sophie Charlotte.

10 Friedrich I's Audienzkammer
The ceiling paintings and Belgian tapestries depict allegorical figures symbolizing the fine arts and the sciences. There are also magnificent lacquered cabinets, modelled on Asian originals.

THE HOHENZOLLERNS AND BERLIN

Friedrich Wilhelm, the Great Elector

In 1412, Burggraf Friedrich of the Hohenzollern dynasty of Nuremberg was asked by Sigismund of Luxemburg to support him in the princely feuding before the imperial election for the throne. When Sigismund became king, he gave Friedrich, in 1415, the titles of Margrave and Prince-Elector of Brandenburg as a reward for his services – this is where the histories of the Hohenzollerns and Berlin first became entwined, a relationship that was to last for 500 years. From the start, the family tried to limit the powers of the town and of the Brandenburg nobility. Culture, however, flourished under the new rulers, especially the Great Elector 200 years later, who invited 20,000 Huguenot craftsmen to Berlin and founded an art gallery and several schools. His grandson Friedrich Wilhelm I, father of Frederick the Great, transformed the city into a military camp, with garrisons and parade grounds, and scoured the town for tall men to join his bodyguard. In the 19th century, however, relations between Berlin and the Hohenzollerns became decidedly less cordial.

**TOP 10
HOHENZOLLERN
RULERS**

1 **Friedrich Wilhelm** the Great Elector (1620–88)

2 **Friedrich I** (1657–1713)

3 **Friedrich Wilhelm I** (1688–1740)

4 **Friedrich II** the Great (1712–86)

5 **Friedrich Wilhelm II** (1744–97)

6 **Friedrich Wilhelm III** (1770–1840)

7 **Friedrich Wilhelm IV** (1795–1861)

8 **Wilhelm I** (1797–1888)

9 **Friedrich III** (1831–88)

10 **Wilhelm II** (1859–1941)

The Great Elector Receiving Huguenot Refugees, **18th-century etching by Daniel Chodowiecki**

TOP 10 ⭐ Kulturforum

The Kulturforum is a unique complex of museums, concert halls and libraries west of Potsdamer Platz. Here, some of the most outstanding European art museums, as well as the famous concert hall of the Berlin Philharmonic Orchestra, attract millions of visitors interested in culture and music. The complex, based in the former West Berlin, has been growing steadily since 1956 as a counterpoint to the Museumsinsel in the former East Berlin. The Kulturforum also contains some of Berlin's best examples of modern architecture.

Gemäldegalerie
Berlin's largest art museum **(right)** holds masterpieces of European art. They are displayed in the modern Neubau, built in 1998 by Heinz Hilmer and Christoph Sattler. The collection includes Bosch, Holbein, Dürer, Gossaert, Vermeer, Brueghel the Elder, Titian, Caravaggio and Rembrandt.

② Neue Nationalgalerie
Based in a building **(above)** by Mies van der Rohe *(Potsdamer Straße 50)*, this holds 20th-century art, with an emphasis on German Expressionism. Highlights are on show elsewhere during the renovation.

③ Philharmonie
This tent-like building **(right)** was the first new structure *(Herbert-von-Karajan-Str 1)* to be built in the Kulturforum in 1960–3. Considered one of the best concert halls in the world, it is the home of the Berlin Philharmonic Orchestra. Kirill Petrenko will conduct in 2019.

④ Kunstgewerbe-museum
Craft objects **(left)** from across Europe from the Middle Ages to the present day are on show at this museum *(Matthäikirchplatz)*, including valuable items like the Guelphs' treasure, Lüneburg's silver and Renaissance faïence.

5 Musikinstrumenten-museum

Concealed behind the Philharmonie is this fascinating little museum of musical instruments. More than 800 exhibits are on show here, particularly early instruments such as harpsichords **(right)** and a 1929 Wurlitzer.

NEED TO KNOW

MAP D4 ■ West of Potsdamer Platz ■ (030) 266 424 242 ■ www. smb.museum

Gemäldegalerie: Matthäikirchplatz 4/6; open 10am–6pm Tue–Sun (until 8pm Thu)

Philharmonie: Herbert-von-Karajan-Str. 1; (030) 25 48 80; Box Office: open 3–6pm Mon–Fri, 11am–2pm Sat & Sun; www.berliner-philharmoniker.de

Kupferstichkabinett: Matthäikirchplatz 8; open 10am–6pm Tue–Sun

Kunstbibliothek: Matthäikirchplatz 6; open 10am–6pm Tue–Sun

St Matthäuskirche: Matthäikirchplatz 1; (030) 262 12 02; open 11am–6pm Tue–Sun; organ concert 12:30pm; adm for concerts; www.stiftung-stmatthaeus.de

Neue Nationalgalerie: MAP D4; www.smb.museum

A day pass for all museums is €16

■ The Kulturforum restaurant and café is a convenient spot for coffee.

Map of the Kulturforum

6 Kammermusiksaal

The smaller relative of the larger Philharmonie, this concert hall is one of Germany's most highly regarded chamber music venues.

7 Kupferstichkabinett

The Gallery of Prints and Drawings holds more than 550,000 prints and 110,000 drawings from all periods and countries, including a portrait of Dürer's mother.

8 St Matthäuskirche

This church **(right)** is the only historical building pre-served in the Kulturforum. Built in 1844–6 by Stüler, it is also a venue for art installations and classical music concerts.

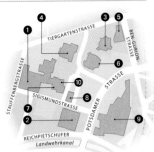

9 Staatsbibliothek

Built in 1978 by Hans Scharoun, the National Library *(Potsdamer Straße 33)* is one of the world's largest German-language libraries, with five million books and journals.

10 Kunstbibliothek

The Art Library has a collection of advertising and art posters, among other items, and also hosts art and architecture exhibitions and design shows.

Gemäldegalerie

1 Portrait of Hieronymus Holzschuher

Albrecht Dürer painted this portrait of the mayor of Nuremberg in 1529.

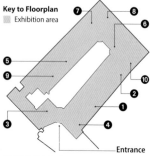

Gallery Floorplan

Holbein's *Portrait of Georg Gisze*

2 Portrait of the Merchant Georg Gisze

This 1532 painting by Hans Holbein, showing the Hanseatic League merchant Georg Gisze counting his money, reflects the rise of the rich citizen during the Renaissance.

3 Madonna with Child and Singing Angels

A 1477 painting by Sandro Botticelli, this depicts the Madonna and Child, surrounded by angels carrying lilies.

4 The Birth of Christ

Martin Schongauer's (1445/50–91) altar painting (c.1480) is one of only a few religious paintings by the Alsatian artist that have been preserved.

5 Victorious Eros

Caravaggio's 1602 painting follows Virgil's model and shows

Eros, the god of love, trampling underfoot the symbols of culture, glory, science and power.

6 Portrait of Hendrickje Stoffels

In a 1656–7 portrait of his lover Hendrickje Stoffels, Rembrandt's focus is entirely on the subject.

7 The French Comedy

This painting by Antoine Watteau (1684–1721) belonged to the collection of Frederick the Great.

8 The Glass of Wine

A skilfully composed scene, Vermeer's *The Glass of Wine* (1658–61) shows a couple drinking wine.

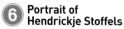

Detail, Botticelli's *Madonna with Child*

9 Venus and the Organ Player

Painted by Titian in (1550–52), this piece reflects the playful sensuality typical of the Italian Renaissance.

10 Dutch Proverbs

Pieter Brueghel the Elder (1525–69) beautifully incorporated and literalized more than 100 proverbs into this 1559 painting.

ARCHITECTURE IN THE KULTURFORUM

The tent-like roof of the Berlin Philharmonie

The Kulturforum was planned to fill the area between Potsdamer Straße and Leipziger Platz that had been destroyed during the war. The idea for a varied townscape of museums and parks is credited to Berlin architect Hans Scharoun, who had designed plans for this between 1946 and 1957. It was also Scharoun who, with the building of the Philharmonie in 1963, set the character of the Kulturforum: the tent-like, golden roofs of the music hall, the Kammermusiksaal and the national library, designed by him and – after his death – realized by his pupil Edgar Wisniewski, are today among Berlin's top landmarks. All the buildings are characterized by the generous proportions of their rooms and, although controversial when they were built, are today considered classics of modern architecture.

TOP 10
KULTURFORUM ARCHITECTS

1 Hans Scharoun
Philharmonie

2 Mies van der Rohe
Neue Nationalgalerie

3 James Stirling
Wissenschaftszentrum

4 Heinz Hilmer
Gemäldegalerie

5 Christoph Sattler
Gemäldegalerie

6 Friedrich August Stüler St Matthäuskirche

7 Edgar Wisniewski
Kammermusiksaal

8 Rolf Gutbrod
Kunstgewerbemuseum

9 August Busse altes Wissenschaftszentrum

10 Bruno Doedens
Henriette-Herz-Park

The auditorium of the Berlin Philharmonie

TOP 10 ⭐ Zoologischer Garten

Berlin's Zoological Garden in the Tiergarten district is the oldest zoo in Germany and, with nearly 1,500 different species, one of the best-stocked in the world. Animals have been kept and bred here since 1844. Today, the zoo hosts about 19,500 animals, ranging from jellyfish to Indian elephants. Many, such as the polar bears and baby gorillas, have become celebrities, and with numerous other fascinating enclosures to explore, a zoo trip is a favourite day out for Berliners and visitors alike.

1 Penguin House
Playful Antarctic king and rockhopper penguins inhabit this cool haven, complete with realistic cliffs, illuminated "heavens" and a giant skylight. Happier in warmer climes, Humboldt **(left)** and African penguins swim and waddle outside.

2 Monkey House
Monkeys and apes are at home in this house, and here you can watch gorillas, orangutans and chimpanzees playing and swinging from tree to tree. The Eastern Lowland Gorillas are very popular.

3 Polar Bear Feeding
The 10:30am public feeding of the polar bears attracts big crowds. Check all the animal feeding times online or at the entrance on arrival.

4 Giraffe House
The 1872 North African-style Giraffe House **(below)** is the oldest enclosure. Visitors enjoy watching as the giraffes nibble the leaves of a tree or slowly bend down to drink.

5 Nocturnal Animal House
Located in the Predatory Animal House, this shelters the creatures of the night, including reptiles and birds. Here you can admire striped bandicoots, fruit bats and slender loris **(above)**. Asleep during the day, they have superb hearing and eyes that light up eerily in the dark.

⑥ Elephant House

These huge, good-natured pachyderms have a healthy appetite: Indian elephants **(left)** devour up to 50 kg (110 lb) of hay a day. Since 1998, 16 elephants have been born here.

Aviaries ⑦

Nowhere else in the city can you hear such singing, tweeting and whistling – cockatiels, parrots, hornbills and herons **(right)** sound off in the Bird House.

⑧ Hippo House

Glass domes arch over an aquatic habitat **(left)** at one of the world's most remarkable modern zoo enclosures. An underwater viewing area lets you admire the hippos as they swim with seemingly weightless balletic grace. The animals also have access to an outdoor pool.

⑨ Aquarium

The greatest draw in the aquarium, where fantastic Caribbean and Amazonian habitats have been re-created, are the green morays and blacktip reef sharks, as well as a jellyfish cylinder allowing 360-degree views of the shimmering aquatic beauties.

⑩ Amphibians' Section

Poisonous snakes, bird spiders and reptiles as well as other amphibians crawl and slither around behind glass **(below)** on the second floor of the aquarium. A particularly spectacular event is the feeding of the spiders.

NEED TO KNOW

MAP C4 ▪ Hardenbergplatz 8 and Budapester Str. 34 ▪ (030) 25 40 10 ▪ www.zoo-berlin.de

Open mid-Mar–Sep: 9am–7pm daily (winter: until 5pm daily)

Adm €15.50; €21 combined entry for zoo and aquarium

▪ There is a café and self-service restaurant with a terrace inside the zoo, to the right of the Elephant Gate.

▪ A day at the zoo is not complete without a visit to the aquarium. The basins and terraria teem with life, as do the zoo enclosures.

Top 10 Berlin sights
see pp282–313

Top 10 Restaurants

1. **Alpenstück**
   Hearty German fare

2. **Bocca di Bacco**
   Italian

3. **Zum Paddenwirt**
   Traditional local cuisine

4. **Facil**
   Michelin-starred dining

5. **Refugium**
   International and German

6. **Café Einstein**
   Traditional Viennese café

7. **Café Wintergarten**
   Atmospheric café

8. **Lutter & Wegner**
   German and Austrian

9. **Reinhard's**
   International dishes

10. **Marjellchen**
    Prussian

Top 10 Prague

Historic buildings in Prague's Old Town Square

Exploring Prague

There is a wealth of things to see and do in Prague. Whether you're here just for the weekend or have the luxury of a couple of extra days, these two- and four-day itineraries will help you to plan your time and make the most of your visit.

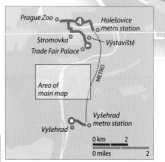

Charles Bridge links the Old Town and Malá Strana quarters of Prague.

Two Days in Prague

Day ❶
MORNING
Marvel at the **Old Town Square** (see pp328–31), taking in the Astronomical Clock. Ramble through the tiny lanes towards **Charles Bridge** (see pp332–3).
AFTERNOON
Meander through Malá Strana, pausing at St Nicholas Church (Malostranské náměstí). Hike up Nerudova – note the house signs – to **Prague Castle** (see pp322–5), where you can tour the Old Royal Palace and **St Vitus Cathedral** (see pp326–7).

Day ❷
MORNING
Begin at Josefov and the Jewish Museum (U Staré školy 141/1). Don't miss the **Old Jewish Cemetery** (see pp336–9). **The Convent of St Agnes** (see pp342–3) nearby houses the National Gallery's medieval art.
AFTERNOON
Take in **Wenceslas Square** (see pp344–5), the heart of the New Town. Admire the National

Astronomical Clock

Museum (Václavské náměstí 68) before walking down Národní towards the river to the National Theatre (Národní 2).

Four Days in Prague

Day ❶
MORNING
Visit the Powder Gate and Municipal House (náměstí Republiky 5) before making your way to the **Old Town Square** (see pp328–31). Then stroll to **Charles Bridge** (see pp332–3).
AFTERNOON
Wander through Malá Strana via Nerudova to **Prague Castle** (see pp322–5) and its Old Royal Palace, **St Vitus Cathedral** (see pp326–7) and Golden Lane.

Day ❷
MORNING
Spend time at the Jewish Museum (U Staré školy 141/1), focusing on the

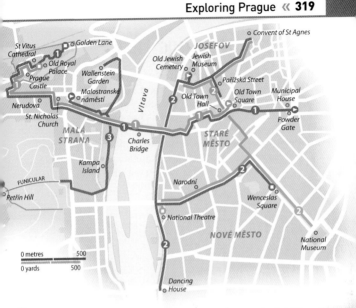

Key
— Two-day itinerary
— Four-day itinerary

The Wallenstein Garden is free for the public to enter, and hosts various cultural events during the summer.

Old Jewish Cemetery (see pp336–9). Explore exclusive Pařížská street then stop by the **Convent of St Agnes** (see pp342–3).

AFTERNOON
Head to the river and walk south along it to the National Theatre (Národní 2) and the Dancing House (Jiráskovo nám. 1981/6). Then take stately Narodní to **Wenceslas Square** (see pp344–5).

Day ❸
MORNING
Start at Malostranské náměstí. Amble through Malá Strana's green spaces, such as Kampa Island and Wallenstein Garden (Letenská). Make for **Petřín Hill** (see pp346–7) and ride the funicular up.

AFTERNOON
From Petřín, head to Strahov Monastery (Strahovské nádvoří 1/132) and to The Loreto (see pp334–5). Be sure to stroll down tranquil Nový Svět.

Day ❹
MORNING
View the National Gallery's modern and contemporary art at the **Trade Fair Palace** (see pp340–341). Then check out Výstaviště and nearby Stromovka. From here you can walk to Prague Zoo (U Trojského zámku 3/120).

AFTERNOON
Explore Vyšehrad, the city's spiritual home. Be sure to visit the Slavín Monument, Casemates and Sts Peter and Paul Cathedral.

TOP **10** Prague Highlights

At the heart of Europe, Prague's beautiful cityscape – from the Gothic exuberance of its castle and cathedral to the dignity of the medieval Jewish Cemetery and the 19th-century opulence of the "new" town – has been created and sustained by emperors, artists and religious communities. Under Communist rule, Prague was off the tourist map, but since 1989 the Czech capital has seen a surge of visitors eager to take in this spectacular city.

1 Prague Castle

Visitors can spend a day exploring this hilltop fortress of the Přemyslids, now home to the Czech president *(see pp322–5)*.

St Vitus Cathedral 2

The glory of the castle complex, St Vitus took nearly 600 years to build. Don't miss the exquisite stained glass and delightful gargoyles *(see pp326–7)*.

3 Old Town Square

The city has few finer charms than watching the moon rise over the Old Town Square between the towers of the Church of Our Lady before Týn *(see pp328–31)*.

The Loreto 5

Pilgrims have visited this Baroque shrine to the Virgin Mary since the 17th century. Visitors can admire the priceless ornaments held in its treasury *(see pp334–5)*.

Charles Bridge 4

The huge crowds can make it hard to appreciate the beautiful statues on this bridge that links the city's two halves, but a visit is a must when in Prague *(see pp332–3)*.

6 Old Jewish Cemetery

This jumble of tombstones in the former Jewish ghetto gives little indication of the number of people buried here (see pp336–9).

7 Trade Fair Palace

One of Europe's first Functionalist buildings, the Trade Fair Palace now houses the National Gallery's collection of modern art (see pp340–41).

8 Convent of St Agnes

The oldest Gothic building in the city is now home to the National Gallery's collection of medieval art (see pp342–3).

9 Wenceslas Square

From a humble horse market, the square has grown into a modern hub, with monuments recalling its role in the nation's history (see pp344–5).

10 Petřín Hill

Perched above Malá Strana, the hill is crisscrossed with footpaths offering some of the city's best views. The Ukrainian church is wonderfully romantic (see pp346–7).

TOP 10 ⭐ Prague Castle

Crowned by St Vitus Cathedral, Prague Castle *(Pražský hrad)* is the metaphorical and historical throne of the Czech lands. Around AD 880, Prince Bořivoj built a wooden fortress on this hilltop above the river, establishing it as the dynastic base of the Přemyslids. In the 14th century the castle became the seat of the Holy Roman Empire. Much of it was rebuilt by Empress Maria Theresa in the latter half of the 18th century, giving it a formal Neo-Classical look. Today the castle is the official residence of the Czech president.

1 Old Royal Palace
While Prince Bořivoj made do with a wooden structure, subsequent residences were built on top of each other as the tastes of Bohemia's rulers changed. Halls are decorated with coats of arms **(above)**.

2 South Gardens
Emperor Ferdinand I and his son Maximilian II gave the castle some greenery in the late 16th century, and First Republic architect Josip Plečnik created the lined paths, steps and grottoes that extend to Malá Strana.

3 White Tower
The castle's White Tower was once used as a prison and torture chamber. Today, shops here sell grisly souvenirs. The gangways from which archers once watched over the moat are lined with replicas of weapons.

4 Lobkowicz Palace
The only privately owned building **(below)** in the castle complex, this rival to the National Gallery holds works by Bruegel, Canaletto, Dürer, Rubens and Velázquez in its collection.

Prague Castle and the Vltava

5 St George's Convent
Prince Boleslav II, with Princess Mlada, established the first Czech convent for Benedictine nuns here in AD 973. The Romanesque building is not open to the public.

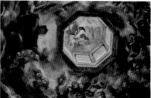

6 St George's Basilica
Prince Vratislav built the basilica around AD 920. The 13th-century chapel of St Ludmila, St Wenceslas's grandmother, is decorated with beautiful 16th-century paintings **(above)**.

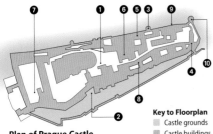

Plan of Prague Castle

Key to Floorplan
- Castle grounds
- Castle buildings

CASTLE GUIDE

Most of the grounds are free to enter, but tickets to see the interiors are sold at the information centres in the second and third courtyards. The shorter circuit takes in Golden Lane, the Old Royal Palace, St George's Basilica, St Vitus's and Daliborka Tower; the longer tour circuit adds the Powder Tower and the Rosenberg Palace. Tickets for other castle areas are also available.

8 Rosenberg Palace

This 16th-century palace has had multiple uses during its history: as an 18th-century residence for noblewomen, as part of the Ministry of Internal Affairs of Czechoslovakia and as modern presidential offices.

9 Golden Lane

In order to avoid paying guild dues in town, goldsmiths lived in these colourful little houses **(below)** that were built into the castle walls.

7 Chapel of the Holy Cross

Built by the Italian architect Anselmo Lurago in 1763, this chapel **(left)** houses the Treasure of St Vitus, which includes the sword of St Wenceslas.

10 Daliborka Tower

When captured, Dalibor, a Czech Robin Hood figure, became the first prisoner of the tower that now takes his name.

NEED TO KNOW

MAP B3 ■ Hradčany
■ 224 372423, 224 372434
■ Adm (various combination tickets available; check on the castle website) ■ www.hrad.cz

Old Royal Palace, Golden Lane, St George's Basilica, Rosenberg Palace, Powder Tower, Daliborka Tower & Picture Gallery: open Apr–Oct: 9am–5pm daily; Nov–Mar: 9am–4pm daily

Chapel of the Holy Cross, Great South Tower: open Apr–Oct: 10am–6pm daily (Nov–Mar: until 5pm)

Lobkowicz Palace: open 10am–6pm daily; www.lobkowicz.cz

Grounds: open 6am–10pm daily

■ The change of guard ceremony takes place on the hour and at noon in the first courtyard.

Old Royal Palace Features

Vaulted ceiling of the Vladislav Hall

1 Vladislav Hall
Here, Benedikt Rejt created a mastery of Gothic design with the elaborate vaulting. It has been used for coronations and jousting tournaments, and, since the First Republic, the country's presidents have been ceremoniously sworn in here.

2 Louis Wing
Only ten years and a few steps separate the southern wing from the main hall, but in that brief space, Rejt moved castle architecture from Gothic to Renaissance. Bohemian nobles met here in an administrative body when the king was away.

3 Bohemian Chancellery
In 1618 Protestant noblemen threw two Catholic governors and their secretary from the east window, sparking off the Thirty Years' War. Their fall was broken by a dung heap – or an intervening angel, depending on who you ask.

4 Old Land Rolls Room
The coats of arms on the walls belong to clerks who tracked property ownership and court decisions from 1614 to 1777. Until Maria Theresa, records were unnumbered, identified only by elaborate covers.

5 Diet
Bohemian nobles met the king here in a prototype parliament. The king sat on the throne (the one seen today is a 19th-century replica), the archbishop sat on his right, while the estates sat on his left. The portraits on the wall show, from the left, Maria Theresa, her husband Franz, Josef II, Leopold II and Franz I, who fought Napoleon at Austerlitz.

6 Chapel of All Saints
A door leads from Vladislav Hall to a balcony above the Chapel of All Saints, modelled by Petr Parléř on Paris's Gothic Sainte-Chapelle. After fire destroyed it in 1541, it was redesigned in Renaissance style. Of particular artistic note is Hans van Aachen's *Triptych of the Angels*.

7 Soběslav Residence
Prince Soběslav built the first stone palace in the 12th century.

8 The Story of Prague Castle
This informative and entertaining exhibition covers the history, events, personalities and arts and crafts relating to the main castle complex.

9 Busts from Petr Parléř's Workshop
These impressive effigies, created in the late 14th century, include the grandfather-father-grandson set of John of Luxembourg, Charles IV and Wenceslas IV.

10 Riders' Staircase
The low steps and vaulted ceiling of this stairway permitted mounted knights to make grand entrances to the spectacular jousting tournaments held in Vladislav Hall.

The rib-vaulted Rider's Staircase

PRAGUE'S DEFENESTRATIONS

Prague's first recorded instance of execution by hurling the condemned people from a window occurred at the outset of the Hussite Wars in 1419. Vladislav II's officials met a similar fate in 1483. Perhaps as a tribute to their forebears, more than 100 Protestant nobles stormed the Old Royal Palace in 1618 and cast two hated Catholic governors and their secretary out of the window. Protestants said the men's fall was broken by a dung heap swept from the Vladislav Hall after a recent tournament, while Catholics claimed they were saved by angels. The incident is often cited as the spark that began the Thirty Years' War (1618–48). After the defeat of the Protestants by the army of the Holy Roman Emperor Ferdinand II at the first skirmish at White Mountain, 27 of these nobles were executed in the Old Town Square *(see pp328–31)*.

**TOP 10
RULERS OF PRAGUE**

1 **Wenceslas** (around 907–935)

2 **Ottokar II** (1233–78)

3 **Charles IV** (1316–78)

4 **Wenceslas IV** (1361–1419)

5 **Rudolf II** (1552–1612)

6 **Tomáš Garrigue Masaryk** (1850–1937)

7 **Edvard Beneš** (1884–1948)

8 **Gustáv Husák** (1913–1991)

9 **Václav Havel** (1936–2011)

10 **Václav Klaus** (b.1941)

The Battle of White Mountain (Bílá Hora) in 1620 played a role in the Counter-Reformation and the re-Catholization of the Czech lands.

The Defenestration of Prague, 23 May 1618 **(1889)** by Václav Brožík depicts the Protestants' attack on the Catholic governors. Painted 271 years after the event, it illustrates how the event remained in the Czech consciousness.

TOP 10 ⭐ St Vitus Cathedral

The spectacular Gothic *Katedrála svatého Víta* is an unmissable sight in Prague, not least because of its dominant position on Hradčany hill, looming over the Vltava and the rest of the city. Prince Wenceslas first built a rotunda here on a pagan worship site and dedicated it to St Vitus *(svatý Vít)*, a Roman saint. Matthew d'Arras began work on the grand cathedral in 1344 when Prague was named an archbishopric. He died shortly thereafter and Charles IV hired the Swabian wunderkind Petr Parléř to take over. With the intervention of the Hussite Wars, however, work stopped and, remarkably, construction was only finally completed in 1929.

1 Great South Tower

The point at which the Hussite Wars halted construction of this 96-m (315-ft) tower is clear. When work resumed, architectural style had moved into the Renaissance, hence the rounded cap on a Gothic base **(left)**.

2 Royal Crypt

The greatest kings of Bohemia are buried in a single room beneath the cathedral, including Charles IV, Wenceslas IV and Rudolf II.

Cathedral Floorplan

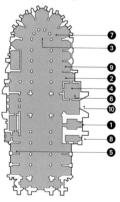

3 High Altar

Bounded by St Vitus Chapel and the marble sarcophagi of Ferdinand I and family, the high altar and chancel follow a strict Neo-Gothic philosophy **(above)**.

4 Wenceslas Chapel

This stands on the site of the first rotunda and contains St Wenceslas's tomb. The frescoes of Christ's Passion on the lower wall are surrounded by 1,300 semi-precious stones. To celebrate his son Ludvik's coronation, Vladislav II commissioned the upper frescoes of St Wenceslas's life **(right)**.

5 New Archbishop's Chapel

Czech artist Alfons Mucha (1860–1939) created the Art Nouveau window of the Slavic saints for the chapel **(left)**. Despite appearances, the glass is painted, not stained.

6 Bohemian Crown Jewels

You'd think there would be a safer place for the crown and sceptre of Bohemia, but the coronation chamber of Wenceslas Chapel is said to be guarded by the spirit of the saint.

PETR PARLÉŘ

After the death of Matthew d'Arras, Charles IV made the Swabian Petr Parléř his chief architect. Parléř undertook work on St Vitus Cathedral, Charles Bridge and numerous other Gothic monuments that still stand in Prague. He trained numerous artisans, and his talented sons and nephews continued his work after his death in 1399.

8 Sigismund

One of four Renaissance bells in the Great South Tower, the 18-tonne bell affectionately known as Sigismund is the nation's largest and dates from 1549. It takes four volunteers to ring the bell on important church holidays and at events.

9 Royal Oratory

The royals crossed a narrow bridge from the Old Royal Palace (see p322) to this private gallery for Mass. The coats of arms represent all the countries ruled by Vladislav II.

7 The Tomb of St John of Nepomuk

The silver for this 1,680-kg (3,700-lb) coffin came from the Bohemian mining town Kutná Hora, signified by the miners' statues to the left of the tomb.

10 Golden Portal

This triple-arched arcade **(above)** was the main entrance to the cathedral until the western end was completed in the 20th century.

NEED TO KNOW

MAP B3 ■ Third Courtyard, Prague Castle ■ 224 372423/34 (castle information centres) ■ Adm (only combined tickets with the castle available; buy at the information centres in the castle courtyards) ■ www.katedralasvate hovita.cz

Cathedral: open 9am–5pm Mon–Sat, noon–5pm Sun (Nov–Mar: to 4pm)

Great South Tower: open 10am–6pm daily (Nov–Mar: to 5pm)

■ The entrance (western) areas of St Vitus Cathedral can be visited for free – you'll see about a quarter of the building. Admission is charged for other areas.

■ The Royal Crypt may be entered with a guide, and you can see the basilica.

TOP 10 ★ Old Town Square

As the heart and soul of the city, no visitor should, or is likely to, miss the Old Town Square *(Staroměstské náměstí)*. There was a marketplace here in the 11th century, but it was in 1338, when John of Luxembourg gave Prague's burghers permission to form a town council, that the Old Town Hall was built and the square came into its own. Today, it has a lively atmosphere, with café tables set out in front of painted façades, hawkers selling their wares and horse-drawn carriages waiting to ferry tourists around.

1 Dům u Minuty

The "House at the Minute" **(below)** probably takes its name from the not-so-minute *sgraffito* images on its walls. The alchemical symbols adorning Staroměstské náměstí 2 date from 1610. Writer Franz Kafka lived in the black-and-white house as a boy, from 1889 to 1896.

2 House at the Stone Bell

Formerly done up in Baroque style, workers discovered the Gothic façade of this house as late as 1980. On the southwestern corner is the bell which gives the house its name. The Municipal Gallery often hosts temporary exhibitions here.

3 Church of Our Lady before Týn

This Gothic edifice **(below)** began as a humble church serving residents in the mercantile town *(týn)* in the 14th century. Following architectural customs of the time, the south tower is stouter than the north one; they are said to depict Adam and Eve.

Prague's beautiful Old Town Square

4 St Nicholas Cathedral

Prague has two Baroque churches of St Nicholas, both built by Kilian Ignac Dientzenhofer. The architect completed the one, called the cathedral now, in Old Town **(above)** two years before starting Malá Strana's. Regular concerts here are worth a visit.

Jan Hus Memorial 5

Hus was burned at the stake in 1415 for proposing radical Church reform. The inscription below the figure of Hus **(right)** at the 1915 memorial reads "Truth Will Prevail".

JAN HUS

The rector of Prague (later Charles) University, Jan Hus was dedicated to fighting against corruption in the Church. He was declared a heretic by the Church, and was summoned to Germany where he was burned at the stake. Czech resentment turned into civil war, with Hussite rebels facing the power of Rome. But the Hussites split into moderate and radical factions, the former defeating the latter in 1434. Hus is still a national figure – 6 July, the day he was killed, is a public holiday.

7 Ungelt

The courtyard behind Týn church was home to foreign merchants in the 14th century, but today it houses smart boutiques and cafés.

8 Štorch House

At Staroměstské náměstí 16 **(left)**, the focal points are Art Nouveau paintings of St Wenceslas (the patron saint of Bohemia) and the three Magi.

6 Marian Column

On Czechoslovakia's declaration of independence in 1918, this former column reminded jubilant mobs of Habsburg rule and they tore it down. A plan is afoot to rebuild it.

9 Kinský Palace

This ornate Rococo palace now houses the National Gallery's temporary exhibitions. It was once home to the haberdashery owned by Franz Kafka's father, Hermann.

Malé náměstí 10

The ornate wrought-iron well in the centre of the "Small Square" doubles as a plague memorial. The elaborate murals of craftsmen on the façade of Rott House **(right)** were designed by Mikoláš Aleš. From the 19th century to the early 1990s, the building was an ironmongery.

NEED TO KNOW

MAP E4 ■ Old Town

Old Town Hall: Staroměstské náměstí 1; 236 002629; Halls & Cellars: open 9am–7pm daily (from 11am Mon); Tower: open 9am–10pm daily (from 11am Mon); Adm (combined, family and reduced tickets available); www.staromestskaradnicepraha.cz

■ Climbing on the Jan Hus Memorial or trampling the flowers could earn you a fine as well as embarrassment.

Old Town Hall Features

1 Astronomical Clock

During the day, bells ring, cocks crow and 15th-century statues dance on the hour while crowds of tourists watch from below.

Apostles in the Astronomical Clock

2 Apostles

Marionette artist Vojtěch Sucharda carved the 12 wooden figures that emerge from the clock every hour – they replaced the ones destroyed by German artillery in 1945.

3 Art Gallery

On the Old Town Hall's ground floor is an exhibition space which features temporary shows.

4 Dukla Memorial

Behind a brass plaque marked with the year 1944 is a pot of soil from the Dukla battlefield. German artillery gunned down 84,000 Red Army soldiers in this Slovak pass in one of the most grievous military miscalculations of World War II.

Dukla Memorial

5 White Mountain Memorial

In the pavement on the town hall's eastern side are set 27 crosses in memory of the Bohemian nobles who were executed for their role in the Thirty Years' War. After the Battle of White Mountain, the men were publicly hanged, beheaded or drawn and quartered here.

6 Gothic Chapel

The small chapel adjoining the Mayors' Hall was consecrated in 1381 in honour of Sts Wenceslas, Vitus and Ludmila. Wenceslas IV's emblem and his wife Eufemia's initial adorn the entrance portal. In the nave is a model of the Marian column *(see p329)* which stood on the square until 1918 and may be rebuilt.

7 Lift

The striking lift to the viewing gallery of the tower won a design award in 1999. Oddly enough, its space-age design works harmoniously with the stony surroundings. It also permits wheelchair access to the top of the tower – a rare consideration in Prague.

8 Viewing Gallery

The parapet under the Old Town Hall's roof affords visitors a unique view of the square and the Old Town below. A little pocket change will buy you two minutes on a miniature telescope, with which you can admire the Prague Valley.

9 Gothic Cellars

The cellars of the Old Town Hall were once ground-floor rooms. The town was subject to flooding, so more earth was added to keep the burghers' feet dry. The spaces were used as granaries as well as debtors' prisons.

10 The Green

Retreating German artillery unloaded their guns on the Old Town Hall's north wing to avoid carrying the shells back to Berlin. After the war, the wing was torn down. Now the area is lined with stalls selling Czech handicrafts.

BUILDING THE OLD TOWN HALL

Prague's Old Town received its charter and fortifications from John of Luxembourg in 1338, but its town clerk had to wait nearly 150 years for an office. The Old Town Hall was cobbled together from existing houses over the centuries until it comprised the five houses that stand at Staroměstské náměstí 1–2 today. The town hall's eastern wing once stretched to within a few feet of St Nicholas Cathedral *(see p328)*, but in 1945 German artillery bombardment reduced it to rubble. The 69.5-m (228-ft) tower was built in 1364, and in 1410 the imperial clockmaker Mikuláš of Kadaň created the basic mechanism of the Prague Orloj, or Astronomical Clock. In 1552 Jan Táborský was put in charge, and by 1566 the clock was fully mechanized.

TOP 10
FEATURES OF THE ASTRONOMICAL CLOCK

1 Solar clock
2 Lunar clock
3 Josef Mánes Calendar
4 Apostles
5 Angel and the Sciences
6 Vanity, Avarice, Death and Lust
7 Rooster
8 Hourly shows
9 Mikuláš of Kadaň
10 Dial

The Astronomical Clock not only tells the time, but also displays the movement of the sun and moon through the signs of the zodiac, and of the planets around the earth. The calendar plate below the clock has paintings by 19th-century Czech artist Josef Mánes.

TOP 10 ⭐ Charles Bridge

The spectacular Charles Bridge *(Karlův most)* has witnessed processions, battles, executions and, increasingly, film shoots since its construction between 1357 and 1402. Architect Petr Parléř built it in Gothic style to replace its predecessor, the Judith Bridge. The bridge's most distinguishing feature is its gallery of 30 statues. The religious figures were installed from 1683 onwards to lead people back to the Church. Some, such as Bohn's Calvary, are politically controversial; others, such as Braun's St Luitgard, are incomparably lovely. Today all the statues are copies, with the originals preserved in museums across the city.

1 Old Town Bridge Tower

From the parapet of the Old Town bridge tower, you can see the gentle S-curve that Petr Parléř *(see p327)* built into the bridge to obstruct invaders, as well as a jaw-dropping panorama of the city.

Charles Bridge and the Old Town bridge tower

2 Calvary

This statue will cause double takes among students of Hebrew. According to a nearby apologia, the words "Holy, holy, holy is the Lord of Hosts" were added in 1696, paid for by a local Jewish man who had been accused of profaning the Cross.

3 The Lorraine Cross

Midway across the bridge is a brass cross (below) where John of Nepomuk's body was thrown into the river. It is said that wishes made at the cross will come true.

4 Statue of St John of Nepomuk

At the base of the statue of St John (right) is a brass relief showing a man diving into the river. Rubbing it to attract good luck is an old local tradition; petting the adjacent brass dog is a new one.

5 Statue of Sts Cyril and Methodius

Greek missionaries who brought both Christianity and the Cyrillic alphabet to the Czech and Slovak lands, Cyril and Methodius are revered figures in both countries to this day. Karel Dvořák created this statue in 1928–1938 at the peak of Czechoslovakia's National Awakening following independence.

6 Statue of Bruncvik

Peer over the bridge's southern edge to see the Czech answer to King Arthur. Bruncvik **(left)**, a mythical Bohemian knight, is said to have had a magical sword and helped a lion fight a seven-headed dragon. He and his army are promised to awaken and save Prague at the city's most desperate hour.

7 Our Lady of the Mangles

The portrait of Mary hanging on the house south of the bridge is tied to an ancient tale of miraculous healing. Seeing the light go out on the balcony below is supposedly an omen of imminent death – don't stare too long.

8 Statue of St Luitgard

Matthias Braun's 1710 depiction of a blind Cistercian nun's celebrated vision, in which Christ appeared to her and permitted her to touch his wounds, has a timeless appeal **(right)**.

NEED TO KNOW

MAP C4 ■ en.muzeum prahy.cz/prague-towers

Malá Strana bridge tower: 607 050434

Old Town bridge tower: 724 379677

Open Apr–Sep: 10am–10pm; Nov–Feb: 10am–6pm; Mar & Oct: 10am–8pm (both towers)

Adm (both towers)

■ The Malá Strana bridge tower houses an exhibit on the bridge's history. The Old Town bridge tower has an exhibit on Charles IV and the bridge.

WHEN TO VISIT CHARLES BRIDGE

During summer, and increasingly year-round, the bridge is well nigh impassable throughout the day, crowded with artists, tourists and the odd Dixieland jazz band. It is best seen in the early hours as the sun rises over the Old Town bridge tower. A late evening stroll gives a similarly dramatic view, with the illuminated cathedral and castle looming above.

9 Antonín

One of many artists on the bridge, the popular Antonín mostly painted portraits of himself as the devil. His proximity to the Čertovka (Devil's Canal) may have been the key to his choice of subject.

10 Statue of the Trinitarian Order

This religious order was set up to ransom prisoners of war from the Crusades and buy Christians back their freedom, hence the depiction of a bored Turk keeping guard outside a cell **(left)**.

★10 ⭐ The Loreto

At the heart of this sparkling 17th-century Baroque pilgrimage site is its claim to fame and most proud possession: a replica of the original Santa Casa in Loreto, Italy, believed to be the house where the Virgin Mary received the Incarnation. Construction of the grandiose church and the surrounding chapels coincided with the Counter-Reformation, and one of Prague's first Baroque buildings was intended to lure Czechs back to the Catholic faith.

Loretánské náměstí ①

This square is said to have been a pagan burial ground. The stucco façade of The Loreto (right) is dwarfed by the Černín Palace opposite, home of the Ministry of Foreign Affairs.

Plan of The Loreto

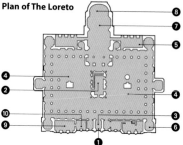

② Santa Casa

The stucco reliefs on the outside of this replica (above) of the Holy Family's house in Nazareth depict scenes from the life of the Virgin Mary. Inside stands the miracle-working statue of Our Lady of Loreto.

③ Bell Tower

The carillon was the gift of a merchant of Prague whose daughter was healed by the intercession of the Lady of Loreto. An automated mechanism chimes a Marian hymn every hour.

Inner Courtyard ④

In this courtyard, visitors can admire two Baroque fountains (right). The south fountain depicts the Assumption of the Virgin; the north features a sculpture of the Resurrection.

5 Arcade
Before and after visiting the Santa Casa, pilgrims passed through the arcade and prayed at its chapels dedicated to the Holy Family, the Holy Rood, St Francis Seraphim, St Antony of Padua, St Anne and Our Lady of Sorrows.

6 St Wilgefortis Altar
The Chapel of Our Lady of Sorrows contains the altar of a bearded, crucified woman. Wilgefortis (Starosta in Czech) was said to be a Portuguese maiden who prayed for a masculine appearance in order to preserve her chastity.

SANTA CASA

The Santa Casa was the house in Nazareth in which the archangel Gabriel is believed to have announced to the Virgin Mary that she would conceive the Son of God. In the 13th century, the Greek Angeli family moved the house to Loreto, Italy. As the Marian cult spread, copies of the Italian Loreto started emerging all over Europe – the 17th-century Prague site is believed to be the truest representation of the original structure.

8 Altars of Sts Felicissimus and Marcia
On either side of the altar in the Church of the Nativity are large reliquary displays containing the remains of these two Spanish saints.

9 Treasury
The Communists created this exhibit of sacred items **(right)** to show how the church brought peasants to obedience with a "cheap promise of happiness beyond the grave".

7 Church of the Nativity

Originally a small alcove behind the Santa Casa, the church **(left)** was expanded into its present size in 1717. The Rococo organ stands opposite the altar, over a crypt to Loreto benefactors.

NEED TO KNOW

MAP A4 ■ Loretánské náměstí 7 ■ 220 516740 ■ www.loreta.cz

Open Apr–Oct: 9am–5pm daily; Nov–Mar: 9:30am–4pm daily

Adm (under-6s free, family tickets available); audio guides can be hired

■ At Kapucínská 2 nearby is a memorial to people tortured by secret police in the former Interior Ministry building.

10 Prague Sun
The silver monstrance **(left)** for displaying the host – created in 1699 by Johann Bernard Fischer von Erlach – is gold-plated and studded with 6,222 diamonds. The Virgin looks up at her son, represented by the host in the receptacle.

TOP 10 ⭐ Old Jewish Cemetery

The crumbling Old Jewish Cemetery (Starý židovský hřbitov) is a moving memorial to the once considerable Jewish community of Prague. This was one of the few burial sites available to the city's Jews, and graves had to be layered when the plot became full. Estimates put it at about 100,000 graves, with the oldest headstone dating from 1439 and the final burial taking place in 1787. The Old-New Synagogue, built in the 13th century, is situated across the street.

1 Avigdor Kara's Grave
The oldest grave is that of this poet and scholar, best known for his documentation of the pogrom of 1389, which he survived.

2 Mordechai Maisel's Grave
Mordechai Maisel (1528–1601), the mayor of the Jewish ghetto during the reign of Rudolf II, funded the synagogue that bears his name.

3 Grave of Rabbi Judah Loew
The grave of Rabbi Judah Loew ben Bezalel, to whom legend attributes the creation of the Prague Golem, is located here **(left)**.

Gravestones, Old Jewish Cemetery

4 Gothic Tombstones
The eastern wall has fragments of Gothic tombstones rescued from another graveyard near Vladislavova street in 1866. Further graves at another site were found in the 1990s.

GRAVE SYMBOLS

A Hebrew tombstone (matzevah) as a rule contains the deceased's name, date of death and eulogy. In addition, the grave markers here often included symbolic images indicating the lineage of the deceased. Names are often symbolized by animals, according to biblical precedent or Hebrew or Germanic translations – David Gans's tombstone features a goose (gans in German). Some professions are also represented: scissors may appear on a tailor's tombstone, for example.

5 Klausen Synagogue
Mordechai Maisel also commissioned the building of the Klausen Synagogue (U Starého hřbitova 39/1) on the cemetery's northern edge **(above)**. It now houses exhibitions on Jewish festivals and traditions.

6 Nephele Mound
Stillborn children, miscarried babies and other infants who died under a year old were buried in the southeast corner of the cemetery.

8 David Gans's Tombstone

Gans's headstone **(left)** is marked with a goose and the Star of David, after his name and his faith. A pupil of Loew, Gans (1541–1613) was the author of a seminal two-volume history of the Jewish people. He was also an accomplished astronomer during the time of Johannes Kepler.

9 Grave of Rabbi Oppenheim

Rabbi David Oppenheim was the first chief rabbi of Moravia, and later chief rabbi of Bohemia and finally of Prague, where he died in 1736.

10 Zemach Grave

The gravestone of the printer Mordechai Zemach (d. 1592) and his son Bezalel (d. 1589) lies next to the Pinkas Synagogue *(Široká 23/3)*. Mordechai Zemach was a co-founder of the Prague Burial Society.

NEED TO KNOW

MAP D4 ▪ Josefov

Old Jewish Cemetery:
U Starého hřbitova 3; 222 317191; open Apr–Oct: 9am–6pm Sun–Fri (Nov–Mar: to 4:30pm); closed Jewish holidays; Adm (ticket valid for 1 week, includes entrance to various synagogues); audio guides available; www.jewishmuseum.cz

Old-New Synagogue:
Červená; open 9am–6pm Sun–Fri (Nov–Mar: to 5pm); Adm (under-6s free); www.synagogue.cz

▪ In the synagogues, it is customary for men to wear a *yarmulka* (skull cap). Look for them at the entrance; return them when you leave.

▪ The Museum of Decorative Arts' east windows *(17 listopadu 2)* offer excellent crowd-free views of the cemetery.

7 Hendl Bassevi's Grave

This elaborate tombstone **(below)** marks the resting place of the "Jewish Queen", Hendl Bassevi. Her husband, mayor Jacob Bassevi, was raised to the nobility by Ferdinand II and permitted a coat of arms, which can be seen on his wife's gravestone.

Entrance

Plan of the Old Jewish Cemetery

Old-New Synagogue Features

 Rabbi Loew's Chair
Topped with a Star of David, the tall chair found by the eastern wall has been reserved for the chief rabbis of Prague throughout the history of the synagogue.

2 Jewish Standard
Prague's Jewish community was permitted a banner in the 15th century as a symbol of its autonomy. The copy hanging above the bimah replicates a 1716 original, featuring a Jewish hat within a six-pointed star and bearing the legend "Shema Yisroel".

The nave of the synagogue

3 Nave
Twelve narrow windows, evoking the 12 tribes of Israel, line the perimeter walls, which are unadorned save for the abbreviation of biblical verses. Two central pillars are modelled on the façade columns of the Temple of Jerusalem.

 Ark
Behind the curtain on the eastern wall are the Torah scrolls, which are kept in the holy ark. The tympanum features foliage and grape motifs, which are also found in the nearby

The roof and attic of the synagogue

Convent of St Agnes (see pp342–3), and date from the synagogue's construction in the late 13th century.

 Entrance
The biblical inscription "Revere God and observe His commandments! For this applies to all mankind" admonished worshippers as they were entering and leaving the synagogue.

6 Vaulting
To avoid forming the sign of the cross, a fifth rib was added to the nave's vaulting, which is decorated with vine leaves and ivy.

7 Women's Windows
Women were not permitted in the nave of the synagogue, but sat in the vestibule. Narrow openings in the wall allowed them to follow the services being conducted within.

 Bimah
A pulpit stands on this dais in the centre. From here the rabbi reads the Torah and performs wedding ceremonies.

9 Josefov Town Hall
Adjacent to the synagogue stands the Jewish Town Hall (Maiselova 250/18). The hands of the clock on the façade run anticlockwise – or clockwise if you read Hebrew.

10 Attic
Legend has it that Rabbi Judah Loew stashed the remains of the Golem he had created under the synagogue's large saddle roof.

THE JEWS IN PRAGUE

Prague's Jews have suffered anti-Semitic behaviour almost since their arrival in the 10th century. Zealous Christians destroyed an early settlement in what is now Malá Strana. Such pogroms were not uncommon – the most infamous is the Passover slaughter of 1389, in which rioters killed more than 3,000 Jews, including those who had taken refuge in the Old-New Synagogue. But there were also high points. Prominent Jews, notably Rabbi Loew and Mordechai Maisel, enjoyed influence in the court of Rudolf II; Charles VI recognized the community's autonomy in 1716; his descendant Joseph II ended many discriminatory measures; and in the late 19th century Jews were active in the National Revival. However, anti-Semitism still lurked. In 1899, Leopold Hilsner was accused of ritual murder; his legal counsel was Tomáš Garrigue Masaryk, future president of independent Czechoslovakia. Although the interwar years were a golden age for Czech Jews, among them Franz Kafka, the 1938 Munich Agreement paved the way for Hitler to take possession of Czech lands, and the Jews were restricted to a ghetto before being deported to Nazi concentration camps. Synagogues were turned into archives for looted Jewish artifacts. Hitler reportedly even planned to create a museum of the Jews as an extinct race in Josefov. By the end of the war nearly 80,000 Jews from Bohemia and Moravia had died in the Holocaust.

TOP 10
JEWISH LEADERS

1 Eliezer ben Elijah Ashkenazi (1512–85)

2 Judah Loew ben Bezalel (c. 1520–1609)

3 Mordechai Maisel (1528–1601)

4 Mordechai ben Abraham Jaffe (1530–1612)

5 Ephraim Solomon ben Aaron of Luntshits (1550–1619)

6 Joseph Solomon Delmedigo (1591–1655)

7 David ben Abraham Oppenheim (1664–1736)

8 Yechezkel ben Yehuda Landau (1713–93)

9 Solomon Judah Lieb Rapoport (1790–1867)

10 Efraim Karol Sidon (b. 1942)

Terezín was a holding camp north of Prague to which the capital's Jews were moved by the Nazis during World War II. From there, many were later transported to Nazi-run extermination camps in occupied Poland.

⭐ Trade Fair Palace

Surrounded by the Art Nouveau tenement buildings of Holešovice, the austere Trade Fair Palace *(Veletržní Palác)* is a daring work of art in itself. It was the first official Functionalist building in Europe, and even Le Corbusier was impressed when he visited Prague in 1928. In 1979, plans were launched to turn the former trade fair complex into the home of the National Gallery's modern and contemporary art collection. The space was inaugurated in 1995, with works by prominent Czech artists alongside a rich array of international masters from the 19th, 20th and 21st centuries.

1 House in Aix-en-Provence

The National Gallery's impressive collection of French art was begun in 1923, when Czech president Tomáš Masaryk helped found a small collection. This bright work showing a large tan house (c. 1887) by Paul Cézanne (1839–1906) was one of those original 25 pieces.

2 Bonjour, Monsieur Gauguin

Paul Gauguin (1848–1903) originally painted this simple, flat self-portrait **(above)** as a decoration for the panel of a dining-room door in an inn in Le Pouldu, Brittany. The much-admired 19th-century French artist painted this enlarged copy in 1889.

3 Green Wheat

Van Gogh's encounter with Impressionism was a decisive moment. Charmed by the southern French countryside, he created bright canvases such as this 1889 landscape **(above)**.

4 Anxiety

Otto Gutfreund (1889–1927) paved the way for modern Czech sculpture. This bronze 1912 work captures the apprehension of man in the early 20th century.

5 St John the Baptist

Auguste Rodin's (1840–1917) 1878 sculpture is a study of spiral motion; the natural movement is heightened by his visible muscles, from the tension of the anchored feet to the head turned away from the dominant gesture of the hand **(right)**.

6 Jaguar Attacking a Horseman

Delacroix (1798–1863) often visited zoos to study predatory animals whose movement inspired him. This 1855 canvas, striking for its interaction of colour and motion, is an example of his research and French Romanticism in painting.

7 Self-Portrait

One of 14 Picassos donated in 1960 by former National Museum director Vincenc Kramář, the almond-shaped eyes and triangular nose of this 1907 work testify to the influence of Iberian art.

8 Head of a Young Girl

Henri Laurens's (1885–1954) 1926 bronze sculpture is a synthesis of Cubism and the Classical ideal of form and beauty. It was added to the collections in 1935.

NEED TO KNOW

MAP F1 ■ Dukelských hrdinů 47, Holešovice ■ 224 301122 ■ www. ngprague.cz

Open 10am–6pm Tue–Sun

Adm

■ The ground floor and mezzanine house the temporary exhibits. The exhibits shown on these pages are part of the regularly changing medium-term exhibitions throughout the building. Call ahead for further details.

9 At the Moulin Rouge

Toulouse-Lautrec (1864–1901) thrived on depictions of Paris nightlife such as this oil tempera **(above)** on cardboard. One of the dancing women is his muse, Jane Avril. Oscar Wilde is one of the figures in the background.

Myself, Self Portrait 10

With the city of Paris and the elements of modern civilization in the background, Henri Rousseau's (1844–1910) self-portrait with a palette in hand in the foreground, painted in 1890, depicts the artist as a self-assured personality **(right)**.

🔟⭐ Convent of St Agnes

The 13th-century Convent of St Agnes of Bohemia *(Klášter sv. Anežky)* is an impressive Gothic building closely tied to Czech statehood. Daughter of Czech King Přemysl Ottokar I, Princess Agnes chose a spiritual life and founded a convent here in 1234 for the Poor Clares, an order of nuns associated with the Order of St Francis. However, it was Agnes's diplomatic skills and work in establishing the convent which raised Bohemia in the eyes of Rome, as much as any courtly efforts to do the same. Restored in the 1980s to its original splendour, the convent is now part of the National Gallery and exhibits its collection of medieval and early Renaissance art.

1 Strakonice Madonna
This larger-than-life, 700-year-old statue of the Virgin and Child is the Czech National Gallery's most prized possession. The gestures of the Madonna are strikingly rigid, and evoke the Classical French sculpture found in places such as Reims Cathedral.

2 Zbraslav Madonna
Bohemia's most celebrated Marian painting is evocative of Byzantine icons in its style. The ring on the Madonna's left-hand finger symbolizes the church through the mystical marriage between Christ and the Virgin Mary. The work was moved to the Convent of St Agnes from the Cistercian Zbraslav Monastery where the majority of the Přemyslid kings were laid to rest.

3 Vyšší Brod Altarpiece
The 14th-century cycle begins with the *Annunciation*, then proceeds through the *Adoration of the Magi* to *Pentecost* **(right)**. The creator of these beautiful panels is unknown.

4 Works of Master Theodoricus
Parts of an altar set on loan from Karlštejn Castle, these works include *St Charlemagne*, *St Catherine*, *St Matthew* **(left)**, *St Luke*, *St Ambrose* and *St Gregory*.

ST AGNES OF BOHEMIA

St Agnes of Bohemia was a powerful figure in medieval politics. Gregory IX granted special privileges to her convent and his successor Innocent IV sent priceless relics to be housed there. Agnes died in 1282, but her influence on Czech statehood was felt centuries later when, in 1989, Pope John Paul II canonized her; five days later, the Velvet Revolution began.

5 Třeboň Altarpiece

Only three of the five double-sided panels of the 14th-century retable Třeboň Altarpiece **(left)** have survived to the present day.

6 Capuchin Cycle

The origin of these 14 panels is unknown. The Virgin Mary is flanked by St Peter on the left and Christ on the right.

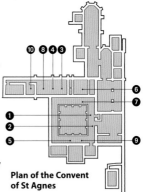

Plan of the Convent of St Agnes

7 Velhartice Altarpiece

Originating in south Bohemia around 1500, this is a rare example of a completely preserved altar **(right)**. Beneath the Madonna, cherubs hold the *vera* icon.

8 Martyrdom of St Florian

Albrecht Altdorfer (1480–1538) created this painting **(below)** as part of a multipanel altar featuring scenes from the legend of St Florian. Other pieces from the series are in Florence.

NEED TO KNOW

MAP E3

◼ U Milosrdných 17

◼ 778 725086

◼ www.ngprague.cz

Open 10am–6pm Tue–Sun

Adm: check website

Gardens open 10am–10pm daily (Nov–Mar: to 6pm)

◼ Visitors can visit and relax in the two renovated cloister gardens that are complemented with sculptures by leading artists. Entry is free.

9 Puchner Altarpiece

St Agnes gave up a life at court to pursue a spiritual vocation. On this 15th-century altarpiece, she is typically depicted nursing the sick.

10 Apocalypse Cycle

Although Albrecht Dürer is considered the foremost German Renaissance artist, he is best known to many for his woodcuts, such as this series of 15 **(left)**, which date from 1498 and reveal a strong Gothic flavour.

TOP 10 ★ Wenceslas Square

This former medieval horse market began to be redeveloped in the 19th century, rapidly becoming the commercial hub of Prague. In 1848 it was renamed Wenceslas Square *(Václavské náměstí)* in honour of Bohemia's patron saint. The majority of the buildings seen today date from the early 20th century, and their beautiful Art Nouveau façades illustrate how keenly this style was embraced by Czech architects of the time. The square has often been the scene of historic events, most recently in 1989, when large, jubilant crowds gathered here to celebrate the end of Communism.

1 National Museum

Invading Warsaw Pact troops shelled the Neo-Renaissance building in 1968, mistaking it for the country's parliament (you can still see the pock-marks). The small entry fee is worth it, if only to see the grand marble stairway **(left)** and pantheon of Czech cultural figures *(Václavské nám 68)*.

2 St Wenceslas Statue

The Přemyslid prince sits astride a horse flanked by other Czech patrons **(right)** in Josef Myslbek's 1912 sculpture. The area "under the tail" is a traditional meeting place for locals.

3 Communist Memorial

In front of St Wenceslas is a memorial to the victims of Communism, such as the two men who died protesting against the 1968 invasion.

Wenceslas Square

4 Palác Lucerna

Václav Havel's grandfather designed and built this building, now home to an art gallery, cinema, cafés, shops and a ballroom.

5 Palác Koruna

Built in 1912 in Geometric Modernist style, this "palace" **(right)** held offices, homes and Turkish-style baths. The listed building now hosts the Koruna Palace shopping centre, which boasts several cafés and luxury stores.

HISTORIC DEMONSTRATIONS

Wenceslas Square saw its first demonstration in 1419 when Catholic reformer Jan Želivský led a procession to St Stephen's Church. On 28 October 1918 the area witnessed Czechoslovak independence. In 1969, student Jan Palach set himself on fire here as a political protest against the Soviet occupation. It is still the scene of political protests today.

Grand Hotel Evropa
It's gone to seed over the years, but the Art Nouveau building **(right)** preserves its original façade and decor. Although it is closed for renovation until 2020, its architectural features can still be seen.

7 Upside-Down Statue
Hanging in the central passage of the Palác Lucerna is David Černý's take on Czech patron saint Wenceslas.

9 Franciscan Garden
A stone's throw from Wenceslas Square, this former monastery garden **(below)** provides much-needed peace from the city bustle (*Jungmannovo náměstí*).

10 Svobodné slovo Balcony
During the Velvet Revolution, Václav Havel addressed supporters from the balcony of the *Svobodné slovo* newspaper building. When the deposed Alexander Dubček joined him, the crowds knew that Communism was over.

NEED TO KNOW

MAP E5 ■ New Town

■ Cafés line both sides of the lively square from top to bottom.

■ Owing to the high volume of tourists, Wenceslas Square is where pickpockets are most active. Be especially wary at the square's north end.

---

8 Church of Our Lady of the Snows
Founded by Charles IV upon his coronation in 1347, this beautiful church **(above)** was to have been more than 100 m (330 ft) long, but it was never completed.

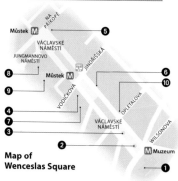

Map of Wenceslas Square

Petřín Hill

Covered with forests and orchards and dotted with strolling lovers, Petřín Hill is a soft counterpoint to the spires of Hradčany on the Vltava's left bank. Rising more than 300 m (1,000 ft) above sea level, the area began life as a vineyard in the 15th century, but has been a public park since 1825. Early chronicles say it was the site of pagan rituals to the god Perun, and believers still practise ancient rites here on 1 May each year. Above all, however, it is the perfect escape from the bustling city crowds.

Observation Tower ①
Modelled after the Eiffel Tower in Paris, Petřín Hill's 63.5-m (210-ft) *Eiffelovka* stands only one-quarter as high as its inspiration. The tower was created for the Jubilee Exposition of 1891. A climb of 299 stairs leads to the viewing platform **(right)**.

② Strahov Stadium
It may be ugly, but Strahov Stadium **(below)** is the largest arena of its kind in the world. It was built for Sokol, a physical exercise organization, and used for gymnastic rallies. Today it is a rock concert venue.

NEED TO KNOW

MAP A5 ■ Malá Strana

Funicular: open 9am–11:30pm daily; adm; www.dpp.cz

Observation Tower & Mirror Maze: open Apr–Sep: 10am–10pm; Mar & Oct: 10am–8pm; Nov–Feb: 10am–6pm, adm; en.muzeumprahy.cz/prague-towers

Strahov Monastery: open 9am–noon & 1–5pm daily; adm; www.

strahovskyklaster.cz

Church of St Michael, Church of St Lawrence: Closed to the public except during Masses (Sun, Mon or Fri)

Štefánik's Observatory: opening hours vary throughout the year; adm

■ Nebozízek restaurant (Petřínské sady 411) offers spectacular views.

■ There is also a café in the entrance hall of the Observation Tower.

③ Strahov Monastery
Founded in 1140, Strahov houses the nation's oldest books in the Strahov Library **(below)**, while still functioning as a monastery. The Theological Hall, with its frescoes and statue of St John, is a must-see.

6 Karel Hynek
Mácha Statue
Mácha is a national poet, best loved for his Romantic poem "May". On 1 May, admirers lay flowers at his statue.

4 Hunger Wall
The 14th-century wall **(above)** was once part of the city's southern fortifications. Charles IV is said to have ordered its construction as a project to feed the poor during a famine.

7 Church of St Michael
Still used for services, this lovely little 17th-century wooden church **(below)** was moved to Prague when the Ukraine valley it stood in was flooded by a dammed-up river.

8 Štefánik's Observatory
Operating since 1928, the observatory **(below)** was named after M R Štefánik, a Slovak diplomat and co-founder of the Czechoslovak Republic, as well as a scientist and astronomer.

5 Mirror Maze
After laughing at the distorting mirrors in the labyrinth, take in a bit of history with a diorama depicting the final battle of the Thirty Years' War on Charles Bridge.

9 Church of St Lawrence
Facing the mirror maze is this onion-domed church, built on a pagan shrine in the 10th century and rebuilt in Baroque style in the 18th century.

STRAHOV MONASTERY EXHIBITS

Strahov has suffered pillaging armies, fires and totalitarian regimes. Josef II dissolved most local monasteries in 1783, sparing Strahov on the condition that the monks conduct research at their library. Today the majority of the research involves paper preservation. On display are old books, pictures, ornate gospels and miniature Bibles.

10 Funicular
If you want to save your breath, do as visitors have done since 1890 and take the funicular railway to the top of the hill and walk down. The cable car offers outstanding views of the castle to the north.

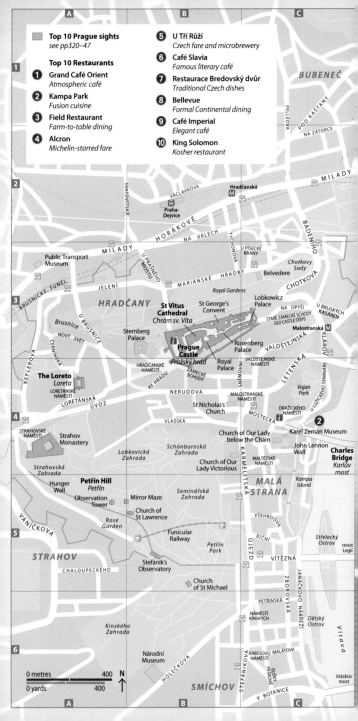

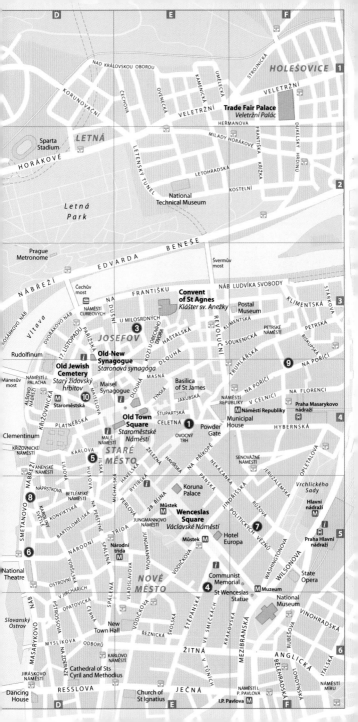

A 1

E

F

HOLEŠOVICE 1

NAD KRÁLOVSKOU OBOROU

KORUNOVAČNÍ

KAMENICKÁ

UMĚLECKÁ

STROJNICKÁ

VELETRŽNÍ

ČECHOVA

OVENECKÁ

VELETRŽNÍ

Trade Fair Palace
Veletržní Palác

HEŘMANOVA

DUKELSKÝCH HRDINŮ

LETNÁ

Sparta Stadium

MILADY HORÁKOVÉ

FRANTIŠKA

HORÁKOVÉ

LETENSKÝ TUNEL

LETOHRADSKÁ

KŘÍŽKA 2

KOSTELNÍ

Letná Park

National Technical Museum

Prague Metronome

EDVARDA

BENEŠE

Švermův most

NÁBŘEŽÍ

NÁB LUDVÍKA SVOBODY

Vltava

FRANTIŠKU

Convent of St Agnes
Klášter sv. Anežky

Postal Museum

KLIMENTSKÁ 3

STAROVA

Čechův most

NÁMĚSTÍ CURIEOVÝCH

NA DUŠNÍ

U MILOSRDNÝCH

KLIMENTSKÁ

PETRSKÉ NÁMĚSTÍ

PETRSKÁ

BISKUPSKÁ

REVOLUČNÍ

17. LISTOPADU

PAŘÍŽSKÁ

DVOŘÁKOVO NÁB.

JOSEFOV ❸

KOZÍ U OBECNÍHO DVORA

HAŠTALSKÁ

SOUKENICKÁ

TRUHLÁŘSKÁ

NA POŘÍČÍ ❾

NA PORÍČÍ

Rudolfinum

Old-New Synagogue
Staronová synagóga

DLOUHÁ

MASNÁ

Mánesův most

NÁMĚSTÍ J. PALACHA

Old Jewish Cemetery
Starý židovský hřbitov ❿

Maisel Synagogue

Staroměstská

MASARYKOVO

KŘÍŽOVNICKÁ

PLATNÉŘSKÁ

MALÁ STRANA

TÝNSKÁ

Basilica of St James

JAKUBSKÁ

NÁMĚSTÍ REPUBLIKY

V CELNICI

NA FLORENCI

Praha Masarykovo nádraží 4

Alšovo NÁBŘEŽÍ

NÁMĚSTÍ REPUBLIKY

Old Town Square
Staroměstské Náměstí ❶

ŠTUPARTSKÁ

CELETNÁ

Powder Gate

Municipal House

HYBERNSKÁ

Clementinum

KŘÍŽOVNICKÉ NÁMĚSTÍ

MALÉ NÁMĚSTÍ ❺

OVOCNÝ TRH

STARÉ MĚSTO

ŽELEZNÁ

HAVÍŘSKÁ

NA PŘÍKOPĚ

NEKÁZANKA

SENOVÁŽNÉ NÁMĚSTÍ

OPLETALOVA

JERUZALÉMSKÁ

Vrchlického Sady

ANENSKÉ NÁMĚSTÍ

SMETANOVO NÁBŘEŽÍ ❽

NÁPRSTKOVA

BETLÉMSKÉ NÁMĚSTÍ

KARLOVA ❺

LILIOVÁ

HUSOVA

MICHALSKÁ

RYTÍŘSKÁ

28. ŘÍJNA

Můstek Ⓜ

Koruna Palace

PANSKÁ

JINDŘIŠSKÁ

POLITICKÝCH VĚZŇŮ

RŮŽOVÁ

Hlavní nádraží

Praha Hlavní nádraží 5

SMETANOVO NÁBŘEŽÍ ❻

KAROLÍNY SVĚTLÉ

KONVIKTSKÁ

PERLOVÁ

JUNGMANNOVO NÁMĚSTÍ

Wenceslas Square
Václavské Náměstí ❼

WASHINGTONOVA

WILSONOVA

State Opera

NA PERŠTÝNĚ

BARTOLOMĚJSKÁ

TŘÍDA

Národní třída Ⓜ

Můstek Ⓜ

Hotel Europa

National Theatre

VÍTĚZNÁ

VORŠILSKÁ

OSTROVNÍ

NÁRODNÍ

SPÁLENÁ

JUNGMANNOVA

VLADISLAVOVA

VODIČKOVA

NOVÉ MĚSTO

Communist Memorial ❹

St Wenceslas Statue

Muzeum Ⓜ

National Museum

VINOHRADSKÁ

Slovanský Ostrov

MASARYKOVO

V JIRCHÁŘÍCH

PŠTROSSOVA

OPATOVICKÁ

ČERNÁ

ŘEZNICKÁ

New Town Hall

VODIČKOVA

ŠKOLSKÁ

ŠTĚPÁNSKÁ

VE SMEČKÁCH

KRAKOVSKÁ

MEZIBRANSKÁ

BĚLEHRADSKÁ

ANGLICKÁ

LONDÝNSKÁ

ITALSKÁ 6

Dancing House

JIRÁSKOVO NÁMĚSTÍ

MYSLÍKOVA

NA ZDERAZE

ODBORŮ

KARLOVO NÁMĚSTÍ

RESSLOVA

Cathedral of Sts Cyril and Methodius

ŽITNÁ

V TŮNÍCH

JEČNÁ

Church of St Ignatius

NÁMĚSTÍ I. P. PAVLOVA

I.P. Pavlova Ⓜ

NÁMĚSTÍ MÍRU

D

E

F

General Index